The Art of the Personal

The Art of the Personal

A Selection and Interpretation of the Writings

of

PATRICK GRANT

Permission has been received from the State University of New York Press
to reproduce excerpts from *Buddhism and Ethnic Conflict in Sri Lanka* (Albany: SUNY, 2009).
The portrait by David Goatley, *Personally Yours. Patrick at Eighty* is reproduced by
permission of the artist, davidgoatley.com.

Matador
Unit E2 Airfield Business Park,
Harrison Road, Market Harborough,
Leicestershire. LE16 7UL
Tel: 0116 279 2299
Email: books@troubador.co.uk
Web: www.troubador.co.uk/matador
Twitter: @matadorbooks

ISBN 978 1 80313 511 3

British Library Cataloguing in Publication Data.
A catalogue record for this book is available from the British Library.

Printed and bound in Great Britain by TJ Books Limited, Padstow, Cornwall

Typeset in 11pt Minion Pro by Troubador Publishing Ltd, Leicester, UK

Matador is an imprint of Troubador Publishing Ltd

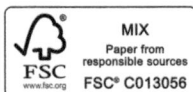

For the many helpers, whose voices I hear still
with gratitude throughout these pages.
"For in this way, while you are far from me, I who
am absent speak to all of you."

Benedictus de Spinoza
Letter to Simon de Vries
March, 1663

* * *

Gloria
In memoriam

CONTENTS

Preface   ix

Abbreviations   xi

Introduction   xiii

Part I   Form   **1**

1. Persons, Individuals, Collectives   3
2. Culture   52
     (a) Myths, Narratives, Ideas   68
     (b) The Sacramental View: The Middle Ages   88
     (c) Disenchantment and Discovery:
         Renaissance and Reformation   109
     (d) Secularism and Modernity   150
3. The State Apparatus and the Rule of Force   178
4. Language, Desire, and Suffering   221

Part II   Impulse   **263**

5. Dialogue   265
6. Imagination   296
7. Method in Art and Science   332
8. The Encompassing and the Perennial Philosophy   360

PREFACE

The following book is a distillation of positions arrived at by way of some twenty, mostly academic, book-length studies published during the past fifty or so years. The connections between these academic enquiries and the personal circumstances informing the choice and treatment of their subject matter remain central to the present project, the broad aim of which is to set out a personalism fitting for the times in which we live. Briefly, today instrumental knowledge, predatory global capitalism, rapid technological advances in communication, declining levels of literacy and a widespread debasement of public discourse have brought about a general devaluation of what it means to be someone whose individual good is inseparable from the common good returned as the good of each – which is to say, what it means to be a person.

According to the view of the person I want to propose, the other whom we meet remains not fully accessible and yet through the event of our meeting, the other is already to a degree constitutive of ourselves. Seen in this light, personal relationships reach beyond the merely instrumental provision of mutual benefit that the all-too familiar free enterprise and social contract theories promote by placing an over-riding value on individual self-interest. A person is not sufficiently accounted for as either a self-sufficient individual or a faceless item within a collective, and what I am calling the art of the personal takes shape in what goes between these poles. Just so, in the following compilation each excerpt makes a particular, let us say individual, statement even as the excerpts are shaped by topics of common, or general concern, so that the form of the book mirrors its governing theory. In addition, a series of interconnected, interpretive essays, together with an autobiographical introduction provide a narrative dimension, but without determining how the excerpts are to be read or how they might be re-combined. The book therefore invites a dialogical response, and, as I will suggest, dialogue is quintessentially the art of the personal, a fact that art itself invites us to experience and understand.

On the following page, I provide a list of the published materials on which the excerpts draw and to which they are keyed by way of the identifying initials provided. The excerpts are printed without footnotes, which can be consulted in the original versions.

ABBREVIATIONS

DA   *Dialogue in the Digital Age. Why it Matters How We Read and What We Say* (London: Routledge, 2021), 110 pp.

RV   *Reading Vincent van Gogh. A Thematic Guide to the Letters* (Edmonton: Athabasca University Press, 2016), 184 pp.

PW   *"My Own Portrait in Writing". Self-Fashioning in the Letters of Vincent van Gogh* (Edmonton: Athabasca University Press, 2015), 183 pp.

LV   *The Letters of Vincent van Gogh. A Critical Study* (Edmonton: Athabasca University Press, 2014), 239 pp.

IM   *Imperfection* (Edmonton: Athabasca University Press, 2012), 227 pp.

SL   *Buddhism and Ethnic Conflict in Sri Lanka* (New York: SUNY, 2009), 146 + xiv pp.

HD   *Hardened to Death. Literature, Rhetoric and Violence in Northern Ireland, 1968–98* (London: Palgrave, 2001), 193 + xii pp.

BE   *Breaking Enmities. Religion, Literature and Culture in Northern Ireland, 1967–97* (London: Macmillan, 1999), 239 + xi pp.

PP   *Personalism and the Politics of Culture* (London: Macmillan, 1996), 211 + viii pp.

SD   *Spiritual Discourse and the Meaning of Persons* (London: Macmillan, 1994), 202 + x pp.

PV   *Literature and Personal Values* (London: Macmillan, 1991), 255 + x pp.

NT   *Reading the New Testament* (London: Macmillan, 1989), 161 + ix pp.

DM   *Literature and the Discovery of Method in the English Renaissance* (London: Macmillan, 1985), 193 + ix pp.

DD   *A Dazzling Darkness. An Anthology of Western Mysticism* (London: Collins, 1985), 366 pp.

LM   *Literature of Mysticism in Western Tradition* (London: Macmillan, 1983), 195 + x pp.

SA   *Six Modern Authors and Problems of Belief* (London: Macmillan, 1979), 199 + x pp.

II   *Images and Ideas in Literature of the English Renaissance* (London: Macmillan, 1979), 243 + xiii pp.

TS   *The Transformation of Sin: Studies in Donne, Herbert, Vaughan and Traherne* (University of Massachussets Press, 1974), 240 + xiii pp.

OC   *Out of Contradiction* (London: Pentland, 1994), 62 + x pp.

KF   *The Kung-Fu Diaries* (Leicestershire: Book Guild, 2018), 213 pp.

BH   *Brieven aan Hans* (Amsterdam: Offsetdrukkerij Jan de Jong, 2018), 120 pp.

INTRODUCTION

Looking back, I found myself wondering if what I had written during the past fifty or so years might be a single project informed by a coherent and developing set of ideas. The shift from one research topic to the next felt natural at the time, but there was no overall plan. Occasionally, I imagined that if a plan were in the making it would declare itself by and by, and so it was better not to take stock prematurely. Meanwhile, as Herman Hesse puts it, 'each man's life represents a road towards himself, an attempt at such a road, the intimation of a path', and I felt that an intimation would be enough to be getting on with until some further design might become apparent.

As I discovered by and by, Hesse was strongly influenced by Carl Gustav Jung, from whom, by happenstance, as a teenager I learned a great deal. Jung – echoed here by Hesse – held that the achievement of personality is a process that is never completely realized. Also, he maintained that the symbol systems universally developed by human cultures are a means of helping people on the way towards the personal integration and meaning that they desire, even if they never fully achieve it.

In 1959, when I was eighteen, I accidentally came upon John Freeman's interview with Jung on the television series *Face to Face*.

I was passing through the small living room of the Belfast house and the erratic black-and-white television was turned on, though I am not sure anyone was watching it, and an old man was being interviewed. I caught only a fragment of what he was saying, but I was arrested and stopped to listen. I had never heard of Carl Gustav Jung and I did not fully grasp what he was getting at, but what I heard was a revelation.

For the first time, that is, I understood how symbolism in religion, art, and culture might help people to organize their lives in a purposeful way. I am not sure how much I learned from the interview itself as distinct from what I read afterwards, spurred on by what I had heard. But in broad terms Jung enabled me to see the toxic, quasi-religious ethnic divisions in Northern Ireland in a new light. Previously, I had thought of religion within a framework of argument and controversy in which believers made a case for the truth claims to which they were committed. In Northern Ireland, these claims were in large part antagonistic and mutually exclusive, and the often-stereotyped otherness of the opposed groups ('Catholic' and 'Protestant') typically went a long way to confirming a person's identity. But for me, as the child of Presbyterian and Roman Catholic parents (a rarity in Northern Ireland at the time), the question of belonging to either cohort was problematic. I was educated in one government ('Protestant') and two Catholic schools, and in all three religious prejudice was so deeply ingrained as to be normalized to the point that the generally well-intentioned adults in charge were beyond recognizing it. Dominic Murray's fascinating study of two primary schools in Northern Ireland shows how in the 1980s this kind of unconscious prejudice continued to prevail.

From a very early age I had recognized all too well the phenomenon Murray would later describe, though I had no words then to explain it. Still, I knew it not least because the domestic interior in which I grew up was not so much a refuge from the prevailing malaise as an incubator that reproduced it in a plumper, more richly virulent hot-house variety. This luxurious overgrowth was fed not so much by openly declared antagonisms as by closely harboured, intimate resentments, aggressions, and attitudes of contempt reflecting the grievances of the culture at large, so internalised as to have become matters of perception rather than reflection. I am still unable to decide how much to attribute to the generically formed 'Catholic' and 'Protestant' identities of the two principals responsible for my unfortunate begetting as distinct from their own irreconcilable differences. But the upshot was that the domestic interior was a microcosm, not a sanctuary, and even as an adult who had long since emigrated I could never re-visit the Belfast house without feeling such a sense of discomfort that I wonder still at not being able to handle it better.

And so in my late teens the happenstance encounter with Jung was profoundly significant because it offered me a way to understand religion other than as a marker of identity within a disturbingly intractable ethnic conflict zone. In addition, as I recognized quite clearly at the time, a path had been prepared for my welcoming response to Jung by yet another chance encounter that occurred a year or two previously.

On a bleak, rainy day I had gone into the Belfast Central Library to get out of the weather, and to justify my presence I selected a book at random from the open shelves. It was a biography of Vincent van Gogh – I have no idea which one – with extensive excerpts from the letters and cheap reproductions of a selection of his paintings. Some two hours later I left, still clutching the book.

Today, it is difficult to recollect the impact of that discovery, except to say that I was astonished that such a person could exist, that such courage should be able, at such personal cost, to break with an oppressive upbringing while also re-shaping the positive aspects of that upbringing in a visionary way through painting and writing (Van Gogh was an extraordinary and voluminous letter-writer). Also, Van Gogh's persistence and defiance together with his compassion for the poor and marginalized were deeply moving and were also to leave a lasting impression. And yet, although Van Gogh's example was inspiring, I could not see how to follow it until the encounter with Jung re-adjusted the picture, so to say, by way of a set of observations and ideas more amenable to my aptitude for academic enquiry and writing than was the painterly practice at the heart of Van Gogh's life and work. And so, in summary, Van Gogh declared that art could be a replacement for a defunct religion, and Jung that religion can (and should) be artistic. It seemed then that art, culture, and religion might combine in the shaping of a meaningful human life, and in that light I had already begun to feel, however faintly, something of Hesse's 'intimation of a path'.

Although I have remained appreciative of Jung, I have also been wary because it is easy to be overwhelmed by the grand Victorian, monumental structure of his thought – too easily taken over, as it were. Eventually, I came to think of Jung's vast body of writing as a record of his own path towards personal integration, an example of his advice that we have to find a way appropriate for each of us. Consequently, although I have read Jung and written about him, I have stopped short of becoming a Jungian, and I have even convinced myself that he might well approve of that.

As far as Van Gogh is concerned, I promised myself in those teenage years that by and by I would come back to him, but I resisted doing so for fear of breaking the spell of that first, incandescent encounter. More than fifty years later, I did at last come back to Van Gogh in order to write the first full-length critical assessment of his achievements as a writer. I need not have feared the spell being broken; if anything, the impact has gone deeper.

In the 1990s, during the last phase of my career, I returned also to Northern Ireland in order to write about the Troubles there in relation to the literary renaissance that took place during the same period, roughly between 1968 and 1998. And so, indeed our ends are in our beginnings, as T.S. Eliot says, but there was also an intervening journey that for me lay through the investigation of a series of questions and problems engendered by the circumstances I have so far described.

This journey began at Queen's University in Belfast, where I read English Literature and became interested in the devotional poetry of the seventeenth century. Laurence Lerner was influential as an undergraduate teacher, and would become a lifelong friend and an unfailingly engaging – and testing – interlocutor. From Queen's, I followed Laurence Lerner to Sussex University where I wrote a doctoral thesis, which he supervised, on the seventeenth-century devotional poets. During the seventeenth century, the most powerful minds in Europe were engaged with religious and cultural problems that were still alive and well in modern Northern Ireland, and it seemed to me that studying that period was a way of shaping an approach to the phenomenon of religiously based ethnic conflict in which I was interested for personal reasons.

My dissertation was the basis of *The Transformation of Sin. Studies in Donne, Herbert, Vaughan and Traherne* (1974), which dealt with literature and cultural transformation in the Renaissance and Reformation. A second book, *Images and Ideas* (1979), extended the enquiry to include Spenser, Shakespeare, and Milton, as well as the influence in England of some aspects of French devotional literature. In the process of writing this second book, I became increasingly aware of the strong continuities among literature, science, and religion, especially in relation to the development of secularism. As a way of throwing light on the complex shaping of the modern world in light of these several cultural and social concerns, I wrote *Six Modern Authors and Problems of Belief* (1979). Meanwhile, I had come to see that the innovations of the scientific revolution had a more powerful shaping influence on literature and culture than I had allowed, and

I needed to take further account of that. The result was *Literature and the Discovery of Method* (1985).

As a consequence of these studies, I found myself wondering about the truth claims of religion itself, and especially about the status of religious discourse for readers in a scientific and secular age. And so the core spiritual traditions of Western Christianity became central to the next two books, *Literature of Mysticism in Western Tradition* (1983) and *A Dazzling Darkness* (1985), in which I argued that the spiritual classics have their own kind of poetry and offer a humane understanding of our shared condition. By and large, that is, the literature of mysticism presents belief as a response to the exigencies of desire rather than as mainly a matter of doctrine.

With some feeling of inevitability, I moved from these books to the New Testament, which, in *Reading the New Testament* (1989), I described as presenting the problems of belief imaginatively, while also, paradoxically, declaring the inadequacy of the fictive imagination. I suggested that the cross, which is central to the gospels, is a sign that declares the insufficiency of signs. It does so especially by confronting us with the problem of innocent suffering, and faith is embraced or refused in response to this impasse, or *aporia*.

What, then, might be concluded about the interinvolvements of language, art, science, religion and culture in light of these several loosely interwoven but independent lines of enquiry? The next three books attempted an answer, focusing on the idea of the person as a means of consolidating, as well as further exploring, the implications of what I had so far concluded. These enquiries into personal agency were conducted and synthesized by way of a broad range of modern theorists, and in keeping with other commentators on the topic I suggested that the personal is experienced by direct encounter but eludes definition. That is, the idea of the person is grasped by default, by way of a sort of *via negativa*, in so far as a person is neither wholly an individual nor an item subsumed within a collective, but rather is shaped through a dynamic interplay between these poles. That is, persons are social beings because it is impossible fully to extract the other from the self, and yet personal presence is grasped through a recognition in each individual other, not only of a kindred interiority, intentionality, and ability to communicate, but also of an irreducible strangeness and singularity. As Martin Buber says, the personal is encountered in what goes between and therefore is fundamentally dialogical. In turn, as Plato understood from the beginning, dialogue is an art, of which art itself is both a symbol and efficacious means. These concerns are explored in *Literature and Personal Values* (1992), *Spiritual Discourse and the Meaning of Persons* (1994), and *Personalism and the Politics of Culture* (1996).

From the vantage point of this central massif, as it were, I returned to Northern Ireland to write about the Troubles that occurred there between roughly 1968 and 1998, and about the literary renaissance that played a progressive but not sufficiently acknowledged role in relation to the prevailing political concerns. In dealing with literature and the annexation of religion to ethnic exclusivism and violent conflict, the two books, *Breaking Enmities* (1999) and *Hardened to Death* (2001), return to my earliest concerns, interpreted by way of the analytical tools developed in the preceding studies, and especially by my conclusions about personalism, personal values, and dialogue.

The books on Northern Ireland were followed by a study of an analogous conflict zone in Sri Lanka, in which religion also played a key role. I undertook the project on Sri Lanka partly in an attempt better to understand the common factors in these two conflicts, as well as their differences. But I wrote also from a growing conviction that because persons are fundamentally dialogical they are perpetually on the boundary, as Bakhtin says, and should attempt therefore to remain open-ended in their relationships with others. Along the same lines, Simone Weil writes that persons should deliberately place themselves on the boundary between what they know and everything that is different or resistant. With these points in mind, I thought it advisable – indeed, exigent – to acquire some knowledge of and imaginative sympathy with another major wisdom tradition in addition to the one with which I was most familiar. For me, this other tradition was, and remains, Buddhism, and the book that I wrote as a dialogical companion to the books on Northern Ireland is *Religion and Ethnic Conflict in Sri Lanka* (2009).

The main positions explored in the studies I have so far described remain formative in a retrospective collection of essays dealing with art, politics, and religion. The collection is entitled *Imperfection* (2012), and contains chapters on Van Gogh and Jung. In the course of writing the chapter on Van Gogh, I discovered that the massive corpus of his letters, which are highly regarded both in the Netherlands and elsewhere for their literary distinction, had received no fully developed critical exegesis. The task of supplying this omission led to three books in which a dialogical approach to the self-fashioning dynamics of the letters as literature proved fruitful. The books are *The Letters of Vincent van Gogh. A Critical Study* (2014), *My Own Portrait in Writing* (2015), and *Reading Vincent van Gogh* (2016). As can readily be imagined, there was some gratification in bringing the accumulated results of the intervening years of study to bear on the earliest source of inspiration for the entire journey, and to which I had once promised myself to return.

The immediate predecessor of the present book, *Dialogue in the Digital Age* (2021), deals with rapid developments in today's information technology and how these developments pertain to a widespread erosion of public discourse as well as to a troubling general decline of literacy. The values by which a humane culture might resist the encroachments of a depersonalizing, stultifying barbarism fuelled by a predatory and anarchic neo-liberal economy are, I take it, worth stating. Put simply, the core conviction underpinning the book on dialogue is that people have a right to develop meaningful lives in the shaping of a common good that is also their own good as persons.

Faced with the challenge of reducing Emmanuel Mounier's bulky personalist study, *Traité du caractère* (1947), to one third of its length, his English editor and translator, Cynthia Rowland, remarked that the original version was more like a 'mandala' than a systematic study. Mounier's 'peculiarly personal work', she writes, comprises a variety of patterns and elaborations that suggest a developing sense of coherence, as in a mandala, which, she reminds us, citing Jung, is 'a symbol of integration and individuation'. Initially, her job of editing and selecting seemed to Cynthia Rowland 'an invitation to a massacre' but, as she explains, her solution was to reproduce in her edition something of the mandala design of the original, so that the result would not be just a collection of chopped-up excerpts, but would itself be an example of the emergent, meaningful coherence that is central to Mounier's view of the person.

I mention Cynthia Rowland's approach to Mounier because it describes very well what I attempt also to do in the following pages. That is, I choose excerpts from the books I have now described, arranged in patterns to suggest the design of the personalism that is my main topic. The result is not without an element of bricolage, something of the 'coherent deformation' that Maurice Merleau-Ponty describes, referring to art. Still, there is a clear design. The first of the two main sections, 'Form', sets out the book's governing ideas or principles; the second, 'Impulse', deals with the interpretive agency without which formal structures lack energy. The interaction between Impulse and Form is fundamental also to dialogue, the hallmark of the personal that I take art to symbolize and to require as a pre-condition of its reception. Something of this symbolic dimension is represented in how the structure of the following book itself invites, and I hope provokes, further discussion.

In addition to these formal considerations, I maintain throughout that a dialogical view of the person entails a politics that is at the very least socialist. And in so far as one might choose to address the encompassing mysteries of life and death, the following pages invite an affirmation – the 'eternal yea', as Carlyle says – declared (as long as we have the strength for it) in defiance of the unanswerable scandal of innocent suffering that remains the foundation of a tragic view of life. Finally, as Alain Badiou says, a person is the other of the other through whom each one is a self, and so in dialogue the other is neither exclusive nor excluded, because nothing then would go between. Nothing would be discovered. There would not even be an intimation of a path to take.

PART 1

FORM

1 PERSONS, INDIVIDUALS, COLLECTIVES

Some 200,000 years ago *Homo sapiens* acquired a capacity for the rapid symbolic speech that makes us distinctive. Other species can not duplicate how, through the representative and reflective aspects of symbolic language, humans are able to represent what they know and also to reflect on what they know.

Moreover, through language we can construct counterfactuals – imagined entities and events based on actually existent things but not confined to them. For instance, because we are familiar with birds and horses we can imagine a winged horse, and by the exercise of this aspect of our linguistic capacity we can invent stories about imaginary places and events, and pose questions about the future and speculate about answers, holding perhaps several possibilities before our mind's eye. On the one hand, then, we represent things and reflect on our representations; on the other hand, we imagine how things might or ought to be, and the values and standards by which we shape our lives emerge from an interplay between these two modes of representation.

While engaged in the process of thinking, people also often have a strong sense that their reflections are conducted by themselves and that their thoughts are their own. But in fact language is not anyone's individual property, and our thoughts are not entirely private, if only because they depend on a collective lexicon. Language, rather, is a threshold phenomenon bridging the gap between the individual and collective, the actual and possible. This is the case also with the human person, who, likewise, is neither an isolated individual nor an anonymous item within a collective, and I will want to maintain that the idea of the personal is best grasped by reflecting on the complex networks of discourse by which its threshold status is constituted, even though not defined.

The following excerpts deal with these topics by focusing on individual self-consciousness in relation to the social dimensions of personal identity, as well as with the evolution of the idea of the person from the ancient world through Christianity to modern psychology and phenomenology.

1.

The meaning of the word person has evolved, and remains controversial. John Locke's (1632–1704) statement in *An Essay Concerning Human Understanding* (1690) has especially influenced the direction of modern debate by stressing the importance to personal identity of consciousness. According to Locke, a person is

> *a thinking intelligent being, that has reason and reflection, and can consider itself as itself, the same thinking thing, in different times and places; which it does only by that consciousness which is inseparable from thinking, and, as it seems to me essential to it.*

Here Locke emphasizes not just consciousness (which elsewhere he links to memory), but also *unity* of consciousness. In so doing, he shows himself an inheritor of the Cartesian *cogito*, as do Hume and Kant even when they criticize Locke's main positions. In short, much discussion of the idea of the person subsequent to Locke thematises consciousness and the unity of the thinking subject. Yet, as Charles Taylor and Kathleen Wilkes point out, it is misleading to think of the person solely within the Lockean tradition. Consciousness is a problematic concept and the radical interiorizing – or privatizing – of the person that follows upon a strong emphasis on individual consciousness has the effect of uprooting the person from history. Not surprisingly, theories identifying the person with the private consciousness of each of us arose in England simultaneously with religious toleration, insisting likewise on the privacy of religious belief.

Some capacity for self-reflection is indeed a marker of the personal, but this capacity needs to be seen as one element among others. Persons also are agents who engage with matters that they deem significant, and they are able to make plans and set standards. In short, persons are members of communities and their identity is formed through their relations with others in the light of shared goals and through the medium of language and culture. Consequently, a person is not just an isolated individual; nor is a person devoid of interiority and autonomy. Rather, there is a continuing interchange between the personal and the communal, as is the case with language itself. Language is, as it were, a mold in which we are cast; yet human speech is highly unpredictable and the varieties of personal meaning expressed through language are infinitely nuanced. This is the central point of Noam Chomsky's criticism of B.F. Skinner's *Verbal Behaviour* (1957), in which Skinner explains the acquisition of language on behaviourist principles. Yet, however forceful the argument that signification is a functional state of a neuro-physiological system, no explanation in neuro-physiological terms, or in terms of reinforcement, stimulus generalization and so on, comes close to accounting for the range and flexibility of meanings that occur in everyday speech, let alone in literature. Partly for this reason, speech is especially an index of the personal, and something of the complex creativity of speech is stabilized and made amenable to reflection in the kind of writing we call 'literature'. Literature, that is, foregrounds its own discourse, and draws attention to the inexhaustible ranges of connotation and distinctive nuance that mark personal utterance.

SD, 10–11

2.

Kathleen Wilkes points out that there is an uncertain overlap and interpenetration between conscious and unconscious thinking, as is evident in such ordinary experiences as divided attention (we can drive a car and talk at the same time), or choosing between contending desires, or in the fact that we can hold inconsistent beliefs. Much that Wilkes demonstrates in these and many further examples from less common experiences (such as epileptic automatism, fugues, the results of commissurotomy, and so on) confirms the general principles underlying Michael Polanyi's important study, *Personal Knowledge*, arguing that conscious knowledge emerges from processes of adaptation and discernment, by way of skills acquired by repetition so that they become habitual. Polanyi points out that an expert musician or athlete or medical doctor can achieve the knack of making right decisions without quite knowing how this is done. As Wilkes (though she does not mention Polanyi) concludes, 'whatever Locke may have thought –

and opinions differ on this – we want to allow that there must be some gaps in the continuity of consciousness'. Indeed, few people today would argue for the identification of the person with consciousness alone, and yet, as I have said, one distinguishing mark of the human person is a capacity for self-reflection – for having thoughts about oneself, however undefined the boundaries and dynamics of these thoughts are. A great deal about human cognition indeed remains puzzling, and people characteristically are a disconcerting amalgam of shifting personas, contradictions, gaps, and inconsistencies. It is fashionable today to insist on all this, and, as Wilkes says, our 'judgements of "sameness of person" must allow for disunities and discontinuities on a large scale'. That is, we should realize that people are not consistent, even though for practical purposes we depend on a sufficient degree of stability and autonomy in the behavior of individuals, enabling us to treat each of them as 'a single intentional or rational system'. We need something (someone) to relate to, even though there is no question of defining personal identity adequately or of denying the strangeness and peculiarities of human knowledge and its complex overlap and kinship with the animal world.

SD, 12

3.

As Kathleen Wilkes goes on to show, in many cases – as with infants and fetuses, or in certain kinds of brain damage or multiple personality – the use of the word 'person' is so uncertain that there is no clear fact of the matter. In such cases, claims upon our behavior become important, as we take into account such things as future interests, the consequences of loss, and so on. Nonetheless, when we are talking about a person – or even a quasi-person as in these borderline cases – we need a referent. 'We need some specific entity to talk about: *its* interests, prospects, characteristics, future, our relationship and obligations to *it*'. In short, the personal is relational, and in the larger context persons are to a significant degree 'what society thinks persons ought to be'. It follows that the idea of the person to some extent evolves over historical time.

In displacing discussions of the person away from the problems of consciousness and identity, and re-locating the person within social relationships, Wilkes corroborates Polanyi's theories about tacit knowledge (the range of skills we learn by practice, and which are mediated socially), and also Taylor's argument that the idea of the self is inseparable from the kinds of human good valued by different human societies in different historical circumstances.

SD, 13

4.

Characteristically, in attempting to articulate the place in which we stand and what matters to us, we construct narratives – stories that at once describe and constitute what we take ourselves to be. Through story-telling we place ourselves in history and we tend to identify ourselves as persons through dialogue which takes place within a field of questions and develops in narrative form. Persons are thus to be understood through the histories of their becoming, which in turn are indexed to the courses of action they have chosen to affirm and pursue as worthwhile.

SD, 14

5.

The Greek word *prosopon* became in Latin *persona*, the mask through which an actor spoke and which was in turn associated with the adoption of sacred functions or prescribed roles. As Mauss points out, the Etruscans used masks in ancestor worship to confirm clan or family identity. Etruscan mask culture remained influential in ancient Rome, where citizens were said to have a civil *persona* entailing the right to the name or *nomen* of the *gens*. By contrast, slaves had no such rights and did not own their bodies, names, ancestors or possessions: a slave, that is, was not technically a person.

And so the word 'person' here indicates a restricted privilege; it is socially confined and describes certain legal rights and duties. Among the Stoics, this restricted notion was extended or universalized in keeping with the general emphasis among Stoics, Sceptics and Epicureans on the law of nature and the importance of everyone's adjustment to it despite the vagaries of fortune and accidents of birth and privilege. For the Stoic, everyone is an autonomous moral centre, capable of self-conscious reflection and choice that enable a rational accommodation to the order of things. But although the Stoics in this fashion affirmed a universal community of humankind, they did not call for social reforms that would reflect their teaching about the essential equality of persons, and despite various scholarly claims to the contrary, Stoicism had little effect on Roman jurisprudence. It was easy, after all, to reconcile a proclamation of universal human freedom with the facts of slavery through *apatheia*, exhorting us to pass beyond the accidents of fortune towards an encompassing harmony with the order of the universe in which we participate through the seeds of reason in each of us. This emphasis on reason helps to distinguish the Stoic idea of what it means to be a person from the Christian, which, however, eventually drew a good deal upon Stoic morality.

SD, 15–16

6.

It is worth noting in this context that the Greek *prosopon* is used several times in the New Testament, mainly to indicate that God is no respecter of persons (1 Peter 1:12; James 2:9; 2:1; Colossians 3:25; Ephesians 6:9; Romans 2:11; Acts 10:34; Galatians 2:6; Matthew 22:16; Mark 12:14). Mainly, we are to understand here that God does not favour persons privileged by rank or social caste, and the restricted social meaning of *prosopon* is counterpointed by the startling, radically universalizing claim about human worth and identity centering on Jesus, as stated in Galatians 3:28: 'You are with respect to the one, neither Jew nor Greek, slave nor free man, male nor female, for you are all one in Christ Jesus.' From the start, that is, Jesus' message was eschatological, and was a means of cutting across social and religious barriers. Although he preached to Jews first, Jesus extended his mission to gentiles, and the early church soon declared its universality. In his unremitting emphasis on righteousness, dignity and responsibility regardless of nationality or social caste, Jesus gave new content to the worth of human individuals: a new identity, we might say, to the human person, embracing the *anawim*, the depersonalized of the Roman Empire, those who were non-persons in the old sense of the word. Learned opponents of Christianity, such as Celsus, were quick to see the insurrectionist potential of such claims, and Christians were widely held in suspicion as a threat to established order. As we shall see, Christians themselves were aware both of the radical nature of Jesus' teachings, and also of the need to co-operate with the Roman authorities. Here, as Troeltsch shows, Christians were to learn a good deal from the Stoics.

One main adaptation by Christianity of Stoic ideas came through the fact that Jesus was interpreted by early commentators as the *Logos*, the formative, creative principle of the universe itself, understood philosophically. As in Stoicism, so also in many of the early Christian Fathers we find the idea that we participate in a universal ontological order through the 'reason seeds' (*logoi spermatikoi*) in ourselves, just as we participate in Christ. Thus, as Justin Martyr (c. 150) says:

> *Christ is the First-born of God, and we have shewn above that He is the Word [logos] of Whom the whole human race are partakers, and those who lived according to reason [logos] are Christians.*

In this context, Boethius (480–524) would eventually offer his influential definition of the person as an 'individual substance of a rational nature'. Boethius was strongly influenced here by Stoicism, and his 'rational substance' is, in effect, an individuated *logos* participating in the universal *Logos*, the intelligent order of creation itself. This ontological view of the person remained authoritative throughout the Middle Ages, helping to produce theological definitions of God as a trinity of persons by analogy with the psychological experience of humans created in God's image and encountering one another in the world.

Here we might also consider the fact that during the Middle Ages the word *persona* has a complex political history. Arno Borst describes how this is so, showing how various senses of the word combined and were modified to serve different political agendas. Thus, in the compilation of the *corpus iuris civilis* under Justinian, *persona* indicates both an individual's private legal status and also the function of a legal officer, who is a *persona publica*. By contrast, the Vulgate uses *persona* to mean any powerful individual (as in the warnings against 'respect for persons'), and also to indicate a representative function, as when Paul forgives his enemies *in persona Christi* (2 Corinthians 2:10). For Paul, Christ's 'person' unites the several parts of the church, and a Christian's true identity is discovered by participation in Christ's *persona*.

These different senses of *persona* combined also in various ways in medieval theories of kingship, definitions of public office, and in the self-definitions of monastic and other communities dedicated to the headship of Christ. For instance, in the Benedictine Rule, *persona* indicates an individual's worldly, exterior condition, whereas among the Carolingians, a monarch's public role is identical or fused with an individual's private identity, so that the king in fact becomes the royal *persona*. During the eleventh century, the Carolingian equation was modified so that office and *persona* were again separated, and the individual *persona* and the *persona* of the office were kept distinct. Debates on such issues were frequently influenced by theological speculations about the divine *personae*, and Abelard, for instance, held the theological meaning of the word to be the only real one. In this context, Otto of Freising, who criticized some of Abelard's teachings about the divine persons, nonetheless stressed that human individuals could not achieve true personhood, so that, as Borst says, 'the human *persona* did not imply constancy and identity: at the most it merely implied the process of the dissimilar becoming similar'. Only with the closure of history itself would the human arrive at true personhood.

These various interlocking meanings and applications of *persona* are of great interest, and by and by I will return to some of them in more detail, though, as I have indicated, my main aim here is not so much to define the conceptual uses of the word 'person' as to assess how the personal is assessed in the different kinds of literature under consideration. For now, it is sufficient to remark that the way to Locke's modern emphasis on consciousness as the key to personal identity lay through Descartes (1596–1650), who continued to use the Boethian and medieval terminology by describing the mind as a 'thinking substance' set over and against a soulless universe, the 'extended substance' of matter. But although Descartes' vocabulary remains medieval, he was busy de-ontologising the universe in a revolutionary way: matter is no longer a 'pure potentiality' as for Aristotle and Aquinas, but a corpuscular mass driven along lines of force. Over and against it, the 'thinking substance' of the human mind alone guarantees our rationality and humanity. Thus, Descartes' division of mind and body marks the beginnings of Locke's equation of the person with a unified consciousness, thereby effectively disregarding the complex history of the concept.

SD, 18–21

The fact that personal knowledge develops through encounter and relationship does not mean that our dealings with others are always personal. This is so because some degree of depersonalization is necessary for the conduct of day-to-day life. Still, the consequences of a persistent objectification and instrumentalising of others are harmful, especially in a free-enterprise system that places a high value on competitive individualism. In the interest of promoting personal values, some basic understandings and conditions need to be agreed upon and implemented, as the following excerpts suggest.

7.

As Mounier and Maritain point out, a certain amount of depersonalizing is necessary for the day-to-day operations of society. Yet persons grow and develop in relation to others, and so the liberation of each is accomplished through the liberation of all, if only because persons are ineradicably social. Still, there is no easy resolution of the tension between the claims made by society upon the individual, and the personal aspiration to a measure of autonomy. At the very least, the 'personalist socialism' explored a generation ago by Berdyaev, Mounier and Maritain sets minimal conditions for addressing this problem. Today, such a view of personal agency is re-configured by a widespread, post-modern sense that different initiatives are appropriate for different groups in the 'associative interweaving of sociopolitical micro-units' described by Michel de Certeau, intimating a flexible, personalized socialism for the times, which as yet has found no sufficient cohesion as a political force and to which the neo-liberal economic order stands resolutely opposed.

As I mentioned earlier, Karl Marx very effectively describes the processes of depersonalization by which capitalism produces widespread inequality. Ironically, however, capitalism sought to remake society by valuing the same material achievements as its Soviet communist adversaries who likewise promoted vast industrialization at the cost of the good of human persons. As Emmanuel Mounier said in 1938, the 'régimes and programs of the right and of the left all converge towards this unfettered materialism which is the real Leviathan of our epoch'.

PP, 18–19

8.

Without common goals and in the absence of solidarity, success is widely equated today with occupying a position sufficiently powerful to get you what you want, pitched against your rivals. Yet such an attitude produces a mere parody of community, which is to say, it produces a society built on negative interdependence, where equality consists mainly in the right to affirm difference. Although this right is valuable, an exclusive emphasis on difference is debilitating, and an excessive stress on individualism ironically promotes its opposite, namely authoritarianism, if only because strong regulation is required to keep the babel of special interests in order.

The same is true, analogously, of persons. Post-modernism is keen to assert the fragmentation of human identity and the fictional, provisional nature of the self. But if the principle of fragmentation is pushed too far, we end up denying that persons can act coherently over time, or shape their lives on values, the pursuit of which gives them an identity and a social function or vocation. In this context, personalism offers a way to acknowledge differences, and also to affirm equality.

PP, 173

9.

In summary, I take 'personal' in a traditional sense to indicate a way of understanding human beings and the cultural and political means by which they organize their common life. That is, individuals are said to enter into personhood through relationship entailing a recognition in the other of a sentience and intentionality akin to one's own, together with a shared sense of strangeness, or difference. Because the personal develops always from and through the inter-personal, it follows that in the social sphere the good of all is returned as the good of each, so that the realization of communal goals is also the self-creation of those agents, or persons, who bring them about. The analogue of this process in the realm of verbal discourse is what I mean by dialogue.

DA, 10

Within the perennially unresolved tensions between individualism and the common good, literature especially helps us to understand how personal values are shaped through dialogue and narrative. 'The self is a telling', as Robert N. Bellah says, and the following excerpts deal broadly with literature in this context.

10.

Elsewhere, I have dealt in some detail with recent literary theory in order to propose a view that literature awakens us to experiences with which we are familiar, but which are occluded and dulled by habit or convention. Literature, that is, discloses and discovers aspects of our relationships with the world and with one another which we recognize as true and compelling. This view has recently been argued by A.D. Nuttall, George Steiner, and Northrop Frye, among others, and in the foregoing pages I take 'literature' to mean a kind of writing that awakens us to the lively interpenetrations between ourselves and the world, ourselves and one another.

In this context, the idea of the person is relevant because the fact that we can be awakened to new recognitions of our belonging together entails that we habitually exist to some degree in a state of mutual alienation – a fact to which we also can be awakened. And so people are drawn to the future by aspirations arising in the context of present alienations, which are in turn understood through the intimations of belonging and mutuality that offer a release from such constraints. No description of what it means to be a person amounts to a definition revealing ourselves to ourselves transparently, outside the history that inhabits us as we inhabit it. Consequently, persons are understood through the narratives of their becoming, the stories we tell.

SD, 158–9

11.

The development of the secular teaching of literature in England and America during the twentieth century offers an evaluation of the personal that might counteract the ills of technologizing facelessness and of the negative interdependencies resulting from an all-but sacralized individualism, the law of each against all. Today, it is a moot point in America and England alike whether or not the 'literature industry' has been assimilated by the systems against which it might best countervail. At any rate, as I have argued, literature's singular contribution is to enable us to encounter in a heightened form the forces by which persons are constituted, taking up a position in history, called to transform the situation within which they find themselves, at once belonging and alienated. And yet, literature in itself prescribes no specific political policy or practice.

SD, 173

The following pages consider two authors, Nicolai Berdyaev and John Henry Newman, who exemplify the points set out in the previous two excerpts.

12.

Under the new communist regime, Nicolai Berdyaev was elected professor by the faculty at the University of Moscow, despite the fact that he had no degrees. Not surprisingly, he soon found the revolution too authoritarian and materialistic, and he spoke out against its brutality, which he thought in some respects worse than the old regime. He was arrested twice, and was exiled from Russia. He was lucky to escape with his life, and before leaving was required to sign a document proclaiming that if he returned he would be shot. In 1922 he departed for Berlin.

Berdyaev stayed in Germany for two years and in 1924 moved to Paris, where he remained for the rest of his days. With the rise of National Socialism in Germany, he took a stand against Hitler and the collusions of Pétain. He deplored anti-Semitism, and attacked the Nazis as more dangerous and wicked than the Bolsheviks. Yet again, he was arrested and interrogated, and again his life was in jeopardy, though he was eventually released, unrepentant.

In the years preceding the outbreak of war in 1939, Berdyaev wrote his most compelling books, including *The Destiny of Man* (1931) where he sets out and explores what he elsewhere describes as his main themes: 'uncreated freedom, God's need for human creativity, objectivization, the priority of personality and its tragic conflict with society and the world order'. The links between freedom and the personal remain at the heart of Berdyaev's mature writing, and he developed a philosophy combining his theories of personal freedom with a strong commitment to socialism. In formulating such a position, he avoids the pitfalls of the 'empty' freedom I described earlier, and also the materialist reductionism that would deny to individuals the dignity of personal agency altogether. He was still working on these issues when his sister-in-law, Eugenie, found him dead at his desk on 24 March, 1948.

Despite the spontaneous intuition in which he says it originated, *The Destiny of Man* is the most systematic of

Berdyaev's typically unsystematic works. He begins by attacking 'objectification', by which he means the idea that things can be known without the participatory activity of a knower. This argument is basically Kantian, and Berdyaev owed much to his early reading of the great German philosopher, who persuaded him that 'knowledge is an act in and through which something happens to reality'. In short, we are immersed in a mystery that we can never fully know objectively, and in so far as knowledge awakens us to the mystery, it is spiritual. Also, knowledge enables us to create values, and in so doing to taste the bitter fruit that grows from the distinction between good and evil. Indeed, for Berdyaev, freedom is basically 'man's creative energy resulting in the production of values', and life's tragedy stems from the fact that freedom to choose good entails freedom for evil.

PP, 108–10

13.

Berdyaev prefers to replace the matter-spirit dichotomy with a distinction between choices that liberate and those that enslave. As he everywhere insists, freedom lies in the production of values and must be won by creative action in a world deeply riven by paradox and contradiction. In short, freedom is a task, and persons are called to work at transfiguring their material world instead of remaining passive under its impersonal mechanisms. Also, because human beings do not properly exist apart from others, Berdyaev favours the idea of *sobornost* ('brotherhood'), a close equivalent of the 'communality' espoused by the French personalists. Here he declares himself anti-individualist, condemning the institutionalized selfishness of capitalism as destructive of human community.

Berdyaev goes on to explore what he feels is a perennial conflict between creativity and morality governed by law. He acknowledges that the rule of law is positive in so far as it preserves and protects people from violence, oppression and exploitation. But the law also reduces human behaviour to actions directed by a common or herd mentality, and is powerless to bring about the creativity through which individuals become persons. Here, as everywhere in his work, he singles out Dostoevsky's 'Legend of the Grand Inquisitor' because of its penetrating depiction of how people prefer freedom to socially-legislated happiness, even though freedom can be exercised only at the cost of allowing the possibility of evil. This is the main point at issue between the Grand Inquisitor, who engineers a social utopia, and Christ, with whom he debates.

So far, then, Berdyaev assures us that law has a positive dimension, but also that we need to struggle for social justice against the insufficiencies of legalism. Moreover, the fact that the state produces order by force is contrary to the Gospel; consequently, there can be no Christian state, and the tension between creative freedom and society is to remain until the Kingdom of God is realized, and the state will wither away.

Berdyaev describes himself as a mystical anarchist, but he sees the Kingdom intimated more truly in socialism than in capitalism with its fantastic stock exchanges and fetishisms, its pitiless materialism and heartless complacency. He deplores bourgeois materialism (which he finds also in communism), and argues that we must take seriously the 'partial truth of socialism, at any rate the negative truth of its struggle with capitalism'.

PP, 111

14.

In his account of Newman's philosophy, Edward Sillem notices that its focal point is 'the existence of the self as a human person', and that 'Newman conceived his philosophy in terms of personal thinking'. By this, Sillem means that Newman finds it difficult to deal with ideas 'apart from persons' and consequently there is a strong dialogical and autobiographical element throughout his writing. This is especially evident in the *Apologia*, but it is clear even in a work like *The Grammar of Assent*, an examination of the philosophical problem of certitude, written partly in response to the agnostic William Froude. Newman leaves us with a strong sense that the book is written to persuade a particular interlocutor, and his solution to the problem of certitude focuses on the idea of the person, which Newman engages not just through logic but by way of an assessment of the lived experience of dialogical thinking. In short, Newman's is a philosophy of personal encounter, and in the *Apologia* he assures us that 'It is face to face, "solus cum solo", in all matters between man and his God'. Newman's ability to capture in his writing this sense of a personal 'face to face' encounter is the foundation of his literary reputation, and today the *Apologia* is studied at least as much by students of literature as by students of religion.

SD, 135

15.

Newman especially attacks those who would reduce the person to something that can be defined and assessed in the manner of Descartes and Locke, or who would regard the person merely as a centre of individual feelings on the 'Shelleyean' model, as he says. For Newman, personal certitude emerges in complex ways from feeling states in combination with our thinking processes. For instance, although dogma is deduced by reason, the process of deduction engages our whole personality as thinking and feeling creatures. This position reflects Newman's teaching that although notional assent and real assent remain distinct they also interpenetrate, and his idea of the person takes this into account. Consequently, he everywhere insists on religious dogma against the liberal view that would treat religious belief as a matter of private opinion or subjective feeling. At the same time, he values the person as an autonomous centre of individual experience.

This brief account helps to explain why Newman does not develop a precise definition of the word 'person'. The whole point is that the personal elicits and requires 'real assent', and so must be explored by participation as well as formally described. Indeed, for Newman, one way of arriving at an acceptable idea of the person is precisely by grasping the deficiencies of liberalism, as he brings us to see by attacking a series of formulations in the empirical and rational philosophies deriving from Locke and Descartes. Edward Sillem shows in detail the extent of Newman's engagement with the empirical and rational traditions, but the crucial point for the present argument is, simply, that Newman's thinking about the person would not have emerged as it did had there been no Locke to encounter and rebut.

SD, 140–41

The foregoing reflections on the idea of the person bring us now to two examples of how far-reaching the consequences of what we decide about this topic are. The examples deal with two state executions in the United States.

In 1983, Karla Faye Tucker murdered two people with a pickaxe and was sentenced to death. In the following fourteen years she became a reformed person, and by all accounts was rehabilitated. In 1998, despite protests from across the globe, in Huntsville, Texas, she was executed by lethal injection.

In 1981, Ricky Ray Rector shot and killed a policeman and then turned the gun on himself. He survived but was brain-damaged and incapable of fully understanding his situation. Nonetheless, he also was executed. To what extent can we say that Karla Faye and Ricky Ray were the 'same persons' who committed the crimes, given that they were both profoundly changed over time?

16.

Vindictive self-righteousness is one unfortunate liability of an exaggerated view of the stability and enduring identity of the self, which is presumed to have responsibilities that have eternal consequences. As a moment's reflection makes clear, the self is unstable, volatile, and often fragmented, and the changes that can occur to a person over time can be on the order of a virtual metamorphosis. Yet pushing this point too far also leads to absurdities, because if there were no continuity whatsoever, we could not act purposefully, even in performing the simplest tasks. The challenge is to balance the fact that, on the one hand, our ideas about perfection awaken us to imperfections for which we assume responsibility, striving to do better, and, on the other hand, our imperfections and uncertain self-identity are part of what we are – unstable creatures emerging into more or less adequate ways of knowing, who are volatile and need to understand our mutual insecurities in order to get along without resorting to ego-inflated self-righteousness or callous indifference.

With these points in mind, I would like to consider

two examples in which the interpretation of responsibility in relation to self-identity is, literally, a matter of life and death. These examples are executions conducted in the United States by two governors who would later become president.

IM, 80

17.

Of course, there is continuity: Karla was once a child, and there is a physical and psychological connectedness all the way back. But in 1998, Karla was no longer that child or her juvenile self, any more than a sunflower seed is the sunflower. As Derek Parfit explains, our identity is like a rope, no single strand of which is continuous along the entire length; just so, our connections to our past and future selves are a complex interlacement of overlapping elements. Consequently, we are not so much self-identical individuals as provisionally stable amalgams of psycho-physical effects, values, beliefs, goals, and habits. Parfit cites Hume in suggesting that persons have the same kind of unity as does a nation of commonwealth – such entities exist, but no underlying essence survives when they are dismantled. Likewise, human persons do not have an independently existing soul, and although we might wish for more, the fact is that we do not know what happens to us after we die, and we tell ourselves stories about an afterlife to provide purpose and stability in an imperfect world where there is much suffering and injustice and where we are all at last condemned to perish.

IM, 84–5

18.

As we see, Karla was rehabilitated, and not even her

executioners disputed the fact that she had become a richer, more compassionate human being, a threat to no one. Ricky Ray also was changed, but he was less than he had been (rather than more, as in Karla's case), and no one disputed that he was brain-damaged and irreparably diminished in his capacities. Of course, the justice system in the United States (as elsewhere) recognizes that people change. Diminished responsibility, mitigating circumstances, rehabilitation, and early release for good behavior are familiar currency in the assessment of culpability and punishment. Yet, despite such provisions, judgment remained firm on the assumption that Karla Faye and Ricky Ray were sufficiently the same as they had been and that they therefore remained wholly responsible.

Karla's last words were a promise, now that she was going to Jesus, that she would wait there to welcome her friends (including the warden). Ricky Ray, when given a final meal, thought he would save his dessert for later. In each case, I would want to suggest, the probability is about equal. Meanwhile, the prayerful Bush reassured anyone who cared to listen that 'judgements about the heart and soul of an individual on death row are best left to a higher authority'. That is, God alone knows the secrets of Karla's soul, and Bush humbly submits to God's higher judgment while getting on with the business of taking the life from her body. Leaving God's mercy to God alone while imitating God's vindictiveness affords a two-edged legitimation against which Karla Faye, Ricky Ray, and the nameless and innumerable multitude like them, have stood no chance at all.

The great delusion here is that we can know in the first place about God's intimate concern for each of our immortal souls, or that we have the permission of a perfectly loving God to kill others. Some Christian theologians (for instance, the French Protestant Jacques Ellul and the Irish Catholic James Mackey), as well as many Christian believers across the denominations, refuse to justify the taking of human life in God's name. Yet the moral perceptions of such people are not shared by the more zealously vindictive among their Christian brethren who peruse the Good Book and readily enough find other ways to sow the seeds of God's love on earth.

Certainly, children playing in Baghdad and the Sudan had never heard of Karla Faye or Ricky Ray, any more than they had heard of cruise missiles. Like children anywhere, they probably for the most part looked forward to the adventure of growing up. They could not be expected to imagine how they would become the beneficiaries of yet another act of principled destruction, responsibly and righteously undertaken by the good governors who had put themselves to school in the death chambers of Texas and Arkansas before each, in his turn, became president of the one nation, under God.

IM, 86–7

In the twentieth century, the idea of what it means to be a person was greatly influenced by the development of psychoanalysis. If we think of Newton as secularizing space and Darwin as secularizing time, then Freud can be said to secularize the soul, or psyche. As a result, psychoanalysis parted company with traditional religious belief and observance.

Like Freud, Jung held himself to be secular and scientific, but Jung found a way to re-connect the therapeutic aspects of religion with psychoanalytic practice through his understanding of symbolism. In turn, the arts might likewise be, as he says, 'therapies for the sorrows and disorders of the soul', and for Jung there is a strong continuity between the domains of religion, psychoanalysis, and literature.

One result of the evolution of the practices to which Freud's thinking gave rise is that lengthy analysis has today by and large given way to short-term therapies in which the discernment of the therapist and the co-operative understanding of the patient outweigh doctrinaire convictions about method, orthodoxy, and the like. In short, an increasingly hermeneutic approach has brought psychotherapy closer to the practices of literary discourse focused on the analysis of texts, as, for instance, Jacques Lacan and Paul Ricoeur point out. And so, as Jung proposed, the boundaries between psychoanalysis and literature are not hard and fast, and the therapeutic process is co-operative and is directed at personal integration, however unfinalised that process remains, as the following excerpts indicate.

19.

Anthony Storr's hermeneutic emphasis, stressing the advantages of relatively short-term therapy and focusing on object relations (that is, attributing problems to a variety of interpersonal relationships rather than to traumatic and unconscious repressions in early childhood), overlaps extensively with the interpretations of psychoanalysis offered by Jürgen Habermas and Paul Ricoeur, both of whom agree about Freud's 'scientistic self-misunderstanding'. Both also advocate a hermeneutic approach privileging the patient's self-reflection and insight as criteria for judging the effectiveness of the therapy.

For Ricoeur, the psychoanalytic relationship is mainly verbal and is concerned with meanings that can be 'deciphered, translated, and interpreted'. The aim is to restore to language a capability of speaking the subject's desires, thus overcoming the traumatic blocks that have replaced a free expression of emotion with compulsions to repeat. Remembering, says Ricoeur, must replace repetition, and in bringing about this result, memory constructs a narrative, recovering for the patient a story recognized as coherent and adequate to the facts of the case and to what we know of ordinary life. Psychoanalysis thus has an investigative side and a therapeutic side – that is, a set of relations having to do with meaning, and a set having to do with force. The investigative side has a strong affinity with textual interpretation (the psyche is a complex text to be deciphered); the therapeutic side is concerned with working through the analysis towards self-understanding.

PV, 82–3

20.

For Lacan, one consequence of human prematuration at birth is that infants are physically uncoordinated and helpless, but spend a lot of time gazing and hearing. In this condition, they experience the body as fragmented, but through seeing other people they also imagine the body as a totality. Every human subject thus becomes aware of a unified, external form of a body even while experiencing internal fragmentation and chaos. This 'mirror state' occurs at approximately six months of age, when an infant apprehends others as it would an image of itself in a mirror: that is, as a satisfying unity to which it aspires. Mirror images of the integrated self are subsequently developed in various ways through encounters with other persons and things, but the mother is especially significant because a child's earliest feelings of fusion and unity are centered on her.

Although the period of separation from the mother is traumatic, Lacan reminds us that separation must occur for a child to recognize its cultural obligations and become socially adjusted. This process is what is meant by castration (separation in its various forms) and by the Father (mediator of the Law, the cultural order), who bears the phallus (symbolic agent of separation). Thus, each human infant develops from an early stage of bodily fragmentation, through the *imaginary* identifications and misrecognitions of the mirror stage, and into separation and the *symbolic* order of culture, marked by absence and difference. Emergence from the 'imaginary' to the 'symbolic' occurs especially with the acquisition of language, the key agent of human acculturisation, for the child acquires language at the same time as it experiences separation from the mother and from the 'full' imaginary union that she represents. Metaphoric identifications of the mirror stage are then replaced by a metonymic process whereby words mark the difference or gap between desire and its object. Basically, words signify a lack or difference, and it is easy to see how Lacan draws here on Saussure's ideas about the differential structure of language.

Lacan also draws a distinction between what he calls the 'objet petit a' (*autre* with a small a) representing our identifications with things in the effort to unify ourselves and ground desire, and the Other (*Autre* with a capital A) which eludes description because language cannot grasp it any more than language can grasp the subject, which is, as we see, defined by difference and separation. This unconscious Other is neither subjective nor objective, but leaves its trace in our experience by means of the gaps and dissonances through which the unconscious breaks into discourse, and which Lacan designates the 'real'. The ego then is basically the way a subject presents itself to itself within the threefold imbroglio of imaginary, symbolic and real, and Lacan distinguishes between our conscious construct of ourselves (the *moi*) and the *je* that actually speaks but remains occluded and anterior to *moi*. One task of psychoanalysis is to bring *je* to recognize what a fictional construct *moi* is, and thereby to 'achieve a delineation of the subject'.

The structure of language, in all this, is also the structure of the unconscious because we are acculturised by insertion into a language that always means more than we know and precludes us from saying all that we want. Lacan's own oblique, enigmatic style foregrounds the difficulty of expressing his claim that the unconscious is structured like a language; consequently, as with Heidegger, Lacan combines philosophical self-reflexiveness and metaphoric verve to produce a sense of emergent consciousness shot through with ambiguity, ambivalence, and fugitive illumination.

At this point, we return to the general relationship between psychoanalysis and hermeneutics, for Lacan's originality in interpreting Freud through modern linguistics leads him also to Ricoeur's position that deciphering a text is like deciphering the psyche ('commenting on a text is like doing an analysis'). Moreover, Lacan tells us that an ideal Faculty of Psychoanalysis would teach (among other things) 'that supreme pinnacle of the aesthetics of language, poetics', on the grounds that the search for inferences requires 'a profound assimilation' of a language, and especially the kind 'concretely realized in its poetic texts'. That is, one must be able to respond to the fine shifts and valences expressed through metaphor and symbol, tone and diction, and to how the subject always says more than is consciously intended, as does a poem. Thus, in one description of the mirror stage Lacan reminds us that he is 'developing a metaphor', and that his schematizing coarsens and simplifies a more encompassing, more accurate discourse which, like poetry, 'discloses being'.

For Lacan, then, analysis finds people already taken up and immersed in a language, through which they can be brought to recognize an authentic subjectivity, which is also their history. All this might remind us of Heidegger, by whom indeed Lacan is much influenced. As Anthony Wilden says, 'in making his often implicit rapprochement between Freud and Heidegger, Lacan perhaps leaves too much unsaid, so much of his work is imbued with a Heideggerean viewpoint'. For instance, as Wilden goes on to point out, there is a strong affinity between Heidegger's view of the 'they self' ('everyone is the other, and no one is himself') and Lacan's view of the alienated subject misrecognizing itself in the other. But as Mark Taylor also claims, Lacan explores Heidegger through Freud's *fort/da* in order to correct Heidegger by emphasizing the absence (*fort*) upon which *da* depends. Lacan says 'There can be no *fort* without *da*, one might say, without *Dasein*. But, contrary to the whole tendency of the phenomenology of *Daseinanalyse*, there is no *Dasein* with the *fort*'. For Lacan, fragmentation and cleavage thus subtend the partial unities we experience and desire, so that presence is always also the presence of an absence.

PV, 86–8

21.

Raised upon Freud's foundations, Jung's thought deals especially with the role of the unconscious in human creative activity, and, in this context, Jung distinguishes 'self' from 'ego': 'The self is a quantity that is superordinate to the conscious ego. It embraces not only the conscious but also the unconscious psyche, and is therefore, so to speak, a personality which we *also* are'. Applied to psychology of religion, Jung's definition suggests that religious symbolism is a means by which the creative unconscious makes itself present to the ego in order to preserve and develop the 'whole' human person. In turn, this theory reflects Jung's interest in Eastern philosophy, in which subordination of ego to self is a means of liberating the eternal principle in human nature from all that is transient and illusory. The 'integrated' personality, in short, is one wherein a reconciliation of conscious and unconscious elements results in an experience of release and completeness.

LM, 80

22.

'I, Mine, Me and the like', we conclude, ought not to be rejected because ego-consciousness is bad but because of ego's *libido dominandi*: keen to grasp, ego excludes in order to differentiate, and in so doing proclaims its individuality, which is not personality. The 'individual substance of a rational nature', as Boethius' classic definition of 'person' has it, is aware both of the differentiation between 'I' and its interlocutor, 'thou', and also of their communion. Boethius' definition occurs in a treatise on the Trinity, and it has been the special peculiarity of Christian thought to describe the Godhead itself through the category of persons. Within one divine nature three persons subsist in dynamic interchange of light, life and love in which the creative power of the Father is mediated by the Son in the Spirit.

LM, 82

23.

The gradual, painstaking emergence of Trinitarian theology produced a technical vocabulary that is far removed from the kind of personal encounter the New Testament stories enjoin and express. Yet the debate about the meaning of persons in Trinitarian theology also confirmed in theory the dignity of each human being created in God's image as a centre of infinite worth. The idea of the person has evolved through a dialectic between such attempts at conceptual understanding and the kinds of immediate personal exchange that provoke the need for a further, encompassing understanding; a dialectic, that is, between the *persona* of the theologians and the transfigured *prosopon* of the other whom we meet face to face, a dialectic that is taken up in turn by modern psychotherapy.

SD, 45

Psychoanalysis focuses on the individual person, but for Karl Marx, capitalism produces an especially damaging form of individualism by sacralizing selfishness, the law of each against all in the pursuit of profit and capital accumulation regardless of the wellbeing of others. As we see, psychoanalysis warns against ego-inflation and the distortions caused by the ego's *libido dominandi*, but the main emphasis of psychoanalysis is not on the economic and social questions with which Marx deals. Nonetheless, it is arguable that the most powerful strands of the psychoanalytic and Marxist traditions converge in the shaping of a credible modern view of personal agency. A brief outline of Marx's governing ideas can help to clarify how this is so.

24.

T.S. Eliot once observed that a Christian ought to have good reasons for not being a Marxist. Eliot himself did not dwell much on the reasons, but he recognized the basic challenge Marxism offers to Christian praxis. As history shows, the exercise of charity as the main rule of life has hardly measured up to the theory of charity as selfless giving to others. A Marxist would claim that history shows instead how modern Christianity has been widely appropriated by the competitive and self-serving ideology of liberal individualism, just as it was previously by feudalism. Consequently, to a large degree Christianity has served as the instrument of oppressive forces against which, in theory, it raises its voice. By contrast, Marx approaches history by looking first to the material conditions of production. He tells us that labour is the chief instrument of human self-creation, and control over the means of production confers control over the human beings whose labour produces what is necessary for the satisfaction of human needs. The result is a perennial condition wherein the wealth of a dominant few is founded upon the enforced labour of many. Thus, in the ancient world, slavery was the basis of economic life in a wide variety of civilizations. In the Middle Ages, feudalism developed under Germanic military organization, compelling the labour power of an enserfed small peasantry, and as feudal hegemony spread to encompass the towns it shaped the development of trade guilds and the emergence of a burgher class. Eventually, the rise of manufacture and the development of industrial capital in the eighteenth and nineteenth centuries produced conditions for the economic and political dominance of the modern bourgeoisie and the liberal ideology that still supports capitalism. Under the capitalist system, money no longer symbolizes labour, but has acquired autonomous power. Marx identifies the beginning of capitalism as the moment when the owner of capital encounters the labourer, whose only property is his or her labour power, thereby creating the circumstances in which human labour is treated merely as another commodity, and natural relationships are resolved into money relationships. Marx tells us that communism will abolish this state of things, liberating people from exploitation and anxiety caused by the rule of money. Yet Marx also holds that communism can come about only after full industrial development. Only when the productive forces of labour are maximized by efficient industrial technology can human beings be relieved of alienating work, and human need satisfaction be achieved by all. Increasingly serious collisions between the relations of production and the forces of production will herald an eventual breakdown of the capitalist economy, and whether or not this is happening in the twentieth century is a much-debated aspect of Marxism. The unconvinced point out that Marx's predictions have not taken account of the diversity and flexibility of modern markets, and that many of his economic theories are discredited. Besides, the so-called communist states at the present time are in disarray.

Nonetheless, Marx's attacks on the alienations and oppressions perpetrated by industrial capitalism and its enshrining ideology are highly cogent. The description in *Capital I* of the factory system, the horrors of vagabondage, child labour, addiction to opium, dehumanizing work and working conditions, is an indictment simultaneously blood-chilling and imperative. And in this context, Marx's criticism of religion occupies a special position. Basically, this criticism draws on Feuerbach, whose book, *The Essence of Christianity*, proposed that God is the human species in alienated form, and that veneration accorded to God ought to be directed back to its true object, humankind. For Feuerbach, the Christian claim that the human Jesus is divine is at least a step in the right direction.

In the *Economic and Philosophical Manuscripts*, Marx

develops the Feuerbachian idea that humans are alienated from their own species-being, and he describes communism then as the 're-integration and return of man into himself'. In the *Theses on Feuerbach*, Marx affirms this general position, and praises Feuerbach for resolving religion 'into its secular basis'. Yet, for Marx, Feuerbach's critique remains limited because it stops short of a thoroughgoing, revolutionary 'practical-critical' engagement. Marx points out that religious sentiment 'is itself a social product', and alterations effected in consciousness by means of a mere philosophical critique are insufficient. Rather, the structures that produce religious consciousness must themselves be changed. 'Man', says Marx, 'has found only his own reflection in the fantastic reality of heaven' and we must understand that 'man makes religion; religion does not make man'. This point underlies every effective critique of religion, and, in turn, 'the critique of religion is the prerequisite of every critique'.

The language of religious promises is thus the fundamental example for Marx of how ideologies offer illusory prospects of happiness that turn attention away from attaining real happiness 'of this world'. Here is the well-known paragraph:

> *The wretchedness of religion is at once an expression of and a protest against real wretchedness. Religion is the sigh of the oppressed creature, the heart of a heartless world, and the soul of soulless conditions. It is the opium of the people.*

Although religion here is allowed to protest against an oppressive world, it is also condemned for providing an artificial escape. Yet, in general, Marx's distaste for how the ruling classes manipulate religion to subject the poor outweighs his appreciation of authentic religious protest. 'The abolition of religion as the illusory happiness of the people', he holds first and last, 'is a demand for their true happiness'.

But if we take the critique of religion as the premise of every other critique, and grant that humans are indeed caught up in illusions and self-alienation, the problem of how to describe our true 'species being' becomes pressing. Marx takes us to the heart of the difficulty when he points out that human nature itself changes in the process by which nature is changed through human labour: man 'acts upon external nature and changes it, and in this way he simultaneously changes his own nature'. Marx never relinquished this idea that consciousness is not so much 'natural' as a product of social conditions. Thus, he tells us in the *German Ideology* that 'men, developing their material production and their material intercourse, alter, along with this their real existence, their thinking and the products of their thinking. Life is not determined by consciousness, but consciousness by life'. And in a well-known sentence from the preface to the *Contribution to the Critique of Political Economy*, we are assured that people's consciousness does not determine being, 'but their social existence … determines their consciousness'. It follows that part of the revolutionary and 'practical-critical' activity missing from Feuerbach is an engagement in the class struggle whereby oppressive structures are changed, and false-consciousness discovered for what it is.

However, if consciousness is produced by social structures and if these are oppressive, how are the revolutionaries to escape the ideological net entrapping all the others? And what then can it mean to define communism as the 'return of man to himself'? Lenin's pragmatic solution was to call for a vanguard party to effect changes that would enable the less perspicacious proletariat to see the light of day. Thus, although the masses are blinded by false-consciousness and kept in thrall to the economic *status quo*, a critical minority is apparently able to detect the mechanisms of oppression and resist them. Yet if this is the case, the social determinants must be less than determining after all, and Marxist intellectuals by and large concede the point to some degree. One favourite way of doing so is by insisting on how complex and subtle are relationships between base and superstructure, cultural formations and class struggle, as Marx himself helps to show us in his own complex analyses of actual social change. Thus the Italian Marxist Antonio Gramsci deploys but adapts the notion of a vanguard party to his call for 'organic intellectuals', by which he means an intelligentsia capable of using the resources of a culture to bring to light the real experiences of the masses. Gramsci laments the historical breach between intellectuals and the people, and insists on the importance of bridging the gap. He is also a strong proponent of the view that 'human nature' is not fixed, and that education can reveal tendencies or trends whereby people can recognize their condition and react against oppression. Clearly, for Gramsci the human subject is produced by a many-layered history it cannot observe directly, but which it is able to influence.

Gramsci's line of thinking overlaps with the more stringent and styptic analysis of subjectivity by Louis Althusser, maintaining that social relations shape consciousness to the degree that the very experience of subjectivity is itself ideologically produced: 'empiricism of the subject', we are assured, 'always corresponds to an

PERSONS, INDIVIDUALS, COLLECTIVES

idealism of the essence'. Althusser explains that ideology is so inherent in language as to constitute even our most intuitive or 'obvious' sense of ourselves. To develop this claim, he draws on his one-time psychoanalyst Jacques Lacan, whose theory of the 'mirror stage' (as we have seen) proposes that our earliest sense of personal identity depends on a misrecognition of ourselves in others. For Althusser, ideology is likewise an imaginary misrecognition, and is necessary for the ruling classes to maintain control. Yet such misrecognitions are so much a part of what we take to be 'natural' that we remain unconscious of their arbitrariness: 'those who are in ideology believe themselves by definition outside ideology'.

PV, 179–83

Marx's critique of capitalism is more telling than his account of how a new society is to emerge. His opponents are quick to point this out and to notice in his writings a soft utopianism that stands disappointingly in contrast to his well-defined analysis of the ills of his time (and of ours). Also, capitalism has become more flexible since Marx wrote, and, as with psychoanalysis, allegiance to the founder has developed in a wide variety of directions.

One often-repeated critique of Marx is simply to deny that egoism and selfishness can effectively be suspended in the interest of an ideal common good. According to this argument, we are selfish by nature and capitalism makes the best use of our self-serving, acquisitive impulses. For instance, because the accumulation of capital is sustainable only if there are consumers who have access to money to buy the goods that are produced, society at large benefits from the success of its entrepreneurs and captains of industry, however much the entire system remains unstable and subject to perpetual crises. In the last resort, the disagreement between these two interpretations of selfishness focuses on the nature of human nature itself, and, consequently, on what it means to be a person, as the following excerpts show.

25.

Marx tells us that communism will produce 'man in all the richness of his being, the *rich* man who is *profoundly and abundantly* endowed with all his senses', and, in such a condition, 'the wealth of subjective *human* sensitivity – a musical ear, an eye for beauty of form, in short, *senses* capable of human gratification – [will] be either cultivated or created'. These remarks in the early *Economic and Philosophical Manuscripts* are confirmed by a description in *The German Ideology* of the release of individual talent under communism, and Marx consistently argues for the restoration to individual human beings of capacities and powers of self-expression that have been suppressed or denied. This prophetic side of Marx has exerted a powerful appeal, not least among South American Liberation theologians of the past twenty years; in short, the utopian vision of a liberated humanity expressing itself in work and free to explore its capacities through art and culture remains an important dimension of Marx's thought. Still, Marx's chief concern was the emergence and decline of capitalism, and he consistently attacks liberal individualism. In this context, and following Mounier and others, I will distinguish in the following pages between individuals and persons in order to argue that *persons* are liberated, and not just an aggregate of individual egos. As Carol Gould says, human individuality has to be thought of as also social, and what she describes as a 'social individual' is roughly equivalent to what I mean by a 'person'. This entails that each individual has an inalienable dignity, which should caution us against the extreme of over-regulation I mentioned earlier, even while advising that we remain wary of the opposite danger caused by an unregulated freedom – the liberal individualism Marx attacks.

However, as commentators also point out, many things have changed within capitalism since Marx wrote, and there is now a great deal more social regulation in advanced capitalism than was the case during the nineteenth century. The welfare state, social security, union organization, unemployment insurance and special interest groups of many kinds have had widespread political impact, taking the edge off capitalism's excess. Moreover, as John Milbank argues, capitalism has proven highly flexible and produces not only profits but also consumer desire, mainly by manipulating the imagination through cultural means (advertising, television and so on). Consequently, workers 'can be persuaded to adore the mechanism of seduction', and indeed many of us are actively complicitous with the sensationalism and fake glamour with which we are deluged through so-called mass culture, rather than being merely exploited unconsciously by it. Thus, capitalism seems unlikely to collapse just under the weight of its own internal contradictions, but needs, rather, to be confronted by evaluations that radically challenge its depersonalizing practices.

PP, 4–5

26.

In *A Farewell to Marx*, David Conway argues that people are basically selfish and acquisitive, as the inhabitants of communist states discover when they succumb to the control of power elites, as they invariably have done. Instead, Conway favours the argument proposed by the classical economists, that self-interest is the most powerful human motive, and that people are acquisitive by nature. He points out that 'human beings, as a rule, are disposed to be self-centered in their concerns and to have only strictly limited sympathy', and, consequently, that private property is necessary to avoid inter-personal conflicts. In short, we are to acknowledge the limitations of human nature – its self-centeredness and acquisitiveness – and we should see that capitalism makes the best, most productive use of our imperfect human resources. By contrast, according to Conway, Marxism promotes an illusory, utopian concept of human nature, and this illusion is dangerous because it passes easily into intolerance and self-righteousness. Thus, communists have shown a disastrous willingness to sacrifice people to the Party, and to raise consciousness by repressing those who are held to be insufficiently altruistic. Michael Polanyi adds a further dimension to Conway's analysis by noticing how the doctrine of original sin traditionally reminded believers of an inherited Flaw in the form of unregeneracy and selfishness, thus placing a check on unlimited moral aspirations to bring about a perfect society here and now. In dispensing with original sin and with religion in general, Marxism becomes vulnerable to a messianic fervor in a secularized, supposedly scientific form, a pure moral impulse unwilling (or unable) to compromise, and thus too easily set on a path of destructiveness in the name of liberation.

In so far as the Marxist concept of individualism means selfishness, exploitation, and egoistic prejudice, indeed individualism is properly denounced. But it is less clearly evident that the words 'individual' and 'person' should be conflated. The distinction between them is longstanding in theology and philosophy, and the idea of the person acknowledges (among other things) that the human being is endowed with a degree of freedom to shape an identity in relation to others. A person's ego sustains a sense of identity and continuity, but the ego is not identical with the person. Indeed, equating one's personality with the ego, which by definition is appropriative and grasping, is what theologians mean by sin, and Marxists by 'individualism'. From a broadly Marxist viewpoint, then, literature enables us to better recognize the limitations of ego-consciousness and individualism, and to understand ourselves as both more and less than we habitually think we are.

PV, 188–9

27.

Eve Tavor Bannet objects to the 'epistemic breaks' inserted into the thirty-nine volumes of Marx's *Collected Works* by various interpreters bent on distilling out a set of orthodox positions – whether Engels, the Party, Althusser or the Marxist-Leninist Institute. Rather, she suggests, Marx's 'defining struggle' was precisely 'to overcome in this world the dualism of heaven and earth, of the spirit and the flesh'; throughout, his 'project remains essentially the same: to unite heaven and earth, spirit and matter, idea and reality *in* reality'. In short, Marx was an inveterate enemy of philosophical or religious attempts to divide these realms from one another, and Bannet sees this as linked to his Judaic roots. Both Denys Turner and John Milbank argue for much the same point.

Turner correctly insists on Marx's atheism, and warns against trying to make of him a kind of crypto-theist. Fundamentally, Marx argues that religion effects an ideological split between spirit and matter, sacred and secular, and by such means modern Christianity has brought it about that values regarded as 'spiritual' are conveniently withdrawn from the arena of history. This withdrawal then serves the highly unspiritual interest of capitalism by ensuring that spiritual concerns remain effectively divorced from the day-to-day pursuit of profit and the accumulation of wealth. While pre-empting any full reconciliation of Christianity and Marxism, Turner goes on to argue that it is 'central to an understanding of the role of Christianity in the world' that the split between sacred and secular (or spirit and matter) is rejected, and so, at least on this score, Marx and Christianity (properly understood) are seeking the same goal. Turner thus agrees with Gramsci and Bannet, concluding that Marx 'rejected the terms of the choice itself' between divine and human, and did so in the name of a socialist consciousness that 'has gone beyond the problem'.

Milbank agrees that the Marxist tradition is especially effective in deconstructing the idea of the secular, thereby disclosing the false dichotomy between religious (or spiritual) value and the processes by which we reproduce our lives materially. As Milbank says, Marx 'promisingly calls into question the sundering of the sphere of "making" from the sphere of "values"', and the main lines of his critique should be retained, even though Marx misestimated the resilience of modern capitalism and the complicity of people in the processes by which capitalism stimulates and manipulates desires and longings in order to ensure its own continuance.

Although Gramsci, like Marx, is hostile to religion, he too supports views similar to those espoused by Turner and Milbank. Thus, Gramsci praises the constructive will of individuals directed to 'giving personality to the amorphous element of the masses', and because we modify ourselves to the extent that we modify the whole complex of relationships in which we belong, 'the acquiring of a personality means the acquiring of consciousness of these relationships, and changing the personality means changing the whole mass of these relationships'. In this context, an 'organic intellectual' is one who participates in the process of transformation, remaining connected to the people while making conscious the conditions that liberate or prevent the creation of personality; by contrast, 'traditional intellectuals' erroneously think of themselves as autonomous, a position that ensures they remain pawns of the ruling social class. James Joll describes Gramsci's Marxism as 'personal', and in similar terms, Pozzolini sees Gramsci's position as an 'integral humanism' that does not negate 'personality and freedom'. Nonetheless, Gramsci remained opposed to religion, and although he is favoured by some Latin American theologians today, we should not elide the differences between a Christian view of transcendence and the views set out in *The Prison Notebooks*.

PP, 14–15

28.

Just as Gramsci held Marxism to be a transitional value, so is Christianity: that is, there is no telling, in the condition of a fulfilled humanity, how much from each of these traditions (as well as others) will have taken its place in history as a husk in the process of our emergence and how much will survive, yet changed. In the meantime, I am proposing a view of the human person as inextricable from the meaning and significance of the human body engaged in the choices by which values are shaped. As we have seen, the human is depersonalized if we treat the body as just a material thing; yet, to elevate or rarefy spirit to the extent that we denigrate the material body likewise offends against the meaning of persons, whose needs and fulfillments are also material.

As I have already begun to indicate in my remarks about Edith Wyschogrod, fresh insight into the embodied spirituality of human experience has emerged, during the past decades, from the intense self-reflexiveness of post-modernist criticism. As Philippa Berry points out, deconstruction 'has subtly and unobtrusively dissolved the clear-cut distinction between secular and religious thinking which Kant and the Kantian tradition had carefully secured'. In particular, Jacques Derrida's undermining of conceptual oppositions, and his claims about the 'dissemination' of meaning along chains of signifiers and through endless intertextual traces and crossings have been influential in this respect. Thus, Derrida's exploration of *différance* led him to an interest in the negative way of mystical theology, which has, in turn, engaged the attention of several religious writers. Among these, Mark Taylor has developed an 'a-theology' in which deconstructive play breaks the power of conventional categories and oppositions, effecting an ecstatic, if anguished, liberation. In *Erring*, Taylor suggests that the Death of God in modern thought was accompanied by a virtual deification of the self, the human agent bent on domination, ownership, consumption and utility in a manner that 'erases the difference of the other'. Especially with post-modernist, skeptical deconstructions of the self, the idea of the subject is called into question in a way that opens it anew to its own vulnerability, marginality and contingency. This fracturing of the self allows in turn a fresh opening to others, who cannot simply be accommodated and contained by the homogenizing logic of a utilitarian calculus. Taylor's 'non-centered subjectivity' resembles a similar emphasis among other post-modern theologians on the liminal, communal, and anonymous.

Thus, Don Cupitt celebrates the endless metamorphoses of post-modern culture as a means of liberation. He welcomes the excess, variety and heterogeneity of an unsystematic pluralism that undermines or deconstructs our desire for certainty and stable identity, and he enjoins traditionally religious people to see the spirit anew as an 'endless interrelatedness of everything'. In this context, Cupitt looks to secularism and anti-religious polemic as a means of 'reviving forgotten aspects of faith' by overriding conventional oppositions between secular and sacred.

In a kindred mode, Edith Wyschogrod looks also to post-modern thinking about surplus and excess, not only in *Saints and Postmodernism* but also in *Spirit of Ashes*, where she explores the significance of an idea of the self 'which rests on the primacy of the interpersonal sphere'. Like Taylor, she denounces instrumental views of human agency that lead to domination, and, in the modern period especially, to devastation – the man-made mass death of her subtitle. As an antidote, Wyschogrod looks to language that is a 'calling forth of the others into community' while remaining aware of how vulnerable the non-substantive 'I' is in its 'transactional' attempt to hold in equipoise 'the individuating aspect of the self, the I pole, and the objectified me'. Clearly, depersonalization is a prior condition for man-made mass death, and an adequate view of personal relationship calls for an understanding of how corporeal agency operates in a liminal space, the site of the radical compassion and generosity recommended throughout *Saints and Postmodernism*.

PP, 16–17

Captain Macmorris in Shakespeare's *Henry V* brings vividly, if perplexingly, to our attention how personal identity is bound up with the material and cultural circumstances that shape, but do not determine, it. The other excerpts in this concluding selection likewise emphasise how literature is especially well-ordered to express the complex status of persons in relation to their cultural embeddedness.

29.

Personal identity is established through others, and however highly one values autonomy, it is less than personal if it fails to recognize itself as formed in relation to culture and as part of a common material world.

As Paul Ricoeur points out, symbolism enables our recognition of the fundamental ties between our bodies, the world, and other people, and just as human self-interpretation changes in time, so symbols are formed into myths through narrative. Jonathan Glover likewise stresses the significance of narrative for personal identity, as does the theologian Don Cupitt, and in the same spirit George Steiner describes literary criticism as producing its own 'fables of understanding'. The present book is basically an attempt to construct a kind of fable in Steiner's sense, and my main point is that literature and criticism make available and confirm a view of the person as constituted within the play of presence and absence fundamental to language. This entails an assessment of persons as historically situated and in process of becoming through time; as autonomous and self-creating to a degree, yet shaped by prior commitments. It follows that, as persons, we begin from where we already are, and however far back we look, we find that earlier beginnings are themselves marks of a narrative already under way.

PV, 2–3

30.

In this context, literary analysis suggests two basic things about persons. The first derives from my comparison between Donne's 'The Exstasie' and the last section of Erasmus's *Praise of Folly*. Although the detailed similarities in these texts might suggest that Erasmus was Donne's source, I have resisted this conclusion, preferring instead to allow a difference between the two works that, in the end, escapes analysis. And just as the poem escapes because of its distinctiveness, so, analogously, does the human person; that is, the essence of a person is precisely that which escapes definition even as it goes on opening up new paths of communication and possibilities of relationship. By contrast – and this is the second point – in the exchange that I have described between Beckett and Havel, communication was hampered by Havel's imprisonment as well as by censorship, and although communication did occur, the constraints in this case remind us that, in general, some degree of historical determinism is inevitable. It seems, then, that persons occupy two positions simultaneously: the constraints imposed by history, and the possibility nonetheless of unpredictable kinds of relationship and communication. On the one hand, to remove a person from history reinforces the notion of a private self, which, as we have seen, leaves the body all the more vulnerable to the controlling designs of the politically powerful. On the other hand, to deny the person a radical interiority and inaccessibility pre-empts dialogue and the possibility of creative communication, without which it is all too easy to regard the other as merely an object. As Vaclav Havel writes:

It's a kind of paradox ... that I, of all people, such a

lover of harmony, who wants everyone to like each other and to be kind to each other – must live my entire life, in fact, in conflict, tension and nerve-racking situations.

PP, 101–2

31.

Henry V even has an Irishman in it: Captain Macmorris. At one point, during a conversation with a Welsh Captain, Fluellen, Macmorris declares that he wants action: 'I would have blowed up the town', he says (3.2.92), and, well, in light of recent Irish history we might recognize the flavor of that. Fluellen then tries to put in a word for taking a more orderly approach, and in so doing lets slip the phrase, 'Not many of your nation'. The rebarbative Macmorris (the first stage Irishman) replies: 'Of my nation? What ish my nation? Ish a villain, and a basterd, and a knave, and a rascal. What ish my nation? Who talks of my nation?' (3.2.124–26).

The main idea in these slightly perplexing words is that Macmorris is angry at being identified as Irish, when the whole point about the King's forces is that they unite English, Scottish, Welsh, and Irish soldiers in a grand solidarity. What do you mean by calling me Irish? Macmorris says. Would you call me a villain, or other abusive names? Well, then, don't vilify me by identifying me as an outsider to this group, this band of brothers for whom I am willing to fight and die. Here, Macmorris rejects his representative identity (as Irish) and insists that he is an individual, able to make his own allegiances, and that he should not be stereotyped.

But in Macmorris's anger, a further anxiety shows

through. He realizes that in England he will appear an Irishman, and in Ireland he will appear to have sold out by joining the army of a traditional enemy. He is touchy and sensitive about this ambivalent identity, and we might reflect on how little has changed over the centuries. But there is also a stronger point: the rhetoric of war requires an enemy – whether French or Irish – to be stereotyped in order to be demonized; yet the one Irishman in the play happens to be in the King's army. As is always the case with actual people, Macmorris is not easily pigeonholed, and his personal identity is not univocal, even though the heroes, such as Henry, need to assume otherwise to suit their political purposes.

IM, 103–4

2 CULTURE

'Culture' is a complex word that is often used in confusing ways. In a broad sense, it refers to how societies are organized with reference to their institutions, customs, and the conduct of everyday life, as, for example, 'the cultures of ancient Mesopotamia' or 'the culture of the Dene people today'. In another sense, current especially since the late nineteenth century, 'culture' refers to a social activity providing enrichment and adding value by way of museums, music, literature, and the like. In this sense, 'Arts and Culture' are assigned a special domain but are not widely regarded as central to the main business of society.

In the following excerpts, I do not favour this second use of the word, on the grounds that the personal is always also interpersonal and is therefore inseparable from the shaping of values within the living organism of society as a whole. In this process, creativity and the workings of imagination occur in virtually all walks of life, as creative spontaneity seeks formal expression so that it can be shared in society at large. In turn, this process mirrors and reproduces the interplay between the individual and the collective that is central to personal agency, so that cultural and personal values are inseparable.

The following excerpts deal mainly with culture in the first, broad sense, beginning with an influential analysis of ancient Greece by E.R. Dodds, who draws in turn on the anthropologist Ruth Benedict. The explanatory power of the differences between shame and guilt culture, as set out by Benedict and developed by Dodds, reaches into medieval and modern culture, as the excerpts go on to suggest.

1.

At this point, Raymond Williams can help to clarify and develop the main distinctions I am drawing. Williams says that the word 'culture' suggests both spontaneous natural growth and also the process of tending to (or cultivating) that growth. Applied to human society, the first of these meanings taken in isolation leads to a high evaluation of creativity and encourages individualism. The second meaning taken in isolation places a high value on training and discipline and encourages uniformity. A liability of the first, Romantic, inclination is that it lapses easily into eccentricity or dissipation, whereas the second, Classical, tendency encourages an exaggerated respect for order. Both extremes – whether Romantic volatility or Classical sclerosis – prevent the development of personal values that culture ought to promote, and which cannot be realized through too strong a stress either on spontaneous individualism or on social planning and control.

PP, 2

2.

In distinguishing shame cultures from guilt cultures, Ruth Benedict writes that 'true shame cultures rely on external sanctions for good behavior, not, as true guilt cultures do, on an internalized conviction of sin'. In his discussion of Greek religion and art, the classical scholar E.R. Dodds draws on Ruth Benedict to describe the Homeric Age as a shame culture:

> *Homeric man's highest good is not the enjoyment of a quiet conscience, but the enjoyment of tîmé, public esteem: 'Why should I fight,' asks Achilles, 'if the good fighter receives no more time than the bad?' And the strongest moral force which Homeric man knows is not the fear of god, but respect for public opinion, aidós.*

And so in *The Iliad* loss of face is especially difficult to bear, which explains why 'cases of moral failure, like Agamemnon's loss of self-control' are projected onto a divine agency whereby the dreaded feelings of shame can be transferred to an external source. Moreover, the gods of *The Iliad*, like the men, are 'primarily concerned with their own honour', so that to neglect them or to maltreat their cult is to make them angry. Nowhere in the poem does Dodds find that Zeus is ever 'concerned with justice as such', and this is so because the formulation of conceptual norms against which feelings of guilt are experienced as distinct from the humiliation caused by shame has not yet emerged.

In *The Odyssey*, however, a developing guilt culture is becoming clear, as Zeus shows himself 'sensitive to moral criticism'. He complains near the beginning of the poem that humans are always finding fault with the gods, and the poem as a whole can be read as a vindication of divine justice: 'The suitors by their own wicked acts incur destruction; while Odysseus, heedful of divine monitions, triumphs against the odds'. The moral education of Zeus, which is already beginning in *The Odyssey*, can be followed through Hesiod, Solon, and Aeschylus, and it involves the discovery of moral standards that are transferred to the gods, who increasingly represent the ideals to which people aspire. People then measure their worth against these ideals, and there is a consequent internalizing of conscience. The 'external sanctions for good behaviour' within shame culture are no longer relied upon to enforce morality, and are replaced by 'an internalized conviction of sin', the hallmark of guilt culture.

TS, 3–4

3.

One major effect of the rationalism of the fifth-century Greek philosophers was to loosen the individual from the bonds of family and clan. This process is described in Glotz's *La solidarité de la famille dans le droit criminel en Grèce*, and E.R. Dodds agrees with the major conclusions of Glotz's study. 'With the rise of the Sophistic Movement', Dodds writes, 'the conflict became in many households a fully conscious one: young men began to claim that they had a "natural right" to disobey their fathers'. The young men who listened to Socrates were no doubt stimulated to think about human responsibility in new ways, but in espousing their mentor's equation of virtue to knowledge and his insistence on individual accountabiliy in ethical matters, they found themselves also opposed to the established mores of the guilt culture of their forbears. It is no accident that the trials of Socrates, Anaxagoras, and others were heresy trials. The charges laid against Socrates were that he corrupted the young and defamed the gods. In a guilt culture interpreting the family in a traditional theological context, these charges were one and the same.

As Dodds shows, the archaic-age culture of ancient

Greece was challenged in the fifth-century by an enlightenment that was inspired by the ideals of ethical self-sufficiency and the rule of reason. But this confrontation was not simply a clash of mutually exclusive viewpoints. Long after the liberation of the individual from the bonds of family and clan was established in law, 'religious minds were still haunted by the ghost of the old solidarity'.

TS, 5–6

Every society faces the challenge of maintaining order, and in a later section I will deal with state power and the use of force in relation to this challenge. For now, Dodds' account of the development of ethical individualism shows how assertions of moral autonomy can come into conflict with traditional group norms and practices. Yet, despite the tensions, social order has to be maintained, and, as René Girard points out, stereotyping and scapegoating are perennial, ages-old means for consolidating group identity, because people pull together better when faced by a common enemy. Typically, then, hostile outsiders are accorded a stereotypical or 'representative' identity, whereby the threatened insiders regard each member of the outside group as a representative rather than a person. This process is mirrored in turn by the outsiders, and the result is the endless cycle of mutual recrimination described by the Northern Irish poet John Hewitt as an 'iron circle'.

In contrast to the scapegoat mechanism, the world's main religious traditions since the Axial Age have insisted that only a shared allegiance to universal values can break the entail of the iron circle by teaching that personal identity is not wholly determined by family, clan, nation, and traditional bonds based on kinship. These need to be superseded by allegiance to transcendent principles that in turn require new kinds of solidarity. One of the most urgent challenges of modern times arises from how, in many ethnic conflict zones today, post-Axial, universal moral aspirations are re-deployed to promote the interests of traditional groups whose aspirations are now supercharged with a passionate absolutism taken over from the Axial Age. I describe this phenomenon as 'regressive inversion'.

In a study of two primary schools in Northern Ireland, each of which is identified with one of the two main, opposed ethnic groups, 'Catholic' or 'Protestant', Dominic Murray shows how traditional cultural formations operate unconsciously to strengthen the negative stereotypes that promote regressive inversion. Still, the universalizing, self-transcending injunctions of Christianity were also taken seriously by many people in Northern Ireland during the Troubles, and were often salutary as an antidote to the 'iron circle'.

The volatile mix of ethnic identity, universal aspirations, regressive inversion, scapegoating and stereotyping, together with initiatives for creative change, remain matters of concern in many cultures in the modern world. With this in mind, I return now to my suggestion at the beginning of this section, that arts and culture are not just social embellishments but an integral part of the process of social formation. The remarkable efflorescence of literature during the Troubles in Northern Ireland provides examples of how this is so.

4.

Frank Wright's outstanding book, *Northern Ireland. A Comparative Analysis*, depicts Northern Ireland as an 'ethnic frontier zone' comparable (with variations) to other troubled areas such as French Algeria, the US South, and Prussian Poland. Wright's key idea is that the 'metropolis' (the seat of government) has difficulty disguising the arbitrariness of its power in ethnically divided colonies or satellites under its jurisdiction but geographically remote from the metropolitan centre. In short, the law that goes unquestioned close to home can appear hypocritical and callous on these 'ethnic frontiers', and the metropolis must be careful to avoid having frontier insurrections spill back to disturb the centre. Such disturbances are a special threat because the law always is, in the end, arbitrary, enforced by those who have sufficient power. Normal societies depend on a more or less shared acceptance of such power, which in turn puts the law apparently above the rivalries, violence, and lust for revenge that individuals or groups within society frequently experience. Yet the law does exact revenge, admitting no rivals even though it must seem to be above all rivalry in order to terminate feuds within its own precincts. Thus, the law often conceals its own arbitrariness, but on frontier zones where the metropolitan authority is itself questioned, the law can appear as especially hypocritical and exploitative, rather than as just and impartial.

Wright draws on René Girard to explain how violence lies hidden at the heart of every human society. Among other things, Girard argues that religions have played a key part in concealing such violence, thereby enabling societies to operate smoothly. This is especially evident in sacrifice rituals by means of which a scapegoat is made the bearer of whatever unacknowledged violent energies might otherwise disrupt the social group. According to Girard, human rivalry is basically 'mimetic', which is to say, people tend to desire what others also desire. When mimetic rivalry becomes intense, the original desired object is replaced by a preoccupation with the rivalry itself. Rivals then come to mirror one another, and each opposed faction rationalizes its own violence by accusing its opposite of being the initiator. The chains of mutual recrimination that follow are interminable unless the cycle is broken, as it can be by the enforcement of a transcendent law. Expelling a scapegoat through sacrifice helps to maintain this transcendence, both by helping to conceal its arbitrariness and by preventing internecine rivalries from spiralling out of control. For Girard, the most significant thing about Judaeo-Christian religion is that it thematises the scapegoat mechanism itself, making it increasingly conscious. In the story of Jesus' crucifixion, the hidden dynamic of sacrificial violence and victimization becomes clear, and the key message of Christianity is that, being now aware of how violence operates, people should be better able to understand how to be free of it.

BE, 10–11

5.

I have cited Anthony D. Smith's definition of ethnicity, linking it to myths of descent and shared historical memories. Clearly, ethnicity in this sense is closely linked to culture, if we take culture as broadly defined by Ernest Gellner as 'a system of ideas and signs and associations and ways of behaving and communicating' characteristic of a certain society. With this in mind, Gellner argues that nationalism is a 'theory of political legitimacy' requiring that 'ethnic boundaries should not cut across political ones', and in nationalism the state (as the agency monopolizing the means of legitimate violence) aims at producing 'cultural homogeneity': 'state and culture *must* now be linked', and that is 'what nationalism is about'. Also, because nationalism arises in response to the rapid growth of industrial society, and is inconceivable without a state apparatus, it differs from tribalism, though myths of tribal solidarity and tribal kinship structures might survive to underpin the cultural and ethnic identity on which nationalism depends. Here again, ethnicity and culture overlap, though we might also allow that 'culture' has a broader sense that could apply, for instance, to people assimilated within a nation and who do not share the ethnic identity of the majority. As Gellner says, tribalism, which is based on 'security-giving kin groupings' might survive as nationalism if it adapts sufficiently to modern conditions, but by itself 'tribalism never prospers, for when it does, everyone will respect it as a true nationalism, and no one will dare call it tribalism'. Gellner also insists – and here he is supported by Benedict Anderson – that nations are artefacts, the products of political will and cultural circumstances at a particular historical juncture. Gellner especially opposes the idea that 'nations' are there, in the nature of things, only waiting to be 'awakened'; that is, nations are not, somehow, the natural destiny or inheritance of particular ethnic or cultural groups, even though nationalist propaganda often deploys a *volkisch* mythology based on destiny, awakening, blood-rootedness, and so on. This is what Smith calls 'primordialist' (as distinct from 'instrumentalist') nationalism, and, like Gellner, Anderson insists that nations are imagined communities – invented rather than inherited or awakened by destiny. Anderson also notices that despite the typical 'anonymity' of the modern secular nation state, the idea of national identity can evoke powerful loyalties. People are willing to die for their country, and to explain such passionate feelings, Anderson turns to the vocabulary of kinship (motherland, fatherland, and so on), which suggests natural ties, and to the 'primordialness' of language (the 'mother tongue', presumably) by which we are acculturized into a sense of group identity and which links us affectively with the dead. Clearly, a sense of membership in a corporate body, instilled through language and culture, often engages people profoundly and finds ready support from folk myths about primordial origins, destiny, and mystical blood-rootedness. Consequently, it is easy to see how mythological elements contributing to ethnicity can feed into nationalism, obscuring the degree to which nations are fabrications developed in response to modern capitalism and industrialization. Gellner notices how 'supremely important and interesting' it is that 'some deeply engrained religious-cultural habits' persist as vigorously as they do in modern times, as 'intimate and pervasive values' linked directly to a religious inheritance from earlier ages and surviving with 'limpet-like persistence'.

BE, 12–14

6.

As we have seen, violence depends on a *depersonalizing* of the enemy, who thereby is reduced to the status of an object to be acted upon. To enable this depersonalizing, the enemy is usually treated not as an individual but as a *representative* of a despised or feared group which is accused of some prior fault, justifying the violence that then occurs. A representative victim also readily becomes a *scapegoat*, the bearer of repressed or unacknowledged fears and enmities within the culture of the victimizers, who consequently experience an enhanced solidarity among themselves. In turn, members of the social group to which the victim belongs will see themselves attacked in and through the victim, and will be strongly tempted to reply in kind. Reprisal then opens the floodgates of a *mutual recrimination*, whereby the difference between accuser and accused all but disappears as the opposites come to mirror one another, locked into an *anonymous mechanism* of reciprocal exchange. I will refer to this combination of effects as the 'iron circle', drawing on a poem of the same name by John Hewitt.

HD, 16–17

7.

During the 1970s, I had come across the idea of 'moral inversion' in the writings of Michael Polanyi, who explains modern secular nihilism as a violent recoil of idealism upon the educational and social institutions that gave shape to that same idealism in the first place. The irony by which a liberating discourse might set loose forces that end up destroying liberty I found highly interesting, even though such a process does not quite describe the phenomena of ethno-religious conflict. And so I have proposed the term 'regressive inversion' to describe what happens when a universally liberating religious vision is re-deployed to supercharge the passions associated with loyalty to a group. This process is *regressive* insofar as it reaffirms an exclusionary identity (the very thing that the universal religious vision was designed to transcend). Also, it entails an *inversion* of value insofar as it draws power from the languages of transcendence, informed as these are by aspirations to an absolute liberation.

SL, x

8.

In brief, regressive inversion occurs when a universalizing religious vision is redeployed to support special interests despite the contradiction entailed in doing so. In the political arena, the consequences of regressive inversion are frequently disastrous, as I undertake to show with reference to the recent histories of Northern Ireland and Sri Lanka, two islands on different sides of the world, in both of which religion (Christianity and Buddhism, respectively) has been enmeshed in politics in the unfortunate manner I have described. One result is that the ethnic dimensions of both conflicts are intensified – the very thing that the teachings of Jesus and the Buddha sought to prevent by promoting a universal morality, not dependent on ties to kin, caste, or tribe. And so the gospels tell how Jesus, Prince of Peace, taught universal compassion, forgiveness, and love of our neighbour. Some five hundred years earlier, another Prince – Siddhartha Gautama – found enlightenment as a Buddha and likewise declared a message of compassion and non-violence. In this shared enterprise, Jesus and the Buddha indeed are brothers – but in a spiritual sense in contrast to the biological variety, of which, as it happens, neither Jesus nor the Buddha was especially keen.

In Matthew's gospel, as Jesus fulminates against the 'generation of vipers' around him, his mother and brethren arrive and Jesus is informed. But he is neither courteous not gracious; instead he asks, combatively, 'Who is my mother? And who are my brethren?' To answer his own question he points to his disciples: 'Behold my mother and my brethren. For whosoever shall do the will of my Father which is in heaven, the same is my brother, and sister, and mother' (Matthew 12:48–50).

Jesus's new family was soon to develop into a hybrid collection, comprising people from all nations, including many individuals written off in the eyes of the world as outsiders, pariahs, and rejects. Whoever got the core message, regardless of social status, family ties, or nationality, could belong in this revolutionary family of love.

In an event known as the Great Renunciation, Prince Siddhartha likewise sought a new understanding of human solidarity. In so doing, he abandoned his wife and child, turning his back on family, parents, and princely duties as he set out alone on a spiritual search. Eventually, as an enlightened Buddha, he formed his own band of brothers (and, eventually, sisters): the *bhikkhus*, or monks, brought together as a spiritual family regardless of caste, social status, or tribal affiliation.

Still, neither the Buddha nor Jesus condemned family life outright. After all, the family provides our basic material needs – what the early Marx describes as our 'species being', consisting of such things as food, shelter, security, and a healthy environment. But although they do not ignore our need for basic nurture, the Buddha and Jesus want to instill an understanding that would enable us to transcend our primary loyalties to the family and kin group.

IM, 42–4

9.

Strive as he might, Dominic Murray could not elicit one favourable stereotype from either primary school with reference to the other. Moreover, he discovered that the commonly held negative stereotypes were frequently wrong when measured against the facts.

For example, when asked about a conspicuous religious emblem in the main entrance to the Catholic school, not one teacher could recall what emblem was positioned there. Yet Protestant visitors would notice this emblem straight away, and would read it as a clear signal that they were in alien territory. Likewise, when the Protestant school used the local Presbyterian church hall for school functions, this did not seem out of the ordinary to the participants, but Catholics would see it as a sign of political allegiance. Again, Murray was assured by the Catholic teachers that 'St. Jude's' was 'not really Catholic', but this was contradicted by the pervasiveness of religion during the school day (the angelus, altar boy lists, holidays for ecclesiastical feast days, preparation for communion). Teachers at the Protestant school, 'Rathlin', complained that Catholic education in general was 'priest-ridden', and, among other things, they thought it likely that there would be more singing and dancing at St. Jude's than at their own school. In fact, only one priest visited St. Jude's during Murray's one-year study, whereas ministers of religion frequently visited Rathlin. As it turned out, there was in fact more singing and dancing at Rathlin than at St. Jude's.

Murray's list of preconceptions, sterotypes, and complex antipathies is both fascinating and depressing. Above all, it makes clear the degree to which opinion in each school was shaped by negative images of the other, and to what extent this shaping was unconscious. Not surprisingly, the word 'unconscious' occurs frequently in Murray's account, and his realization of the subliminal grip of ethnic allegiances upon education was a main reason causing him to revise his opinion about reformers, whose ideals are admirable but who have not grasped the tacit dimensions of the problems they face.

BE, 82

10.

As Dunlop says, a 'culture of politeness' in Northern Ireland carefully avoids mentioning certain problems 'outside a safe circle of trusted friends' and, as one of Inge Radford's interviewees remarks, 'on the surface people mix well. We like to paper over the cracks.' The authors of *Sectarianism* likewise notice an 'unspoken code of behaviour' prescribing what topics of conversation should be avoided. That is, 'polite relationships' make day-to-day civic life possible, even though these depend on 'a tacit agreement' to avoid contentious issues, thereby preserving the status quo. The result is 'an uneasy peace – an absence of violence rather than an absence of fear'. But as Ken Logue remarks, sectarianism remains nonetheless 'the ghost at the feast of much polite society in Northern Ireland'.

Still, as Wright says, restraint also is a hallmark of people's efforts to behave compassionately, and many commentators notice the selflessness expressed in repeated requests by victims that crimes against their own family members should not be avenged. It might well be the case that genuine Christianity has done a great deal to prevent Northern Ireland from descending into a total violent anarchy of civil war. In unquantifiable ways, the injunctions of the Great Commandment are often lived out amidst the hypocritical facades that all too easily nurture animosity, not just like the ghost at the feast, but (in another image from the same play) like the serpent beneath the flower.

It seems, then, that conventions of polite avoidance at once enable restraint and also prevent engagement with fundamental issues. There is no easy method for distinguishing between these mixed elements, and in Northern Ireland people experience the conflict in a great variety of ways.

BE, 24

11.

In his book, *An Evil Cradling*, Brian Keenan insists repeatedly on how Irish he is, and how his growing up in Belfast allowed him to understand his terrorist captors in Beirut better than any of the other hostages could. Keenan's knowledge of the deep structues of ethnic conflict, he says, 'was my sword', with which 'I could cut through our captors' aggression, their perversion, their constant humiliation'. In this context, he reflects on the redundancy of Margaret Thatcher's ideas about terrorism, and at one point he confides in his cellmate John McCarthy that he quite understands the men who are holding them, though he does not condone their actions. McCarthy looks puzzled, and Keenan tells him: 'Well in another sense now you know what it is like to be Irish'. Striking the same note, Keenan protests to his captors whenever possible that he has an Irish passport, and they must be mistaken about his identity because an Irish citizen could be of no value to them. For his part, McCarthy seemed well enough aware of the tensions in Keenan's cultural inheritance, and in one of the imaginary phone calls whereby the two men amused one another by pretending to be well-known people, McCarthy assumes the voice of Margaret Thatcher, explaining to Irish Prime Minister Charles Haughey: 'There's an Irishman who's an Englishman who's been kidnapped'. Also, at times when he felt conditions were intolerable, Keenan describes how he copied the behaviour of the H-Block prisoners. For instance, to protest against having no information about why he was being held, he decided not to eat: 'hunger-strike is a powerful weapon in the Irish psyche. It overcomes fear in its deepest sense'. Thus, 'I simply stopped eating'. He tells how he piled his food in a corner for approximately a week, feeling all the time a growing elation and inner strength. Like the H-Block hunger strikers, he came to realize that his actions gave him power: 'I was in control and control could not be taken from me'. His captors were disconcerted, and at last they relented. They brought him copies of *Time* and

Newsweek, and explained that he was being held because the US Air Force had bombed Libya.

BE, 166–7

12.

Edna Longley argues that poets work 'close to the grain', and 'local pathologies' demand from them 'the precision of a bomb-disposal team: delicate dismantling which is also a matter of life and death'. In short, many Northern Irish writers are deeply affected by the Troubles, but many of them know that easy ideological allegiance with one or other of the supposed two sides is a dangerous evasion. Likewise, on the topic of religion many writers do not just avoid the issue; rather, they provide alternative means for understanding the pervasive binary oppositions that cause people to ignore the sources within themselves of the hatred they blame on those others, the traditional enemies. The culture that produces the sectarian toxin therefore also produces some of its own antidotes, not only from within the literary and intellectual communities, but also from within the organized religions. This process of production and counter-production is far from simple, and for that reason it is all the more important to try to understand it without distorting its complexities.

BE, 2

2(a) Myths, Narratives, Ideas

Our oldest surviving literature preserves a small selection of the presumably vast variety of myths and stories that through oral transmission helped to shape the earliest human societies. In broad terms, myths deal with primordial ties between humans and nature, addressing such questions as the meaning of birth and death, the origins of culture, and the primary obligations by which people develop an identity and sense of purpose. As historical continuity became better understood, myths were incorporated into quasi-historical narratives, as we see in Homer's epics and the early Bible stories. Second-order thinking (thinking about thinking) emerged as a major cultural development during the Axial Age (c. 900–200 B.C.E.), giving rise to the world's first conceptually sophisticated philosophical and religious systems. And yet, developments in conceptual thought did not simply replace myth and narrative, and still today we cannot communicate effectively, even about everyday matters, without story-telling and metaphor. The following excerpts suggest how the metaphoric and mythical phases of language continue to co-exist, however uneasily, with our more favoured analytical and instrumental ways of thinking.

1.

In the story of Adam and Eve, Genesis gives us a glimpse of paradise, before going on to tell us about our ejected first parents. The story therefore draws a contrast between what we are now in our mortal state with what we really are in our true nature if we could be restored to our proper habitat where there is no suffering and where beauty and harmony prevail. By showing us what Odyseus suffers on his journey to return to Ithaca, the *Odyssey* also evokes the meaning of home. Genesis 3 does this by showing us a quality of life we have lost, and although the exclusion-pain of Genesis is, in a way, the opposite of the return-pain of the *Odyssey*, both produce in the reader or listener the same feeling: nostalgia – a sense of separation from a lost wholeness and belonging.

How the authors themselves would have thought of these stories of course is uncertain. On the one hand, the actual feelings of an author can only be guessed at, often remotely if at all from autobiographical evidence or similar kinds of testimony. On the other hand, the images (by which I mean not the actual *phantasmata* in an author's mind, but the appeal of the art itself to sense experience as a conveyor of meaning) continue powerfully to elicit our recognition that the person who made this story did basically feel like us. Thus, although the author of Genesis 3 did not think in the conceptual terms of a doctrine of Original Sin, it is much less certain that the ancient author or compiler was not stung by a pang of nostalgia and a sense of loss, rather like those experienced by large numbers of readers through history to the present time. That is, despite the absence of an abstract critical vocabulary, the images still seem to express for us something of how it was to be human in the conditions under which the story was compiled.

II, 1–2

2.

To some scholars, Odysseus has seemed to make his way with remarkably little self-consciousness, and it has been observed that Homer has no notion of a person in the modern sense. For instance, as Bruno Snell claims, Homer has no word for 'mind', but rather a variety of words (*psyche, thumos, nous*) indicating the functions of bodily organs and their affects. Although Snell's thesis needs to be carefully hedged, he correctly points out that Greek speculation discovered the concept of mind in a philosophical sense, and with it the distinction between body and soul. In so doing, the philosophers to some degree left Homer behind, but in the manner of the Biblical redactors of the ancient sagas, they also appropriated in their search for certainty the main themes already implicit in him: the relationships between change and permanence, words and truth, reality and illusion, appearances and judgement. In short, the ancient myths and symbols penetrate to recesses where our bodies take hold of a world, and if the myths and symbols do not touch us where we all belong, they cannot bring us where we desire to go.

Here, then, the argument turns upon itself, for the old stories help us to see that the human ego before the discovery of mind is not simply equatable with the ego we take for granted as naturally our own. 'I' is not given once and for all as a kind of searchlight to look out on things, but is discovered through and among things. Descartes' attempt in the seventeenth century to found himself indubitably in the *cogito* after having called everything in doubt is therefore itself part of a story rather than the beginning of the true story, as he supposed. A retrieval of the antique past and of the shrouded realms of prehistory can therefore add a great deal to our understanding of how 'I' is historically produced, shaped by the uncertain processes of becoming through which knowledge is made. In this process, language gives us a world, though things in themselves reserve their secret as words search out the hidden interiors and culture then is a means to an end, the story of a community *en route*, finding itself out.

As Ernst Bloch says, the human is constituted within a dynamic of 'is and not-yet', for 'is' entails the presence of the past and the fact that knowledge is traditional; 'not yet' that the present is drawn, as by gravitational pull, to a condition that would repair its deficiencies, relieving it of contradiction. Literature and criticism, I want to suggest, are produced also within this dialectic, making us present to one another while confirming also our opaqueness and mutual separations, the conditions of our habitation within the narrative of history.

PV, 4–5

3.

A well-known example of what I mean by 'desirable repeatability' is provided by Marx's admiration of ancient Greek art, though Marx also deplored some aspects of ancient Greek society.

> *A man cannot become a child again, or he becomes childish. But does he not find joy in the child's naiveté, and must he himself not strive to reproduce its truth at a higher stage? ... The Greeks were normal children. The charm of their art for us is not in contradiction to the undeveloped stage of society on which it grew. [It] is its result, rather, and is inextricably bound up with the fact that the unripe social conditions under which it rose, and could alone arise, can never return.*

That is, a certain potentiality for communion between the human and nature, celebrating the body's harmony and the mind's sense of form, was shaped 'in an unconsciously artistic way' in Greek mythology and then reproduced in Greek art. This unselfconscious communion is not recoverable directly in modern society, but is recoverable – that is, repeatable – on a higher plane as an element in a culture that has passed beyond the brutalities of a slave economy. Analogously, we might point to how the intricate interlacements of medieval Romance embody a complex understanding of how, despite the oppressions of feudalism, love is a personal value we might still prize. Or again, with Dickens we might discover the humanising kindness and dignity of those whose imagination informs their sympathy for others, even as we are invited to recoil from the horrors of the industrial revolution.

'Desirable repeatability', then, is the recovery of a certain good from the literature of past times, and in this sense the thing to be repeated can energise our present hopes and aspirations. Thus, we might say, the future of the past is desirable repeatability, the utopian element that works of imagination are especially fitted to engage. However, as we also see in the above examples, evaluating a repeatable good is bound up with the imperfections of history and the experience of negative contrast that desire always and immediately produces. One special distinction of literature is therefore to give us a sense of how the good and what distorts it are engendered together.

PV, 68–9

4.

In a more worldly and pragmatic assessment of how fairy tales address our desires, the Freudian child psychologist Bruno Bettelheim alludes often to Tolkien's theory about fantasy. In *The Uses of Enchantment* (the title itself recalls Tolkien) Bettelheim admires the literary structure and Freudian orthodoxy of some of the world's best-known fairy tales as bringing to bear a traditional wisdom upon the minds of children faced with problems of growing up in a complex and difficult adult world. Sex, death, sibling rivalries, and the achievement of independence from family and parents in order to make one's way are some of the central themes in this literature. Although the Freudian imbroglios were not understood as such by the original compliers, they are expressed nonetheless with a consistency and moving power that shows how imagination can render effectively truths that the analytic mind may not fully grasp.

Whereas Tolkien talks of Eucatastrophe to describe this reassuring function of imagination, Bettelheim argues that the happy turn is an encouragement to a child because it suggests that solutions to problems of adjustment in the adult world are emergent in the course of nature itself. Developing this point, Bettelheim laments the lack of appreciation of faerie in our own day, and, again like Tolkein, he looks to the period of the scientific revolution for the beginnings of our modern disenchantment. He even suggests that 'What seems desirable for the individual is to repeat in his lifespan the process involved historically in the genesis of scientific thought'. In other words, the emergence of a modern post-scientific and critical consciousness from older modes of apprehension more fully steeped in myth and imagination requires a self-conscious recapitulation in the growth of each of us to adulthood. Bettelheim does not say how this is accomplished, but one means of expressing the same intuition is through the self-conscious recapitulation of the development of literature itself in the practice of fantasy exemplified also, for example, by Carroll and Kipling. The rise of scientific method and empirical philosophy is therefore important not only for explaining the rise of fantasy in historical terms, but for understanding the questions the genre poses to people growing up in a scientific age.

SA, 10

The term 'Axial Age' was invented by Karl Jaspers to describe a revolutionary shift in thinking between roughly 900–200 B.C.E., whereby an individual's adherence to transcendent principles, or universals, was given priority over group participation, for instance through cult practice and family obligation. The transformative power of the conceptual, critical thinking of the Axial Age can be traced especially in the cultures of ancient Greece, Israel, India, and China.

5.

The Axial Age marked a revolution in human thought and behaviour because it elevated the moral conscience of individual persons above the traditional demands of cult practice and group morality. Thus, in ancient Greece, Socrates was condemned to death for teaching young people to think for themselves and to explore the idea that universal principles are the measure of morality. He was accused also of defaming the gods – meaning that he transgressed against traditional practice and custom. These two accusations, at first apparently unrelated, are in fact closely linked: universal ethical norms are observed as a matter of conscience, stressing the autonomy of the individual agent; by contrast, the gods are the guarantors of traditional practice, the cult that binds society together not just by ritual observance but also by mutual obligation enshrined in law, social hierarchy, and shared understandings of the world and our place in it. By promoting the moral autonomy of individuals, Socrates therefore could not avoid offering a radical challenge to time-honoured tradition and to the divine authority protecting it.

Similar universalizing breakthroughs were made by Isaiah and Lao Tzu, with the Buddha and Jesus emphasizing the same governing insight as Socrates by calling their followers to realize that a person can be liberated by adhering to universal principles in comparison to which traditional loyalties, ritual obligations and the like are less significant.

Understandably, these Axial Age breakthroughs were not without conflict, not least because the bonds of family and traditional religious observance were not simply replaced by the new universalism. After all, each human being needs to be nurtured within a family or cultural group as a prior condition of achieving moral autonomy. Furthermore, family affection and a sense of family obligation continue to make a claim even on individuals who have liberated themselves from the constraints of a kin group that might have impeded or hampered their full moral and personal development. An entire repudiation of one's roots – the condition of one's primary nurture – would diminish the humanity that the liberating universal vision is supposed to enhance. Consequently, the historical conflicts attendant upon the Axial Age breakthroughs are reproduced in the development of every individual human being who lives in a society that puts a high value on moral autonomy, and where families remain the main providers of primary nurture.

LV, 159–60

As I have pointed out, the tensions between Axial Age universals and older myth-based thinking are not easily resolved. Also, in virtually every country today, traditional observances and the sacred narratives on which they are based find themselves confronted by the secular scepticism and empiricism that have produced the great benefits of modern science and technology. One major challenge of the modern age is to mediate this tension fruitfully, so that religion and art do not regard science as the enemy, and science understands the value of religion and art in helping people to address the crises of life and the over-arching mysteries of birth and death. In the positivism of the Vienna Circle, the empirical and analytical tradition reached a high point of clarity and self-definition, but, ironically, in post-modern theory ever-more intense analysis has gone on to reveal the suppressed metaphoricity of even the most apparently analytical of discourses. One salutary outcome of the post-modern critique is to show that the analytical and metaphoric, the Axial and mythic, are interdependent and not separable into watertight compartments. In short, all that we have been in the process of our evolution we still, in some sense, are.

Tensions between mythology, philosophy, art and religion are of course not confined to the modern era. Already in antiquity and through the Middle Ages, a complex antagonism between mythic and analytical modes of understanding can be seen in various fields, whether medicine, anthropology, or hermeneutics. The following excerpts provide examples of how this antagonism helped to shape the modern idea of the person. In the subsequent sub-sections I provide further examples, divided into three main historical periods: the Middle Ages, which I describe as 'Sacramental'; the Renaissance, Reformation and Enlightenment, which I describe as a period of 'Disenchantment and Discovery'; and the period from the Romantics to the twentieth century, which I describe as the age of 'Secularism and Modernity'.

6.

The main commonplaces of traditional humoral theory are quite straightforward. The ancient Hippocratic scheme, developed by Galen, held that physical health is regulated by a balance within the body of the four humours – blood, phlegm, yellow bile and black bile. As a microcosm or little world, the human being comprises within itself the four elements (earth, water, air and fire), each of which has specific qualities. Earth is cold and dry, water is cold and moist, air is hot and moist, and fire is hot and dry. Galen held that these elemental qualities are distributed in the body through the action of the natural, animal and vital spirits. An imbalance in the distribution of the elemental qualities produces a person's characteristic humour: the choleric temperament has a predominance of hot and dry, the sanguine of hot and moist, the phlegmatic of cold and moist, the melancholic of cold and dry.

Hippocrates connected the humours also with seasons of the year, and (despite Galen's disapproval of Hippocrates' theory on this point) popular handbooks of the Renaissance, such as John Jones's *Galen's Bookes of Elements* (1574), took delight in charting elaborate correspondences between humours and the seasons, the times of day, and the stages of life. Because the humours are fed by what we eat, drink and breathe, this theory was especially concerned to preserve health through diet and the adjustment of an individual to the physical environment – with 'quality of life', one might say – rather than with disease as pathological anatomy.

The foremost example in English of the Galenist regimen is Sir Thomas Elyot's *The Castel of Health* (1541). Replete with advice on purging, bleeding and puking, it is based on the idea that nature is cured by what is contrary ('as cold by heate, heate by cold, drythe by moysture, moysture by drythe'), and provides elaborate advice, together with tabulated schemes on the humoral consequences of different kinds of food, weather and seasonal change. The temperate person, for Elyot, is one whose life is balanced and whose passions are not permitted to engender excessive needs or desires. Behaving decorously – in a gentlemanly way – according to this programme, is therefore a moral matter: intemperance is less a physical compulsion or illness causing one to act destructively, than the result of free will abused by irresponsible action that consequently harms the body.

Admittedly, it is hard to believe that a thoughtful

medical practitioner could long maintain that individuals are justly punished by sickness for their sins. Doctors faced with the array of human afflictions are more likely to want to cure an illness than moralise about how the patient deserves to suffer, and in *The Methode of Physicke* (1583) Philip Barrough makes this point with reassuring explicitness: 'I have bene more curious in prescribing the sundrie curations and waies to helpe the diseases, then in explaining the nature of them ... the former being more necessarie'. Still, traditional humoral theory is sufficiently flexible to permit scientifically inclined physicians to reaffirm their orthodoxy if called upon to do so. But during the Renaissance, and as part of that general upheaval that I am describing as the discovery of method, the scientific side of medical practice developed so extensively that a serious gap opened between those who saw illness mainly as a mechanical malfunction of the body machine, and those who continued to think about it, on the old model, as a qualitative disorder that was theoretically implicated with moral indecorum.

DM, 55–7

7.

In Boccaccio, as in his main precursors from Petrarch to Macrobius, Lactantius, Jerome, Rabanus, Fulgentius, Isidore of Seville, and (Robert Graves's own favourites) Suetonius and Apuleius, one still feels powerfully the experience of language and of history as creative representations of the human condition rather than as descriptions of it. That is, the mythographers wrote in a pre-nominalist framework and, as his modern editor explains, Boccaccio speaks 'at once as poet, critic, and scholar. Nor does he from time to time exchange one function for another, but all three powers of his mind are coactive throughout his discussion, if indeed they are not really one and single'. Consequently, he 'regards poetry, classical antiquity, and mythology, as pretty much one and the same thing, a deep and abiding source of civilisation and spiritual energy; and his task is to defend, explain, and revive this regenerating power'.

SA, 46–7

8.

The term 'hermeneutics' was first widely used in Biblical criticism to set out rules for approaching a text and for distinguishing between its various senses. Biblical manuals typically divide hermeneutics into noematics (the senses of scripture), heuristics (how to discover what sense is appropriate) and prophoristics (how to convey the sense to others). These manuals aim to establish guidelines for fixing a right understanding of sacred scripture in line with shared traditions of exegesis.

A crisis for this kind of hermeneutics occurred during the Enlightenment, when a widespread critical interest in the Bible as a set of historical documents forced interpreters to regard the sacred scriptures not just as revealed, but as one element in a whole complex of cultural experiences. In this context, Friedrich Schleiermacher (1768–1834) made a distinction between special and general hermeneutics, the latter dealing with knowledge in the widest sense in relation to the totality from which it is inseparable. Schleiermacher was particularly interested in relationships between individual speakers and their language: 'accordingly, each person represents one locus where a given language takes shape in a particular way, and his speech can be understood only in the context of the totality of language'. Psychologically, that is, the person is 'a constantly developing spirit', but the inner totality can be grasped only in terms of an inherited language system, with which the speaker interacts by a kind of organic fusion or synthesis.

Schleiermacher's most influential student, Wilhelm Dilthey (1833–1911), developed his mentor's hermeneutical theory by attempting to provide a foundation for knowledge across the entire spectrum of human sciences. Dilthey proposed that understanding is a 'category of life' (*Lebenskategorie*) originating in what we take life to be in the largest sense. Human beings 'understand' life situations by immersion, and react appropriately without being fully conscious of how they do so. Acts of understanding are lived experiences not entirely reducible to language, but, rather, they reflect the complex ways in which we take our place in society, culture and history. These understandings are 'expressed' (a key term for Dilthey) in different kinds of behaviour. Yet Dilthey's work did not come to maturity before he had read Edmund Husserl's *Logical Investigations*, and since Husserl (1859–1938) is usually regarded as the father of modern phenomenology, we might see already in Dilthey's hermeneutics the beginnings of a convergence leading to the so-called 'phenomenological hermeneutics' of Husserl's student, Martin Heidegger.

The etymological root of 'phenomenon' is 'a thing appearing', and a preoccupation with relationships between sensible appearances and real essences has marked the course of Western thinking since Plato's thematising of the problem in his teachings on 'forms' and 'copies'. Throughout ancient and medieval thought, metaphysics remained the regulating science for studying sense perception, and hence also for studying physical nature. From such a perspective, language was held to disclose some aspect of the divinely established order of things.

As with hermeneutics, a major crisis occurred for the medieval, metaphysically-grounded way of thinking in the Renaissance and Enlightenment, when mathematics replaced metaphysics as the governing science for studying nature, thus bringing about what we now call the scientific revolution. In its wake, talk of metaphysical 'substances' or 'essences' and the like was widely regarded as obscurantist. Notions about language participating in a divinely-scripted book of the world were increasingly replaced among those influenced by the new scientific method by a view of language as a tool for controlling a recalcitrant and inert physical nature.

Among the new philosophers, Descartes (1590–1650) pre-eminently was concerned to foreground the mathematico-physical approach to nature, and although he clung still to medieval talk about substances, he used this terminology mainly to confirm a split between human 'thinking substance' and 'extended substance' or matter. Categorically separate from an inert, mechanical world, the Cartesian ego now becomes free to contrive the means to subject and control nature by experiments governed by mathematical calculation. The results would change the face of the Earth more radically, rapidly, and extensively than anything else in history.

I mention Descartes because modern phenomenology has been especially concerned to reject his distinctions between thought and extension, subject and object. Thus, for Husserl, the Cartesian *cogito* is problematic, even though Husserl learned a great deal from Descartes' method of systematic doubt, holding appearances and common sense in suspension. However, in contrast to Descartes, Husserl wants to describe many different modes of understanding, and science takes its place within the varieties of human consciousness, which Husserl regards as a transcendental foundation for different kinds of knowledge.

Franz Brentano (1838–1917) was important for the further development of Husserl's thought, and drew on scholastic philosophy for the notion that mental acts are 'intentional', which is to say, every thought is about something and so 'intends' its object. Consciousness therefore can be said partly to constitute its object, and strict distinctions between subject and object are untenable. Phenomenology for Husserl is then basically an attempt to reduce phenomena to the stream of consciousness, the basic forms of conscious presence. He proceeds by way of the so-called *epoche* or suspension of judgement, until the essential forms or *eideia* are disclosed to reflection in their absolute being.

To explore the mystery of Being, Husserl therefore re-deploys the key scholastic concept of intentionality to address his own specifically post-Cartesian circumstances. But also, in describing Being from a point of view that attacks the separation between subject and object, Husserl is forced to rely on a language that itself evokes the kind of presentness with which he deals. One result is a diminishment of the difference between the languages of philosophy and poetry, a point that returns us to hermeneutics, and especially to Martin Heidegger.

As we have seen, for Husserl the main point of enquiry is consciousness and its contents. Heidegger (1889–1976) carefully redirects this enquiry towards existence, the world of things, 'being-in-the-world', as he says. He does so partly by insisting on a strong identity between hermeneutics and phenomenology: "The phenomenology of Dasein is a *hermeneutic* in the primordial signification of this word, where it designates this business of interpreting'. That is, our understanding of being-in-the-world comes through the process of interpretation, which for Heidegger (as for Schleiermacher) is intimately connected with language. Through language, human beings are uniquely able to question their own existence, and with this power of questioning comes an experience of dread (*angst*), but also of hope, the projection of one's self towards what Heidegger calls authentic existence. By this he means choosing resolutely a fullness of being in face of one's possibilities and temporal limits – which is to say, death. Thus, for Heidegger the process through which hermeneutics discloses being-in-the-world is temporal. Human existence (*Dasein*, 'being there') is thrown into a situation where meaning is discovered through the merging of past, present and future horizons. In this context, Being is not an object set over against a subject, and Heidegger looks especially to the pre-Socratics for an example of authentic speech without the modern subject-object cleavage. He tells us that Western metaphysics has forgotten this original presence of Being to language, and post-Cartesian technology is the worst offender in causing this amnesia.

In *Being and Time*, Heidegger sets out to restore our sense of Being, partly by argument but partly also by breaking through the familiar concepts and mental constructs by which culture has brought about its own amnesia, its forgetfulness of belonging. Typically, Heidegger conducts us by way of powerful indirections whereby language digs back through the sediment of its own conventional sense to a revelatory moment where words give us a world – a sense of Being. The shock and wonder produced by poetry recover this sense also, and Heidegger the philosopher often contrives to produce a poetic effect of felt strangeness as a means of recovering the primordial 'unconcealedness'. By refusing in this way to treat Being as an object, Heidegger also develops the idea (deriving from Dilthey) that our 'thrownness' (*Geworfenheit*) into the world entails a tacit pre-understanding. That is, we belong beyond our conscious knowing, and in the anxious process of interpreting, questioning and choosing, we must learn again to listen to the rich presentness of Being that constitutes us, and not alienate ourselves from it by the designs of control and power.

PV, 15–19

9.

For Jacques Derrida, the binary opposition between speech and writing is especially significant because of what it reveals about the 'logocentric' excesses of Western metaphysics. Derrida claims that Western philosophy has always favoured speech, and, consequently, the immediacy and presence of meaning to a subject. But the effort by philosophers to suppress their own written discourse inevitably fails, for speech keeps turning into another version of writing in the same way as does the signified in the signifier/signified opposition. For instance, in the *Confessions*, Rousseau attacks writing in order to show how civilization has artificially removed us from our natural origins. Yet writing remains Rousseau's way of making his case, and the result is a complex double bind by which the *Confessions* is both riven and constituted. Deconstruction thus proceeds not simply by inverting a received sense, but by stressing the inter-involvements of apparently opposite terms. This is the case not only with speech and writing, but also with metaphor and concept, literature and criticism, and so on.

There are two broad ways to take all this. The first, represented by Frederick Crews, sees deconstruction as fostering irrationalism. By denying that propositions can be true, deconstruction stultifies its own discourse and reduces criticism to a futile exercise, for 'if there is no stable object of enquiry, critical debate is pointless'. If indeed there is nothing outside the text as Derrida says, and if meaning is endlessly deferred (every concept or referential term being a repressed metaphor), then there is no recourse to evidence. Deconstruction thus also precludes the development of fruitful ideas, and is soon monotonous and hermetic, as well as irrationalist. Literary critics, Crews thinks, are abrogating their responsibility by subscribing to such theories.

Derrida's defender, Christopher Norris, turns the tables on Crews' kind of argument by insisting that Derrida everywhere stresses 'the need to keep faith with enlightened reason … even while assaying that tradition's limits'; the irrationalism belongs rather to those who assume that Derrida is irrationalist, without reading him carefully. According to Norris, Derrida attempts to dismantle the Enlightenment model only insofar as it treats philosophy 'as a locus of pure, disinterested enquiry'. Derrida does not call for an end to Western metaphysics, or to 'the old mimetic regime' because he realises that there is no other ground on which to stand, and language 'is marked through and through by referential (or mimetic) assumptions'. Derrida merely would have us see that the 'classical ideas of this referential function have greatly simplified its nature'. Nor does Derrida deny the relevance of authorial intent: rather, as with Rousseau, an author's intention is often declared, but it is important to see how it is contained in a system that it does not dominate. In short, Derrida looks out especially for the signs of stress and omission, elision and marginal comment that indicate how difficult it is to reduce writing to a single or univocal truth.

Reassuring as Norris is, he ends up with a strangely tame Derrida – the lion with his teeth drawn. For of course deconstruction is right to remind us that meaning is not single, that there is more to literature than authorial intent, that there is no univocal, systematic and authoritative hermeneutic, and that we are encompassed by uncertainties and mysteries. But Derrida's sheer contrivance and ingenuity, his rhetorical pyrotechnics, dizzying obscurities and radical claims about undecidability, about there being nothing outside the text, his statements *sous rature*, and so on, lean decidedly towards the attenuation of referentiality and towards the undermining of appeals to evidence based on experience – in short, towards an extreme hermeneutic position that results from Derrida's reading of Husserl and Heidegger.

Admittedly, Derrida is a complex thinker who is aware of the paradoxes in his own expression of the inexpressible, and he is often an amused ironiser of his own arguments. Partly for this reason, he elevates the principle of play, as he explains in the influential essay, 'Structure, Sign and Play in the Discourse of the Human Sciences', describing the interminable pursuit of meaning through a text, 'the joyous affirmation of the play of the world … a world of signs without fault, without truth, and without origin'. By means of interpretation that 'affirms play', he suggests even that we might 'pass beyond man and humanism'. A similar sense of meaning unencumbered and unanchored by objective constraint is a key theme in such other playful intellects as Barthes, Lacan and Hartman, and here too we might be reminded of Feyerabend for whom, as we have seen, science proceeds not by a single method, but through 'play' in which 'anything goes'. Yet, if anything goes, everything goes, and the limitations encroached upon by Feyerabend's anti-realist account of science are much like those entailed by Derrida's non-cognitive relativism. As A.D. Nuttall says of deconstruction in general, 'without the ordinary restraints of objectivism, there is little for the first intelligences of Paris and Yale to do but play – with a sort of sub-Nietzschean hilarity, parsing and reparsing the texts'. Nuttall's point is confirmed by Richard Rorty, who claims that the later Derrida 'simply drops theory' in favour of 'fantasising' about his predecessors, 'playing with them, giving free rein to the trains of association they produce'. There is no message or method here; rather the achievement of a unique 'richness of texture' allowing no distinction between fantasy and argument. This indeed is a wilder version of Derrida than the one Norris offers, but it points to a characteristic, unconfinable and solvent energy by which Derrida celebrates mainly the freedom to refuse commitment, including appeals to common experience and the assessment of evidence that assumes our descriptions refer to a common world.

PV, 59–61

2(b) The Sacramental View: The Middle Ages

A 'sacramental' understanding of the world and our place in it remained ascendent in Europe until the Reformation and the Scientific Revolution, which, as we have seen, by and large rejected the mythical and metaphysical explanations of nature, history, and social organisation promoted by medieval culture. During the Middle Ages, the predominant 'sacramental' view shared with mythical thinking a conviction that persons and nature are, by design, meaningfully interconnected. That is, nature is the bearer of a divinely ordained significance in which human language participates, so that we consciously refer the meaning of the creation, in praise, to the creator. Our minds and the world are therefore not so much separate as implicitly connected, and the experience of felt participation in the inner life and meaning of other people, animals, the vegetable world and the movement and design of the cosmos itself is fundamental to the participatory consciousness underlying the 'sacramental' organisation of medieval European culture.

The sense of belonging within a divinely appointed hierarchy, whether in nature, the family, or the church, is central also to the guilt culture that I described in I, 2, and in this context it is interesting to consider how medieval Christianity appropriated the myths of ancient Greece and Rome. Here again, the principle of hierarchy proved helpful because the pagan myths could be allowed to convey truth as long as they were understood as subordinate to the superior, revealed authority of the Bible. The same solution was offered in dealing with the fact that, since Constantine, the institutions of pagan Rome were a vehicle for the spread and development of Christianity. Although the cities of Rome and Jerusalem remained fundamentally opposed, as with the pagan myths, Rome was allowed a role in furthering the goals of the new religion. The figure of Virgil especially exemplifies the ambivalence with which the cultural and institutional heritage of ancient Rome was regarded in the Middle Ages, within a precarious synthesis of older, mythic ways of knowing and the universal ideals of organised Christianity.

1.

By participation I mean a felt identity between ourselves

and the energies that shape our everyday world, and which language apprehends (the very sense, indeed, that modern phenomenologists would have us recover). This general notion can be grasped through the claim made frequently in medieval literature and philosophy, that thinking is not confined to the human mind, with the ego set over and against an inert material world. Rather, as in Plato's *Timaeus* and Aristotle's *De Anima*, medieval metaphysicians assumed that movement itself manifests spirit. Thus the rotating heavenly bodies as well as every living thing demonstrate a spiritual activity that indicates God's presence and purposes. Moreover, everything in heaven and earth, including ourselves, is directed to appointed ends, to fulfilments appropriate to their created natures. All of which in turn confirms a further confidence that these ends can be known and hierarchically ordered along a chain of being whereby vegetable, animal, human, and angelic natures are arranged on a scale of increasing perfection. Just so, in each human individual, the soul's reasonable part should rule its appetitive and animal parts, so that here also a hierarchy is maintained whereby the human corresponds to and participates in the creation as a whole.

In various ways, these principles were adapted to explain and justify institutions such as monarchy, feudalism, the family, monasteries, guilds, the arts and a host of other – indeed virtually all other – areas of life. Again, I do not suggest that people's behaviour conformed always to the prevailing theory, but, rather, through the multiple symbolic manifestations and endless exegesis of ideas that were presumed to be foundational, a distinctive human world took shape. Thus, from Augustine to Aquinas, and among the encyclopaedists, allegorisers of the classics, commentators on scripture, homilists, spiritual masters, and Galenic interpreters of the human body, the intricate classifications of hierarchies ends, and patterns of participation were worked out according to an infinitely pursuable *analogia entis*, the analogy of being in which God's human creation declared its belonging within a divine plan, and, consequently its hope for meaning in the face of suffering.

PV, 22

2.

Basically, Augustine's doctrines of the fall and original sin established a theory of inherited guilt that remained ascendent in the West until challenged, especially in the Renaissance, by a series of more optimistic assessments of human nature, one aspect of which was a revival of interest in Pelagianism during the sixteenth and seventeenth centuries. Reform creeds such as the Augsburg Confession and the Thirty-nine Articles specifically reject Pelagianism, which calls into question the traditional Augustinian teaching of inherited guilt, claiming instead that people are not prevented by the fall from doing good works. Cardinal Carnesecchi, an early martyr to the Inquisition, confessed his fears that the Catholic church 'returns furtively to the ideas of Pelagius', and Ernst Cassirer sums up the prevailing mood in the following paragraph about Nicholas of Cusa:

> *Although Cusanus never doubted the doctrine of original sin, it seems to have lost for him the power that it had exerted on the whole of medieval thought and on its sense of life. The Pelagian spirit is reawakening now, that spirit so bitterly fought*

*by Augustine, whose polemics became the basis of
medieval religious doctrine.*

TS, 8–9

3.

In Augustine's theory, sin is inherited from the
transgression of Adam, father of us all, and the church,
through which salvation from guilt is communicated,
is modeled on a hierarchical family. This view is present
from earliest Christian times. Saint Irenaeus, for instance,
describes the church as a mother who provides the milk of
spiritual nourishment, and Cyprian represents the church
as a mother who joins her children in a single family. It is
impossible, claims Cyprian, to have God as father unless we
also accept the church as mother: '*habere non potest deum
patrem qui ecclesiam non habet matrem*'. It follows that if
we, as children, separate ourselves from the family unit,
from the protection of our mother and the jurisdiction of
our father, we condemn ourselves to banishment. Anyone
who does so 'is a stranger, he is unholy, he is an enemy'
– an outcast, much as was Oedipus in his sins against an
earlier and not entirely dissimilar family solidarity.

In Tertullian the same themes recur. In his
interpretation of the Lord's Prayer for catechumens,
he makes clear that in the opening words 'Our Father'
we are to understand also the Son and our Mother the
Church. 'Not even the Mother, the Church, is passed by,
that is, if in the Son and Father is recognized the mother,
by whom the names of both father and son exist.' In the
closing sentences of *On Baptism*, the complete family
constellation and its connection with the inherited guilt
of original sin is clearly stated:

> *Therefore ... when you come up from the most*
> *sacred bath of new birth, and in the house of your*
> *Mother (apud matrem) for the first time open*
> *your hands [to pray] with your brethren, ask the*
> *Father, ask the Lord that to the grace [of baptism]*
> *a very special gift may be added, the distribution of*
> *charismata.*

By the grace of baptism, that is, original sin is washed away
and the outcasts and strangers become brethren, sons of
the same father and mother. The language of sin and its
remission is expressly related here to the imagery of family
reunion, within which each person is given an identity that
incurs obligations to the group. Simultaneously, however,
Christianity stresses that each person's conscience is
autonomous, and the ensuing tension between mythic
and Axial modes of thinking runs throughout medieval
culture.

TS, 10–11

Augustine's ideas about language underpin his teaching that
human beings should consciously 'refer' the meaning of created
things in praise to their creator. The *Confessions* records the
author's personal struggle to do this, as he attempts to conform his
experience to a divine providence whose ways remain obscure in a
world that Augustine believes is nonetheless inherently purposeful
and meaningful. And so the sacramental does not preclude the
existential, and Augustine's struggles still engage readers today,
even though the sacramental view of personal agency that informs
his writing is different from our own.

4.

The *Confessions* is St. Augustine's spiritual autobiography, written from the point of view of a converted Christian who believes that God was present in his life from the start even though this presence went unrecognised by the young man wandering, like Vergil's Aeneas, in search of home, or truth. As commentators have noted, Augustine's story is developed by way of a dual vision, at once recreating the young man's confusion and also showing how God's hand was already present, but undetected. Augustine's unusual inventiveness resides in the way he then contrives to open up his personal failings to the larger, typical patterns of divine Providence. Consequently, even apparently insignificant details turn out to conform to an encompassing design, though the reader (like the author as a young man) only discovers this from a vantage point later in the story, when the design is disclosed. Reading the *Confessions* is therefore a reproduction in the form of words of the personal journey towards illumination that the book describes.

PV, 31

5.

Everywhere in Augustine's work, Odysseus still journeys homeward and Israel still searches for the promised land. That is, Greek philosophy combines everywhere with Biblical religion to provide an interpretation of the Christianity that Augustine develops through the images of bride and concubine, mother and child, Eden and the ideal city, as well as through theories about typology, allegory, and the correspondences between the great myths and each person's individual psychology. These elements are massively synthesised and yet remain perpetually in tension as Augustine explores his imperfect understanding of the mystery that our awakening to the problem of suffering and death forces upon us. Certainly, without the literary distinction or poetry of his work, Augustine would be a much less engaging figure, and in those treatises where exploration hardens into doctrine and poetic complexity diminishes, his views are harsh, even repellent. But at its best, his writing develops in Christian terms the explanatory power of the foundational myths of origins and ends, of belonging and fallenness, inherited by Christianity from Greece and Israel. And already we can feel, through his very struggle for adequate explanations, a new kind of literary self-consciousness. Even St. Paul shows little evidence of the perennial soul-searching we find in the *Confessions*. In short, Augustine's spiritual autobiography is more acutely aware than any work preceding it of the internal contradictions of a person seeking to recover a sense of belonging in an inherently meaningful world while simultaneously experiencing a profound alienation.

PV, 38–9

The following excerpts from Aquinas, Bonaventure, and Boccaccio confirm how a participatory view of language underpins the sacramental understanding of the person set out by Augustine in the previous excerpts.

6.

For Thomas Aquinas the creation remains hierarchically structured with God the *fons et origo*, shaping nature according to the divine Ideas. Matter, as in Aristotle, is indeterminate and unimaginable; it is a mere potency determinable by form, which confers identity and intelligibility upon it. Between God and the realm of bodies stands a hierarchy of substances and causes comprising the corporeal, vegetable, animal, human, and angelic, all ascending towards the creator on whom the entire creation depends. Aquinas thus shares with Augustine the basic idea of a fluid, impermanent realm of matter, and of the divine Ideas as exemplars of the created world. Here the two men belong to a universe of discourse more fully divorced from the empirical nominalism which was to develop at the end of the Middle Ages than they are from each other. As Gilson says, although Aquinas's adaptation of Aristotle imparts an existential cast to his theory of knowledge, Thomistic realism remains 'heir of everything sound in the Greek realist philosophies'.

II, 15

7.

Theology, as Petrarch observed, is a kind of poetry about God, and by assuming a conformity between material substance and the Ideas mediated by the analogy-making imagination, Aquinas, like Augustine, concludes that language is a vehicle for revealing God's purposes. The force of the preposition 'in', therefore, as part of my phrase that Aquinas, like Augustine, 'believes *in* his images', is to describe this sense of a speaker's direct participation in the meaning of things. According to this theory the question is not yet whether the images are a special or arbitrary interpretation of material substance. If this were the case, they could no longer provide evidence of a God-ordained design in the world of bodies.

II, 16–17

8.

Just as the creative light pours down into the material world, giving form and shape to things (for Bonaventure, matter itself is a kind of light), so the mind, attending to nature and discovering its significance, is already on the path back towards the 'Father of Light', the supreme originator. Consequently, the human sciences are 'like rays of light descending from the eternal law into our minds. And thus our minds, illumined and suffused by such great radiance, unless they be blind, can be led through themselves alone to the contemplation of that eternal light'.

The creation, in short, is an inexhaustible multiplicity of formal relationships that human intelligence infused with desire for God can detect and admire. In turn, these signs and traces are more or less intensely brilliant and coherently organised according to their closeness or remoteness from the Father of Light, and a good deal of Bonaventure's writing describes the ascent towards the vision of God as steps on a ladder. Because 'the world is itself a ladder for ascending to God, we find here certain traces (of his hand), certain images, some corporeal, some spiritual ... consequently some outside us, some inside'. There are, for instance, stages of ascent, 'to wit, sense, imagination, reason, intellect, intelligence, and the apex of the mind, the illumination of conscience (*Synteresis*)'. These six steps are analogous to the six days of creation, as well as to various other patterns of six, and are an extension of an even more basic threefold structure whereby the human is constituted by body, spirit and mind, mirroring in turn the single threefoldness of the Trinity, which is duplicated also in the threefold way of purgation, illumination and perfection. Because the human being has an inner and an outer aspect, the mind's threefold structure becomes six, bringing us back to the six days of creation. The six stages of ascent then lead to a mystical seventh (or sabbath) and for this reason Bonaventure's book, as he tells us, has seven chapters.

Bonaventure places before us many variations of such patterns, analogies, and correspondences in order to suggest how human crafts and sciences are all part of the plan. The design is intricate, but Bonaventure's conviction is that we can trust the world and language to provide insights into God's design. Nature responds co-operatively to our intelligent gaze, and as we ascend the ladder of knowledge, illumination becomes increasingly intense.

Yet, as I have mentioned, the affirmative way is never quite altogether affirmative, and Bonaventure knows that in the end every image passes before the vision of God, and this also is part of what is meant by the cross: images are imperfect and indicate our imperfect knowledge by faith. Bonaventure points out that the symbolic six-winged seraph 'signifies the six states of illumination' leading to God, but then adds, 'to Whom no one can enter properly save through the Crucified'.

PV, 170–71

9.

According to Augustine and Bonaventure, the human mind does not so much invent signs and images as discover their significance. The creation is a divine poem and we are part of its imagery and rhythm as it moves towards its fully realized form; so the poet can assist God's craftsmanship by disposing and arranging images to help the reader penetrate to some extent the broader truth of things. The poem makes no pretence to autonomous existence, but extends itself into the reader's life for completion, so that 'his way of living may be, as it were, an eloquent speech', as Augustine says. Again he assumes here that there are real likenesses between the forms of material nature, the image-ideas of the artist, and the principles by which God shapes the whole of creation. We must work to discover such likenesses, however, and in the *De doctrina* we can see that Augustine's use of images in the *Confessions* serves a carefully calculated theological purpose, for poetry, we learn, is obscure (as parts of scripture are obscure) to remind us of our darkened reason and thus stimulate us to work out the significant meanings for ourselves.

The techniques of medieval allegory and mythography develop quite naturally from such a theory. The moral beneath the fable, the kernel within the husk, the exemplum under the enigma, have a psychological justification in the pleasure of discovery, and a theological justification in the belief that temporary obscurities will be illuminated in the light of eternity. On this model, allegory is not simply the depiction of a preconceived set of abstractions by a parallel set of images. It is a mimesis of the way in which images participate in the mysterious and imageless fullness of intellectual vision.

Boccaccio, whose *Genealogy of the Pagan Gods* became for the late Middle Ages and Renaissance a veritable handbook of allegorical convention on the Augustinian model, is clear about how the colourful expressiveness of the old pagan stories is really an obscure shadowing forth of the Christian mysteries. Boccaccio argues that poetry (and here he includes mythology) 'proceeds from the bosom of God', and encloses 'the high mysteries of things divine'. He talks of Moses' 'poetic longing' and claims that the myths of the gentile poets share in a garbled and impure fashion the secrets imparted on Sinai. He also confirms Aristotle's precept that the first poets were theologians, and sees the original meaning of poetry as inspired song that 'streamed forth', revealing God's wisdom to the souls of the prophets.

In conflating the inspiration of prophets and poets, Boccaccio confirms the theory of language set out in Augustine's *De doctrina*: that is, the words of the Bible, like those of the orators, are signs to bring us to God. These signs are to be interpreted by exegesis that refers them to the higher mystery. Allegory, according to this theory, is a poetry of faith, depending for completion on the evidence of things not seen and yet disclosed to the illuminated reader.

II, 10–11

10.

The pagan gods exerted an extensive influence on medieval culture, and theories were sought from the earliest Christian times to accommodate pagan wisdom to Christian revelation. There were a number of hypotheses. For instance, the pagan myths were said to be derived from Moses and therefore they contain truths that a Christian could use, even though the myths are not as authoritative as the inspired wisdom of the Bible. Justin Martyr and Clement of Alexandria are examples of this view. There was also a theory that the pagan myths were interpolations wrought by fiends to confuse Christians and lead them astray. Tatian thought this, and there is a strong element of the same view also in Augustine. Another theory was euhemerism. In a satiric commentary on his own culture, Euhemerus argued that religions have natural causes. Christians used this idea to debunk the pagan myths, arguing also that if the stories of the ancients were seen to have human origins, these stories could be adapted in good conscience by Christians to elucidate the superior, revealed truth of the Bible. Tertullian and Arnobius represent this view, which is retained in Isidore of Seville and was popular throughout the Renaissance.

In so far as these several theories opened the door to the riches of the pagan world, it was clear also that the benefits were not to be enjoyed by Christians without qualification, and the most notable consequence in the Middle Ages of the theoretical subordination of paganism to the Bible was the development of allegorical interpretation through which the works of the ancients could be modified to fit Christian precepts. Consequently, in the Middle Ages virtually every available pagan source was inveterately moralized, and the single analogy (tirelessly reiterated) that best describes the rationale of this process of subordination-becoming-allegory is Augustine's description of 'Egyptian gold' in *On Christian Doctrine*.

Augustine states that Christians should appropriate the works of the ancients to explicate the Christian path to salvation, just as the Israelites appropriated the gold of the Egyptians to assist the exodus from captivity. Basically, 'every good and true Christian should understand that wherever he may find truth, it is his Lord's'.

TS, 14–15

11.

As Christianity developed and became institutionalised, it found increasing need to engage co-operatively with the world of politics. Thus, when the Emperor Constantine converted to Christianity in the fourth century, Roman roads, trade routes, and legal institutions helped to transmit the gospel to the far reaches of the Empire, and it was no longer easy just to oppose Rome to Jerusalem. Augustine understood the problem very well, as we see in *The City of God* where he acknowledges that the Roman Empire provides a means of maintaining order, security and justice through which a Christian ruler can promote the cause of peace and well-being proper to a Christian community. Yet Rome was also a ruthless, tyrannical empire that, among other things, persecuted Christians. For Augustine, the two cities therefore stand radically opposed, but they would remain enmeshed nonetheless throughout the course of history and would be separated only at the end time. So also, the contending kinds of love represented by the two cities (the carnal love of this world and the spiritual love of God) are in conflict within each of us.

This theory was frequently repeated in the Middle Ages, and Dante, for instance, declared that the Roman Empire was an agent of divine providence. Moreover, he granted Vergil a privileged place as a forerunner of Christianity, a view already well esablished by Dante's time. According to Eusebius, Constantine had argued that Vergil's fourth Eclogue foretold Christ's birth, and throughout the Middle Ages there was a widespread opinion that Vergil was as close to Christianity as was possible without actually being Christian. St. Paul is even supposed to have asked what he might have done with Vergil had he found him still alive, and a story developed that Aeneas was a contemporary of David, their two lines of descent converging in the *pax Augusta*. Still, as we see in the Augustinian theory, Rome's worldly power aligns it with the unholy Babylon, and despite his providential view, Dante does not admit his beloved Vergil into paradise in the *Divine Comedy*, but consigns him to limbo. Also, a legend persisted throughout the Middle Ages that Vergil was a sorcerer; thus, Michael Scot links him to Simon Magus, and there are many stories of Vergil as a magician or a conjurer of devils, confirmed for instance by Boccaccio. In the Middle Ages, Virgil therefore tends to be regarded with the same ambivalence as Rome itself; consequently, Christian writers are drawn to the *Aeneid* because of how it depicts human civilisation, and yet they are opposed to it because it knows nothing about the holy city of Jerusalem.

PP, 48–9

12.

In his study of modern nation states, *God Land*, Conor Cruise O'Brien looks to Virgil and to early Christianity as foundational to the story he wants to tell. He points out that in adapting to the classical heritage of Greece and Rome, Christianity inserted between the earthly and heavenly kingdoms a 'political layer', represented first by the Imperial Court, which 'provided Christianity with classical legitimation', making 'the Christian Emperor the fulfillment of the classical past'. O'Brien argues that the 'acceptance of Virgil as a central figure in the culture of medieval Christianity' is crucial to this process, and he points out that the *Aeneid* acquired 'quasi-Scriptural status', as indeed it did. But Virgil's promised land remains the earthly city, and in Christianity after Constantine, a new, territorial vision develops, inheriting, as O'Brien says, the 'notion of the transcendent importance of the terrestrial patria'. The subsequent contention within Christendom between the claims of the heavenly and earthly kingdoms was to remain stubbornly durable, and O'Brien points out how readily new Western nations continued to depict themselves as 'true heirs of the Empire'. This is the case with medieval Germans, Revolutionary French, Victorian English, and the American founding fathers, who saw themselves at once as a Biblical chosen people and as 'transfigured Romans'. Though O'Brien does not say so,

Ulster's Protestants and the American founding fathers have a good deal in common, seeing themselves alike as a chosen people, a new Israel under siege, and also as the enlightened champions of civil liberties against the Caesaro-Papism of a tyrannical, paganized Christian church, where the balance of values deriving from ancient Rome and the Bible had, apparently, gone wrong. Thus, the Reverend Ian Paisley preaches regularly on Fridays outside the Belfast City Hall, and the juxtaposition here of reformed evangelical radicalism and Victorian neo-classicism catches exactly the re-combination of traditional elements, as a Christian new Israel and transfigured Roman civic virtue reinforce a certain ideal of Christian liberty.

IP, 11–12

One function of art is to bring to light aspects of experience occluded by the dominant ideology. In so doing, art interrogates the cultural presuppositions that constitute its own frame of reference, or repertoire, as Wolfgang Iser says. And so Augustine's *Confessions* can engage secular readers in the twenty-first century who do not share the fifth-century Christian author's ideological assumptions but who recognise the anxieties, desires, and aspirations to meaning that remain part of what constitutes us as persons in search of understanding and fulfilment in a world where suffering and death are intractable. A comparison between the medieval drama *Secunda Pastorum* (*The Second Shepherds' Play*) and Samuel Beckett's *Endgame* shows how differences between the author's repertoire of assumptions do not prevent the plays from having an enduring appeal.

With this broad point in mind, it is helpful to look briefly at a non-Western cultural tradition with a view to showing how a similar participatory or sacramental view of language and persons obtains also in that tradition at the early stages of its development.

Thus, the poetry and narratives of the early Hindu scriptures assume an interpenetration between subject and object in a world infused with significance. Subsequently, as in Western tradition, this participatory view was modified by way of a universalizing language that was developed in the Upanishads and in the later flowering of Hindu philosophy, with the same complex blending of earlier and later elements.

The course of this kind of development from myth to narrative and then to critical thinking in a variety of cultures has given rise among some thinkers to the question of whether or not a single primordial tradition might underlie the great variety of the world's myths and religions. René Guénon argues for a modern version of this view, and he warns that science and technology have introduced a 'reign of quantity' that has dislocated the modern person from a primordial wisdom without which human culture cannot survive. The idea that all the world's myths have a single source was maintained also during the Middle Ages, and the analogous but different questions raised by Guénon in a modern context can serve as a transition from the medieval 'Sacramental' view of personal identity to the 'Disenchanted' modern view, which is the topic of the next section.

13.

The medieval play, *Secunda Pastorum*, draws upon the broadly Augustinian presuppositions of the culture governing its production, while disclosing also the frequent blindness of that culture to its own un-Christian behaviours. Thus, we can see how Augustinian guilt culture calls for the moral responsibility that Voltaire demanded so imperatively in the eighteenth century. And yet, in *Endgame* a secular nihilism based on the assumption that human beings are responsible for constructing meaning in an empty universe is revealed as (almost) unendurably bleak, and the play is haunted by the desire for a sense of belonging and for participation in meaning not fabricated just by our own performance. And so, from the centre of Beckett's desolate spectacle comes a resistant dignity and pathos, the intimations of an unrelinquished solidarity against the homelessness of humankind. Although Beckett's world is not identifiable *tout court* with Heidegger's, they share a common ethos, as do Augustine and the author of *Secunda Pastorum*. And although the cultural circumstances of Augustine and Heidegger are different, they are joined in a complex history from which, in part, emerges the category of the person as I am attempting to describe it, inseparable from the historical narrative of its development.

PV, 51–2

14.

Today, educated Hindus are likely to regard the gods of the *Rg Veda* as manifestations of *brahman*, but it is difficult to ignore the polytheistic dynamism of these wonderfully various and complex divine figures, powerfully immanent in the world around us and also within ourselves. Thus, Agni, god of fire, is manifest in the natural world but is also an active principle within each human person: 'Agni is head and height of heaven, the Master of earth is he', and, likewise, Agni is 'shared by all men living'. Similarly, Vayu is the wind and also our life-giving breath:

> *Thou art our Father, Vata [Wind], yea, thou art a*
> *Brother and a friend,*
> *So give us strength that we may live.*

Likewise, Indra, the main hero of the *Rg Veda*, is a

divine warrior who fights with demons, chaos monsters from the deep representing nature's destructive forces as well as the archaic fears and terrors experienced at some time or other by every human person.

In short, the gods remind us that we are infused by energies that cross the boundaries between subject and object, pervading both nature and ourselves. This being the case, the sacrifice ritual is not only a means of propitiation, but also a communicative act putting us in touch with the primal energies that constitute the world and ourselves together, enabling us thereby to remake or re-fashion both. That is, by performing the sacrifice, we (like Indra) might be better able to ward off terror and chaos, thereby ensuring ourselves a better, longer life.

SL, 10

15.

Throughout the *Rg Veda*, the connection between human beings and the cosmos is developed by a remarkable mirror imaging whereby the human not only mirrors the cosmos, but the cosmos also mirrors the human to the point, even, where the cosmos is itself depicted as a man who is sacrificed, out of whose parts the world is formed. This 'primal man' (*Purusa*) is identified with the universe itself ('This Purusa is all that yet hath been and all that is to be'), and when the gods 'prepared the sacrifice' they did so 'with Purusa as their offering', thereby giving form to the main social strata of society:

When they divided Purusa how many portions did they make?
What do they call his mouth, his arms?

What do they call his thighs and feet?

The Brahman was his mouth, of both his arms was the Rajanya made.
His thighs became Vaisya, from his feet the Sudra was produced.

The moon was gendered from his mind, and from his eye the Sun had birth;
Indra and Agni from his mouth were born, and Vayu from his breath.

Forth from his navel came mid-air, the sky was fashioned from his head;
Earth from his feet, and from his ear the regions. Thus they formed the worlds.

SL, 11

16.

René Guénon taught that a catastrophic downward spiral of Western civilisation began with the loss of a vital sense of metaphysics. Catholic Christianity in the West had once sustained a link to 'Primordial Tradition', now broken almost beyond hope of repair by a 'reign of quantity' introduced by modern science. Guénon holds out little hope for Western civilisation unless by a revitalising assimilation of the Primordial Tradition from the East, where it is relatively unadulterated (though grievously threatened) by technology and empire-building.

Guénon writes with intellectual penetration and elegance. His central thesis commands attention, though it is scarcely novel; yet originality is Guénon's least concern. Truth is 'original', he claims, only if we take 'original' in a literal sense, for truth is now as always and we can only repeat it, as the great religions have done from time immemorial. And so Guenon posits an intellectual élite who perennially detect the pure metaphysical content of 'original' truth, and he distinguishes these few from the masses immersed in worldly concerns on the plane of manifestation, receiving tradition through picture images and creeds. Although the recovery of an original ur-myth seems unlikely, I will return by and by to the allied idea of a 'Perennial Philosophy' in order to provide some account of the convergent teachings about the meaning and status of persons in the spiritual traditions of the world's main religions.

LM, 6

2(c) Disenchantment and Discovery: Renaissance and Reformation

The end of the Middle Ages marked a transition from what I have called the 'Sacramental View' to the period of 'Disenchantment and Discovery' often referred to as the Renaissance and Reformation, and more recently the Early Modern Period. Although this transition effected a paradigm shift of profound significance for the development of the modern world and our view of ourselves within it, the changes occurred by way of sporadic upheavals, complex continuities and persistent contradictions that were reproduced unevenly along many fronts and continue to endure today. Still, however unevenly realised, the innovations in science, philosophy, and economic life during the period of 'Disenchantment and Discovery' were revolutionary, leading eventually to secularism and to the pre-eminence of technology and capitalism in the world in which we now live, and which has effectively displaced the sacramental view as the governing ideology in shaping personal and social identity.

The following excerpts focus on the dismantling of the sacramental universe under the influence of these revolutionary innovations, but the excerpts also show how older, mythic ways of understanding remain woven into the new paradigm, affirming the value of ways of thinking that are not based on quantification, scepticism, and empirical verification.

Mythology, which was the topic of section I, 2 (a), is helpful in the present context as a means of charting the larger process of cultural change during the period of Disenchantment and Discovery. As we have seen, Augustine's theory of Egyptian Gold subordinated the pagan myths to Christian revelation. During the Renaissance, new information about the mythological traditions of other cultures became increasingly available, either by way of travel or increased access to an ever-widening variety of literary sources. Following the old model of subordination, scholars continued at first to read the new myths as derivations from the single, ancient Hebrew fountainhead. Yet the sheer weight of the new information proved too much for the old subordinationist framework to contain, and it became impossible to argue credibly that all the world's myths and languages were derived from the Bible. And so, by default, the door gradually opened on the modern study of comparative mythology. Likewise, in other fields of enquiry, new attitudes emerged from a growing scepticism about the old hierarchical and subordinationist models and the metaphysical language that justified them and underpinned the sacramental view of the person, now increasingly isolated and without bearings in a universe of vast empty spaces and unimaginable reaches of time.

1.

In the field of mythology, so much new material became

available from remote and exotic sources that it was soon difficult to maintain that it had all been borrowed from the Hebrews. Comparative mythology thus gradually prompted an awareness that the Hebrew myths themselves might be rooted in the same general human experience as the myths of the pagans. Especially in the seventeenth century, in writers such as Lord Herbert of Cherbury, Bayle, Fontenelle, and Spinoza, medieval attitudes of subordination to a special revelation begin to yield to new theories about natural religion.

TS, 18

2.

Early in the seventeenth century, Lord Herbert of Cherbury had outlined the criteria for natural religion, arguing that salvation was a result of our naturally inspired praise of God. Benedictus Spinoza pointed out that mythology and imagination play a part in all religions, and John Spencer's *De Legibus Hebraeorum Ritualibus* (1685) showed that Christian and Jewish customs and rituals were often borrowed from pagan sources. And so, Augustine's Egyptian gold gradually ceased to be a viable currency, and the 'passion for allegory ceased to possess men like a taste for strong drink; myths became myths whether they were Hebrew, Persian, or Greek. The search for an elaborate pattern of a universal theology divinely revealed was ended now that men like Bayle, Fontenelle, and the French rationalists were making themselves heard. The supernatural had begun to lose its prefix'.

TS, 20

3.

In *The Court of the Gentiles; Or, Discourse Touching*

the Original of Human Literature Both Philologie and
Philosophie from the Scriptures and Jewish Church (1669),
Theophilus Gale adopts as his main thesis the idea that the
best philosophy and mythology of the Gentiles, and even
their languages, were derived from the superior revelation
given to Moses. But Gale's book today seems bizarre, as he
attempts to contain a virtual tsunami of information from
Phoenician, Greek, Roman, Egyptian, Syrian, Hebrew, and
other sources within an increasingly flimsy hypothesis.
It is difficult to accept, for instance, that the Phoenicians
brought Mosaic culture to Ireland and that Abraham
invented astronomy.

TS, 20–21

The recovery by Marsilio Ficino of the *Corpus Hermeticum* was
also highly influential in modifying Augustine's theory of Egyptian
Gold. This body of philosophical and mytho-poetical writing
was supposed to have been written by Hermes Trismegistus, who
was thought to be contemporary with Moses and to have shared
the same divine inspiration. In fact, the *Corpus Hermeticum* is a
compilation of Neo-Platonist and Stoic sources dating from the
early Christian centuries, but the authority accorded to it as divinely
inspired helped to undermine the pre-eminence of the Biblical
revelation. Moreover, because the *Corpus Hermeticum* describes
the magical manipulation of nature's occult powers and energies,
it also provided an impetus for the new scientific investigation of
natural causes, thus furthering the movement towards 'natural
religion' described in excerpts 1–3.

4.

In the *Asclepius*, according to Ficino one of the two
'divine' works of Hermes, we are told how the wise man,
through his own reason, can manipulate the energies

of the cosmos – the stars and the planets – in order to animate statues. Although Augustine had condemned this part of the *Asclepius* as idolatrous, Ficino does not do so, and in his own work on magic, the *De vita coelitus comparanda*, he admires the Hermetic magus for having the power to channel and manipulate the energies of the world soul.

Ficino is careful to distinguish, however, between philosophical or natural magic, associated with the *Corpus Hermeticum*, and evil or demonic magic that sought the aid of the devil. He was sure that our God-given reason remained sufficiently divine for us to guide the powers of the cosmos wisely through sympathetic magic, as recounted in the *Asclepius*. And so the aspirations of the magi to control nature provided an important impetus to the scientific endeavors of the period, and Tommaso Campanella's *Magio e grazia*, for instance, contains passages on 'real artificial magic' involving weights and pulleys, vacuums and pneumatic and hydraulic gadgets, suggesting a scientific side to his otherwise occult interests. The Elizabethan John Dee was both a magician and a mathematician. Indebted especially to Pico della Mirandola, he claims that all things can be made known and controlled by numbers. Dee 'is a very clear example', that is, 'of how the will to operate, stimulated by Renaissance magic, could pass into, and stimulate, the will to operate in genuine applied science'. The same tendency is found in the *De harmonia mundi* of Francesco Giorgio, and Copernicus's momentous *De revolutionibus orbium caelestium* refers approvingly to the authority of the prisci theologi and Hermes Trismegistus.

Other pioneers of science such as Paracelsus, Agrippa, and Kepler were also fascinated by Hermetic philosophy and by the influence of the stars and planets on the earth. The cult of the magus extended even to Francis Bacon through Bernardino Telesio, and the single most influential source book for natural magic, the *De vita coelitus comparanda* of Ficino, became part of a textbook of medicine, the *De triplici vita*. As Frances A. Yates concludes, in general the scientific revolution of the seventeenth century found a major impetus in the 'religious excitement caused by the rediscovery of the *Hermetica*, and their attendant Magia'.

TS, 24–5

5.

The basic contention of Pico della Mirandola's *Oration on the Dignity of Man*, besides the claim that 'man' is a most wonderful piece of work, is the idea that all philosophies and creeds contain some degree of divine truth. Pico openly embraces the optimistic spirit of Ficino's *prisci theologi*, beginning his oration with the declaration of Hermes Trismegistus in the Asclepius that a 'great miracle, Asclepius, is man', and going on throughout the work to conflate ancient and biblical sources, often in startling ways. For instance, 'Moses and Timaeus bear witness' to God's plan; 'Empedocles ... expound[s] to us the words of Job the theologian'; and 'Bacchus the leader of the Muses' experiences the same inspiration as Moses. The doctrines of the Cabalists and Moors are paralleled to David, and 'philosophizing through numbers' reveals a hidden tradition linking Moses, Pythagoras, the Egyptians, Plato, and Jesus Christ. Moses is said to contain the docrines of the Trinity, the Incarnation, Original Sin, the Atonement, and the heavenly Jerusalem, as well as the philosophy of Pythagoras and Plato. Although Christianity may indeed contain more divine truth than the Zoroastrians or the Chaldeans, for Pico the truth of Christianity is not essentially different from these other traditions.

As with the other Florentine syncretists, Pico does not abandon the traditional idea that Christianity is superior, but an uncritical enthusiasm for a 'cosmopolitan carnival' of pagan divinities was the foundation for an important transvaluation of values in understanding the relation of Christianity to the religions of other cultures, and so ultimately to human nature itself. All the key innovative attitudes are already present in the *Oration*, which contains a theory of religious toleration, an interest in the empirical control of nature, and an almost Pelagian trust in the self-sufficiency of the human will. The oration itself was delivered as a challenge to the 'reverent Fathers', who, among other things, stood as symbols of an old order that did in fact conduct an inquisition against Pico.

TS, 25–6

When seen in the context of Florentine Humanism, the Reformation appears simultaneously progressive and reactionary. On the one hand, the main reformers broke decisively with the broad Medieval mythic and sacramental view by dispensing with traditional forms of mediation between ourselves and God, thereby emptying the world of analogical significance. The hierarchical authority of the Catholic Church was then replaced by a strong Protestant emphasis on individualism that was to be highly significant for the development of modernity and for a prevailing modern view of personal identiy. On the other hand, the main Reformers re-emphasised the old guilt culture doctrines of the Fall and Original Sin deriving from St. Augustine, and in their denunciations of paganism (including the Hermetic philosophers) they mounted a highly conservative attack on the new spirit of self-sufficiency and the new Pelagianism promoted by the rise of Renaissance Humanism. The cross-currents between Humanism and Reformation are highly complex, but through these complexities the early modern period was forging a new understanding of personal identity itself.

6.

The Reformers stress the pre-eminence of the Bible in relation to the wisdom of the ancients, and Luther mocks at the medieval allegorizers not because he does not believe pagan art is subordinate to Christian revelation, but because he rejects pagan art altogether. Consequently, Renaissance fads such as the *prisci theologi* and the cult of the magus, with their soft distinctions between Christian revelation and pagan wisdom and their optimistic assessments of human nature, are generally repudiated by the Reformers. At the same time, by insisting on individualism and the freedom of individual conscience, and by attacking the universal authority of the church, the Reformation was preparing the way for modern secularism and for the division between church and state.

TS, 29–30

7.

The Augsburg Confession, the Thirty-nine Articles, and the statement of Carnesecchi, which we have already mentioned, make it clear that Reformers, whether in Italy, Germany, or England, felt Pelagianism as a special threat. The same is true of Luther in his debate with Erasmus on the freedom of the will. Luther complains that 'Erasmus by far outstrips the Pelagians', and he 'will not accept or tolerate that moderate middle way which Erasmus would ... recommend to me', because, 'unless you attribute all and everything to free will, as the Pelagians do, the contradictions in Scripture still remain'.

TS, 31

8.

Calvin does not distinguish between two sorts of magic and condemn only the demonic sort; he rejects 'natural' or 'philosophic' magic as well. Indeed, Puritan iconoclasm in general was less a pure anti-art movement than a rejection of the magus in his 'natural' form as artist. As Frances A. Yates points out (in accord with Walker's demonstration of the same point), the power of the magus to contain the *spiritus* in the *materia* was the power sought also by the Renaissance artists who wanted, like Asclepius, to express spiritual truth by giving it a material form. This endeavor extended also to the art of poetry. For instance, in the work of La Boderie and Tyard, the magus Orpheus was a source of inspiration, and the art of the poem and that of the magical incantation are identical.

TS, 34

9.

To many Protestant reformers the magus had seemed merely to usurp and then perpetuate the power of the priest. That is, the manipulation of material nature by a magician seemed akin to transubstantiation, and the priest seemed a kind of secretive adept, or conjurer. And so, Calvin rejects both Catholicism and the magi because the consecration seemed virtually equivalent to a 'magic incantation', just as the Roman church seemed to labour under 'the error of a magical conception of the sacraments'. In the teaching of St. Paul, unlike that of Rome, 'we should not imagine some magic incantation, supposing it enough to have mumbled the words, as if they were to be heard by the elements'. Calvin also repudiates any Neo-Platonist conception (and here we can imagine Ficino and Agrippa and Dee) of the interpenetration of spirit and matter. The clamor of some 'about a secret inspiration that gives life to the whole universe ... is not only weak but altogether profane', and such teachings set up 'a shadow deity to drive away the true God, whom we should fear and adore'. The only time Calvin mentions Hermes Trismegistus in the *Institutes* is to equate him with Servetus, who was burnt at the stake by Calvin as a heretic.

Reflecting this tradition in England, Anthony à Wood tells of Puritan raids on the Oxford Library in 1550, wherein books containing mathematics were burned as magical and were suspected of being 'Popish or diabolical'. Even in the reign of Charles I, when Nicholas Ferrar burned all the 'vain books' in his library, the Puritans thought him to be burning his 'conjuring books' which they associated with his suspected Papist leanings. In the earlier generation, James I maintained this same Calvinist conviction. His condemnation of necromancers in the *Daemonologie* is linked directly to his fear of Papist superstition and idolatry, and he talks of 'much muttring and murmuring of the conjuerers; Like a *Papist* priest, dispatching a hunting *Masse*'. Transformations wrought on natural bodies are 'like to the little transubstantiate god in the *Papistes Masse*', and 'in the time of blinde *Papistrie*', the devil and his minions, the necromancers and witches, walked most freely 'in these Countries'. Still, despite these repudiations, James goes on to confirm the distinction between natural and demonic magic, and he wishes to separate 'vnlawful charmes, without naturall causes' from a philosophy that can 'abide the true toutche of naturall reason'. He describes mathematics in astronomy as 'not onelie lawful, but most necessarie and commendable'. Astrology also uses mathematics and depends on the knowledge of influences and 'the course of the seasons and the weather'. These concerns, again, are 'not vnlawful, being moderately vsed', but are 'not so necessarie and commendable as the former'. Only the trust in such influences to reveal the future is 'vtterlie vnlawful', and James singles out Cardanus and Cornelius Agrippa for censure on this account.

King James I seems to trust, therefore, in mathematics (used scientifically, not as numerology) and in natural reason as supports for his Calvinist critique of the magi. Indeed, the practical Puritan world was, for the monarch, a real concern, and the *Basilikon Doron* is alive to the concerns of the new, middle-class world on which the King knows he has to keep a weather eye. There, a career can be made or broken by an individual's own enterprise: it is the world not of the masque but of the drama, with Machiavellian malcontents and individual portraiture. It is Rembrandt as distinct from Botticelli, and it can be summed up in the figure of Francis Bacon, whose star rose at court no less brightly than that of Inigo Jones in the years between 1605 and 1613.

Bacon himself, it now appears, in desiring power over nature has something in him of the Renaissance magus. But Bacon's direction is away from the Agrippan Neo-Platonist tradition characteristic of Dee and towards the nominalism of a future Royal Society. Like James I, he attacks Agrippa and Cardanus. 'Agrippa ... is not fit to be named a controversialist, but a rivial buffoon, relying on distortion and ridicule', while 'Jerome Cardan ... like Aristotle, is at variance with facts and with himself'. Bacon concludes that 'alchemists grow old and die in the embraces of their illusion', and the 'achievements of the magicians are unsure and fruitless'. In particular, he heaps scorn on the magicians' cult of secrecy. Their sense of being an elect group with arcane powers had led Calvin and James I to compare them to priests and condemn them as idolators. Bacon sees their secrecy also as pride, the root of idolatry. Thus, Paracelsus is 'conspicuous for his braggart air. His presumption calls for a particular reproof', and the whole of natural magic is 'beneath condemnation' because such 'imposture dresses things up to seem more wonderful than they would be without the dress'. Those practices are 'openly convicted of vanity', and the secret and 'remote and lofty tower' of the magician's pride must be abandoned if the magician is to come 'close to things'. The real obstacle, says Bacon, 'lies … in human pride. … It is this pride that has brought men to such a pitch of madness that they prefer to commune with their own spirits rather than with the spirit of nature'.

The 'lofty tower' seems to Bacon also to encourage the magus in a life dangerously remote from the actual world. This tendency, we learn, originates in Plato, who 'turned our minds away from observation' and 'taught us to turn our mind's eye inward and grovel before our own blind and confused idols under the name of contemplative philosophy'. Such philosophy, 'originating in Greece', issues mainly in 'pride and show', and by adopting it, the magus repeats Adam's sin. True philosophy, on the other hand, 'tends to equalize men's wits and capacities', and depends on patience, humility, and discipline, for 'men's wits require not the addition of feathers and wings, but of leaden weights. Men are very far from realising how strict and disciplined a thing is research into truth and nature'. Time, patience, and a sense of one's common humanity are necessary if we are to be 'delivered' from the 'enchanted glass' of our own mind.

II, 77-9

Shakespeare's portrait of Prospero in *The Tempest* provides a fascinating example of the complex strands of thinking with which the foregoing excerpts are concerned, as Prospero's skills as a Renaissance magus contend with conservative political principles and traditional religious values in the context of political insurrection and Machiavellian intrigue.

10.

In *The Tempest,* Shakespeare draws on the appeal of the Hermetic magus when he inserts a magically conjured masque into the play. But we can feel the reservations everywhere. For instance, the figure of Prospero causes us to be wary of the magus as secretive, power-hungry adept (the magician John Dee according to Bacon). We are alerted also to the dangers of the propaganda and despotism that lie not far beneath the surface for a monarch too convinced of divine right (the Stuart use of the masque for political purposes), and to the dangers of secular impulses no less bent on the control of nature for its own sake (Bacon the forerunner of modern science). Yet at last Prospero offers forgiveness to his enemies, and although the play acknowledges the dangers of the titanic magus, it manages also to show the process of Prospero's education as he spans the poles from Dee to Bacon in the context of traditional Christian values.

II, 81

There is no clear starting point for the movement towards 'Disenchantment and Discovery'. This is so because developments within late medieval scholasticism, combined with the Black Plague and schism within the Church in the fourteenth century, had already given rise to new kinds of critical thinking that gained momentum through the subsequent two hundred years, culminating in the critiques of the sixteenth and seventeenth centuries, as the following excerpts show.

11.

William of Occam (c. 1300–50) speaks for the new tendency. A key element in his thinking is a distinction between God's absolute and ordained powers. *Absolute power*, the argument goes, cannot be estimated from things as they are because God could have chosen other kinds of creation. *Ordained power*, by contrast, is what God has in fact willed and brought about.

This distinction is central for William of Occam because, by using it to demonstrate the non-necessary nature of creation, he is able to stress that God intends contingency itself to be part of the process of salvation. The epistemological consequences of this theological emphasis on contingency are evident in Occam's special interest in perception, what he calls 'intuitive cognition'. That is, we know individuals primarily, but concepts are in the mind only ('*in anima et verbo*') and are not essences shared by a thing with other members of a species.

It is easy, at this point, to assume that for Occam universals must be subjective. To the contrary, he argues that there is a foundation for universals in nature, and so on this point he does not break entirely with scholastic realism. But his drift is nonetheless clear: the mind has to decipher and process language that has an attenuated link with things and is therefore constantly in need of clarification and verification. For Occam, that is, as for many of his contemporaries, mental images were in the process of becoming divorced from concepts.

The development of Occam's main ideas during the next century and into the period of Renaissance and Reformation is complex, but its effect in one respect is certain: discontinuity between the mind's images and the transcendent Ideas to which created species were held to conform became a premise of the new philosophy of nature that grew out of nominalism and into the scientific revolution. Descartes stands exactly at the parting of the ways. He held that the realm of extension is real because its primary qualities are pre-eminently measurable. The mind stands opposed to extension, investing it sometimes with fanciful or analogical significance not inherent in the thing itself.

LM, 54–5

12.

The scorn Hobbes heaped on his scholastic forebears is matched only by the power of his demonstration that their substances and essences and quiddities were the inventions of imagination, 'there being nothing in the world universal but names'. He claims also that abstract mental constructs such as forms and substances are dangerous because they easily become the means for a corrupt priestcraft to claim authority based on a special ordained power to mediate on our behalf between time and eternity. Looking to his admired Galileo, Hobbes argues instead that the structure of matter is atomic, adding that ideas, images and thoughts are explainable in terms of the motions of corporeal bodies. Consequently, if universals are always in the end images and images always corporeal (the residual impressions of '*decaying sense*', as Hobbes says), there can be no independent status for essences or universals as we conceive them. This is true even for our idea of God, which is just a name for the conclusion we reach when thinking about the first cause: 'by the visible things in this world, and their admirable order, a man may conceive there is a cause of them, which men call God; and yet not have an idea, or image of him in his mind'.

On these grounds Hobbes advises Christian sovereigns to destroy the images which their subjects have been accustomed to worship. Because an image is merely 'the resemblance of something visible' it follows 'that there can be no image of a thing infinite', and to worship God as somehow 'inanimating' the finite matter of such representations is idolatrous. Hobbes points out that the use of Scriptural images is not sinful unless we take them as mediators of some real higher nature. There is, in short, no means by which corporeally determined mental configurations can ontologically shadow forth a transcendent reality. Nor does Hobbes allow an eternity in the scholastic (and Augustinian) definition of *nunc stans* wherein time as we know it is annihilated. Instead, he describes eternity as an infinitely prolonged time. Thus, if our images cannot mediate universals, and if there is no eternal realm distinct from this world, the Church and its sacraments are revealed as merely the devices of power-hungry, deluded clerics. Instead, says Hobbes, we must look to salvation, not vertically, but horizontally in a future time, the millennium which will take place under material conditions not substantially different from those we experience in our lives now.

As Hobbes makes clear, the real opponent of Plato is not so much Aristotle as Democritus, for whom the world was composed of atoms, the basic components of material nature that were allowed the attributes of substance and motion to account for the evolution of form. In antiquity the main Democritean positions were adopted by the Epicureans, and especially at the hands of Lucretius were used, in a proto-Hobbesian fashion, to dispense with the transcendental machinery of gods and spirits which, Lucretius argued, were responsible for a good deal of human misery and provided a ready tool for the manipulation of the masses by wily politicians. Although Lucretius preserved a place for the gods, he stressed their indifference, and especially during the Renaissance, Lucretius became synonymous in most people's minds with atheism. It is therefore striking that so many scientists during the sixteenth and seventeenth centuries reverted to some form of atomism, threatening as its implications seemed to orthodoxy, in order to promote their investigations of the physical world. And so Bacon favoured Democritus and Gassendi championed Lucretius in support of the new physics as did Giordano Bruno, while Lorenzo Valla's *Dialogue on Pleasure* drew heavily on Epicurus. Even Descartes, though he rejected a full-blown atomic theory (claiming that no matter how small an atom was, God could divide it) settled for something very like it. He substituted corpuscles for atoms, and, positing God as the first mover, argued by way of a theory about vortices that the particular movement of bodies is due to the laws of impact and conduction. This theory extends to Newton's and Boyle's picturably mechanical universe, until at last De La Mettrie, drawing on Descartes and Newton, pronounced flat out that the human being is a machine – *L'Homme Machine*.

II, 18–20

As we see, traditional beliefs came into conflict with the new science along many fronts. The following two excerpts from the field of medicine are of special interest because of how clearly they illustrate this conflict. Despite the high prestige of medicine today, it is perhaps surprising that there is still a widespread interest in cures based on 'traditional', unscientific practices.

13.

In 1599, Cardinal Pierre de Bérulle wrote his *Traité des Energumènes* to scold the civil authorities for interfering with an ecclesiastical tribunal which had found a young woman, Marthe Brossier, possessed by devils. By order of the king, the woman was arrested because she was subject to frenzies in which inflammatory remarks concerning Huguenots were a cause of embarrassment to the government, which had recently extended a toleration to this minority within the French population. The Capucins, who disagreed with the toleration and were keen to evangelise the Huguenots, thought it in their interest to prove an association between Marthe's demons and the Huguenot community. It was therefore to their advantage, when analysing Marthe's babblings (and attempting to reconstruct from them that she was speaking Latin and Greek under Satan's influence), to hear the demon say upon being driven out, 'Alas, I have lost my Huguenots'. In response, the king shrewdly had Marthe arrested by civil order and examined by a group of medical doctors who found her not demonically possessed but physically ill.

The ensuing row between Church and State is significant beyond the specific case of Marthe Brossier. Traditional theories of the affections and passions, backed by ecclesiastical authority, were increasingly being challenged by secular and materialist arguments whereby the passions, as quantifiable and mechanical, were held to determine aspects of human behaviour and morality formerly considered as having to do with the soul and free will. In short, a broad, new understanding of what it means to be a person was in the making.

SA, 26

14.

Doctors were all too readily suspected of conjuring, and their profession was often confused with the illicit arts of cunning men and wise women. Francis Bacon was prepared even to argue that 'empirics and old women are more happy many times in their cures than learned physicians'. Nor were accusations of charlatanism always wrong. Keith Thomas records the case of a physician curing an abdominal pain in a man who thought himself possessed by demons. The cure consisted of letting a bat out of a bag at the moment when a surgical incision was made, and then claiming that the incision had freed a malignant spirit.

The contaminations of science by charlatanism have never quite gone away. Nonetheless, as science attained to increasingly objective procedures, the claims of medicine to be an art based on occult qualities were radically revised as the operations of the body were described as analogous to a machine. And yet, during the Renaissance science was in the process of defining its own domain, and the boundary between religion (the soul's welfare) and physiology (the body's welfare) was the site of much highly-charged contention. There was, for instance, a recurrent debate on whether natural or supernatural causes (such as demonic possession) were responsible for certain kinds of derangements, as in the case of Elizabeth Jackson, who was tried before the Royal College of Physicians in 1602 (they found her guilty of causing fits in Mary Glover, a teenage girl, though the defence argued that the fits were owing to natural causes), or of Marthe Brossier, tried in France a half-century later and found by a panel of ecclesiastics to be possessed. Subsequently, she was acquitted by a panel of doctors who found her ill. One result is that even conventional treatises on the humours, such as Timothy Bright's *A Treatise on Melancholy* (1586), are uneasy in dealing with matters having to do with the body's influence on the soul.

For instance, Bright assures us that no essential alteration can occur to the soul, and yet the soul is not quite free while in the body. To explain how this is so, he argues that the passions can affect the spirits to such a degree that soul gives itself over to the 'grosse, and mechanicall actions of the bodie'. The effects of 'straunge vapours' also can cross 'the soules absolute intention', and climate and diet often seem to 'turne the mind about'. What stability, then, can the mind have, affected by changes such as these? Bright concludes that the 'spirits' in relation to body are as a hand to an instrument, and so the actual operation of the spirits can best be described mechanically. Nonetheless, body and spirit remain under the soul's direction and to that extent are not wholly explainable in mechanistic terms. Although Bright denies that soul is *essentially* affected by body, the very elaborateness of his circumspection shows how uneasy he was in attempting to reconcile the old and new explanations of our human condition.

DM, 58–9

The development of science offered challenges to which some spiritual writers responded by adjusting their thinking to fit the emergent new paradigm. Pierre de Bérulle's 'Copernican revolution' is an example of a theological response to the new assessments of the idea of the person under way during the period of Disenchantment and Discovery.

15.

Writers on the spiritual life did not ignore the challenges posed by the new science, and this is especially clear in France, where Descartes' influence on theology was directly felt.

Descartes' confessor was Pierre de Bérulle, founder of the French Oratorians and later a cardinal whose special, papally-conferred title was 'Apostle of the Incarnate Word'. Bérulle was so impressed by Descartes that he undertook to develop a mystical theology according to Cartesian principles. In so doing, he founded the so-called 'French school', and his encounter with scientific rationalism in the name of the Incarnate Word had a profound influence on the subsequent history of Western spirituality.

This complex story can be reduced to a few central insights deriving from the fact that Bérulle thought it necessary to effect a change in mystical theology commensurate with that which Descartes was effecting in philosophy. Consequently, Bérulle announced his own 'Copernican revolution', insisting on the absolute mystery of divine transcendence while proclaiming the futility of scholastic argument by analogy. Bérulle's follower, Guillaume Gibieuf, went on to argue that God's transcendence implies God's superiority to the causes that we observe at work in nature, and which, for Gibieuf, affirmed the inability of science to explain the divine mysteries. But he did not have to develop Bérulle very far in order to arrive at these conclusions.

Bérulle's theocentricism combines also with a traditional Augustinian insistence that self-mortification is the channel whereby divine grace works secretly in the soul. To explain this, Bérulle looks to the notion of imitating Christ. That is, we are conformed to God in the degree to which it is open for our everyday lives to be Christlike, and in each of us this occurs according to our particular vocations, gifts and aptitudes. These 'capacities' should be refined by selfless adoration, until, at last, they become permanent dispositions. Bérulle acknowledges the importance of God's assuming flesh, but Christ's actions in the body are significant because they are exemplary. The physical (like the ego) must be stripped of appurtenances of naturalism in order to reveal the pure 'state' (état) of the soul's adherence to God, a purely spiritual knowledge.

Bérulle therefore accepts from the new thinkers that God's purposes are not well perceived in the images of material nature, though material nature must not be rejected because Christ assumed it. Rather, Bérulle asserts that the divine mysteries are intuited by the mind's spiritual faculty, a process that depends on supernatural grace and not on the deliberate interrogation of natural images in the book of the world. And so, as with Descartes, the individual person is now set over against a world no longer rich with inherent meaning in which we participate directly. The Cartesian ego and the ego of Berulle's Copernican Revolution are therefore equally singular, equally solitary.

LM, 58–60

Among other things, the development of Humanism during the period under consideration engendered a spirit of critical enquiry that did much to shape the new sense of individualism exemplified by Shakespeare's Hamlet, and which we find also in different ways in

Ficino and Pico, Erasmus and Luther. As we have seen, the translation of the *Corpus Hermeticum* by Marsilio Ficino helped to stimulate empirical enquiry into the laws of nature. But Italian Humanism, associated especially with Ficino's founding of the Platonic Academy in Florence, is a much broader phenomenon than the recovery of the Hermetic philosophy, and it affected education, politics, and religion both in Italy and throughout Europe.

16.

Italian Humanism is especially associated with Marsilio Ficino (1433–99), founder of the Platonic Academy in Florence, and with his mercurial disciple, Pico della Mirandola (1463–94), who challenged the educated elite of his day with his nine hundred theses and *Oration on the Dignity of Man* (1486). The *Oration* is a soaring display, full of a sense of impassioned discovery and aspiring to master every domain of knowledge. Indeed, Pico comes close to suggesting that he had already done just that: 'I have ranged through all the masters of philosophy, investigated all books, and come to know all schools'. Consequently, he proposes a synthesis of the best of human wisdom, and sets his sights on bringing 'into the open the miracles concealed in the recesses of the world ... even so does the *magus* wed earth to heaven, that is, he weds lower things to the endowments and powers of higher things'.

Pico felt that the ancient philosophers, with whose names he so lovingly and showily studs his *Oration*, harboured a secret wisdom now made available through the synthesising imaginations of the thinkers of a new age, such as himself. Here is the well-known passage in which he describes God's first address to humanity:

The nature of all other beings is limited and

constrained within the bounds of laws prescribed by Us. Thou, constrained by no limits, in accordance with thine own free will, in whose hand We have placed thee, shalt ordain for thyself the limits of thy nature. We have set thee at the world's center that thou mayest from thence more easily observe whatever is in the world. We have made thee neither of heaven nor of earth, neither mortal nor immortal, so that with freedom of choice and with honor, as though the maker and molder of thyself, thou mayest fashion thyself in whatever shape thou shalt prefer. Thou shalt have the power to degenerate into the lower forms of life, which are brutish. Thou shalt have the power, out of thy soul's judgement, to be reborn into the higher forms, which are divine.

Alone among the degrees of angels, animals, and vegetative life, the human being is uniquely a 'chameleon', a 'self-transforming nature' free to make of itself what it wishes, a glorious lord of creation, a 'Proteus' in whom lie the 'germs of every way of life' to be cultivated and brought to maturity according to its own pleasure. This extraordinary picture of the human as a self-creating individual rather than as the interpreter of an already-ordained scheme of things, as synthesiser and discoverer rather than analyst and classifier, has the effect of re-casting established ideas in the mould of an imaginative, creative play.

The Spanish Humanist Juan Luis Vives had read Pico's *Oration*, as we see from his treatise *A Fable About Man* (Louvain, 1518), which takes over the central conception of the human creature's ability to choose a place within the hierarchies and even to become Godlike. Vives describes how Jupiter entertains the other Gods by creating the world as a stage on which the human being is the main player. Although humans have something in them of Jupiter's immortality, they wear a mask of flesh to play a part which, as in Pico, is undetermined and open to free-ranging, imaginative interpretation. At the height of their power, humans are free even to transform themselves into Jupiter himself, and are able to act almost as their own providence:

> From religion and memory, foreknowledge is almost obtained, with the prophecy of the future, evidently a spark of that divine and immense science which perceives all future events as if they were present.

The spirit of Pico's Florentine Humanism thus is taken up by Vives' *Fable*, unmodified except for the depiction of the human person as the key player at a game of perpetual, imaginative self-fashioning.

Vives' treatise *Against the Pseudodialecticians* is also relevant here because it shows how well he knew the philosophical consequences of his depiction of imaginative freedom. As is clear even in the brief passages already cited, Vives, like Pico, relies heavily on rhetoric rather than logic – on images rather than ideas – to communicate a sense of what constitutes us as human. Both authors assume that attempts to classify the place of human beings in nature has led merely to logic chopping, which is what Vives means by 'Pseudodialecticians'. Personal freedom within the cosmic hierarchies is thus analogous to freedom from the scholastic habits of mind attempting to construct a systematic, clear order of ideas and topics for human thought to explore.

PV, 130–32

17.

These observations can serve to suggest a series of strong tendencies characteristic of Humanism's attitude to language, which can be summarised as follows:

1. An optimistic conviction about the creative power of human imagination and will.
2. Rhetorical persuasion of the reader, the important thing being to awaken a change of attitude.
3. An attack on obscurantist jargon that would divide and classify human action, rather than affirm its synthesising, creative freedom.
4. A persuasion that common sense and usage tell us enough about language for us to behave morally; demands for too much consistency lead only to undesirable deviations from well-tried truths, the *consensus gentium*.

PV, 133

18.

In this context, let us turn briefly to the *Praise of Folly* (1515), because Erasmus's irony and fun are already intimated by Vives' arguments against the pseudodialecticians. Basically, the *Praise of Folly* is an extended pronouncement, or *declamatio*, by Folly herself, who shows us how full the world is of her devotees, and how she is necessary to make the world go round. What could be more foolish, after all, than the process of human generation?: 'So if you owe your existence to wedlock, you owe the fact of wedlock to madness'. 'Thus', Folly continues, 'from that amusement of mine, drunken and absurd as it is, spring haughty philosophers and their present-day successors who are popularly called monks, kings in their purple, pious priests and thrice-holy pontiffs'. Without Folly, there would be no human world at all, a fact that makes human pretension all the more amusing, all the more foolish. The touch here is playful, and yet the comedy swiftly veers into satire as monks, kings, priests and pontiffs are revealed as Folly's malicious, inadvertent worshippers, prey to their own vanity and duped, mainly, by taking themselves too seriously. The satire is then itself refracted because Folly is the speaker and we must not heed a word that she says. Under the subsequent multiple refractions of point of view, Erasmus contrives to protect himself from accusations of irreverence, and indeed Folly sees life as a play wherein we do best if we assume many masks:

> To destroy the illusion is to ruin the whole play, for it's really the characterization and make-up which hold the audience's eye. Now, what else is the whole life of man but a sort of play? Actors come on wearing their different masks and all play their parts until the producer orders them off the stage, and he can often tell the same man to appear in different costume, so that now he plays a king in purple and now a humble slave in rags. It's all a sort of pretence, but it's the only way to act out this farce.

Join in, participate in the illusion, the metaphoric indirections, and accept the nonsense, for 'this is the way to play the comedy of life'. The metaphor of theatrical disguise and the emphasis on performance help to confirm how imaginative language best teaches Folly's lesson that a clever exhibition is the most important thing. Even so, the concluding section of her declamation is not frivolous in recommending Christ's 'divine foolishness' as a means of leading us away from worldliness towards 'the supreme mind which alone they call the *summum bonum*'. In the world's eyes, this 'transformation' may be foolish, but it is also wisdom. And it is the same transformation of the synthesising, imaginatively free-ranging mind into God as is described in Pico's *Oration* and Vives' *Fable*.

PV, 133–4

Although Desiderius Erasmus was not impressed by Ficino's Hermetic magus or Pico's ambition to master all knowledge, he was strongly influenced by Juan Luis Vives' critical thinking and literary sensibility. Drawing on Vives, Erasmus developed his own ideas about the reform of education and the value of the Humanist enterprise in fostering a spirit of individual enquiry in a manner that overlaps with the aspirations of the new scientific enterprise and the associated attacks on metaphysics.

19.

Erasmus' central positions remain consistent. They are based on his concern for 'grammar' and *bonae litterae*: for the study, that is, of the ancient languages, especially with a view to providing scholarly texts of the Bible and the Fathers. Philology, Erasmus held, in providing insight into the precise meaning (and, therefore, the spirit) of Christ's message, enables the development of a true *philosophia Christi* based on the practice of a Christ-like life rather than on explicit doctrine or rules – on morality rather than argument – and calling for the reform of the interior life. True followers of Christ are tolerant, peace-loving and charitable; they disavow violence and pursue openness, clarity and co-operation. The study of *bonae litterae* teaches them how to express themselves concisely while preserving the tact and refinement necessary to deal undogmatically and sympathetically with those whose perspectives are different. Underlying all this is a conviction that, if people think about language and literature in Erasmus's fashion, and if they could manage to imitate his style (or at any rate his advice about style), society would be better off; certainly, less prey to tyranny and war.

Part of Erasmus's thinking therefore calls simply for large-mindedness and common sense. Truth, he argues in *The Paraclesis*, is more powerful when simple and plain; be without guile, he advises, and have a 'pious and an open mind'; 'Christ wishes his mysteries published as openly as possible', and true philosophy calls for co-operation, so that even 'a common labourer or weaver' can be considered a theologian. According to Beatus Rhenanus (his contemporary biographer), Erasmus's own 'great openness' occasioned the rebuke of some scholars who accused him of 'divulging our secrets', but Erasmus wanted to make truth accessible to all.

Erasmus therefore combines an optimistic belief in progress with a democratic attitude to knowledge such as might remind us of Francis Bacon. And yet we need to read Erasmus's advice in context: unlike Bacon, he makes no attempt to separate theology from other branches of knowledge, but sees the main end of *bonae litterae* as the nurture of his labourer theologians. Like Thomas More, he retains an allegiance to the general ideal of Christendom and does not countenance (however much his thought anticipates) progress as embracing either secularism or Protestantism. Rather, he holds the main enemy to be scholasticism (or what he, and many other Humanists, considered scholasticism to be).

DM, 36–7

20.

Erasmus' case against scholastic metaphysicians takes a distinctive turn when he associates their love of abstraction and their obscurantism with war and tyranny. If priests and schoolmasters, he argues, would inculcate the 'vulgar doctrine' instead of 'that erudition which they draw from the fonts of Aristotle and Averroës, Christendom would not be so disturbed on all sides by almost continuous war'. The philosophy of Christ therefore should be made as 'simple as possible and accessible to all'.

DM, 37

21.

As Paul Oskar Kristeller has shown, Renaissance Humanism is best understood in the context of a cycle of studies, the *studia humanitatis*, based on grammar, rhetoric, history, poetry and moral philosophy. The emphasis here is in sharp contrast to medieval university curricula stressing logic, natural philosophy, metaphysics, theology and law. The development of *studia humanitatis* in late fourteenth-century Italy was closely connected to the training of letter-writers and composers of documents who wished to acquire a gracious style for diplomatic and other official purposes. This in turn involved the reading and assimilation of ancient authors who provided the best models. As is well known, studies of the ancients were invigorated in fifteenth-century Italy by an extensive recovery of Greek and Latin literature which had been lost to the Middle Ages (including, for instance, the works of Plato and Plotinus, as well as the *Corpus Hermeticum*). Not surprisingly, the new documents stimulated a desire among scholars to learn Greek and to appreciate anew the elegance and power of ancient Latin as distinct from what was increasingly held to be its debased medieval form. Yet the new philological expertise soon proved to be an unexpectedly powerful critical tool for furthering the reformist energies already at work on a wide front in late medieval christendom. For instance, Lorenzo Valla (1405–57), a priest and teacher of rhetoric, criticised the papacy and the corruptions of monasticism. He also produced an influential grammar and manual of style entitled *Fine Points of the Latin Language*. The philological and reforming aspects of his work came together more remarkably when his study of the Latin of the *Donation of Constantine* revealed the document to be a forgery. The *Donation* was an official underpinning of the Church's secular power and was supposed to have been issued from the emperor's hand. Valla's philology thus became a weapon against certain aspects of time-honoured tradition, and a means of attacking the papacy. But this was a mere preparation for the more searching implications of Valla's *Annotations on the Vulgate*, pointing out errors in the Latin translation of the New Testament and calling into question that St. Jerome had translated it. When Erasmus discovered Valla's *Annotations* in a monastery near Louvain in 1504, he hastened to arrange publication and became a disciple of Valla's method, which he developed in a more thorough-going way in his own editions of the Greek New Testament, accompanied by a fresh Latin translation and voluminous notes.

As Erasmus reports in a letter, he was accused of laying the egg that Luther hatched. Certainly, the reformist energy of the Erasmian '*philosophia Christi*' (as he called it, borrowing a patristic term) inspired a similar zeal in Luther, who proclaimed the primacy of the individual in contrast to the corporate interdependencies and mediations of the old Sacramental dispensation during the Middle

Ages. Eventually, however, the two men disagreed, each expressing dismay at what the other had become.

SD, 90–91

The Pelagian spirit of self-sufficiency, which Humanism promoted and which was vigorously attacked by the main Reformers, was taken up also during the Renaissance in a current of thought emphasizing the innocence of childhood. This development stood sharply in contrast to guilt culture assertions about the human being as a *massa damnata*, as Augustine says. The new note of optimism about our fundamental innocence was to have far-reaching influence on the idea of the person, as we see especially in the Romantic period.

22.

Humanism and the scientific revolution are bound together by the critical spirit with which they question the idea of our fallenness and our capacity for self-improvement. Not surprisingly, in this context, during the Renaissance and Enlightenment a fresh interest developed among poets and philosophers in the state of childhood. For instance, Thomas Traherne breathlessly describes his infancy as a time when he was as innocent as Adam, until corrupted by the 'Dirty Devices of this World'. Henry Vaughan writes of the soul's pre-existence in a world of purity and light still accessible to children, as does John Earle. With Rousseau, the idea that we are born good but are corrupted by civilization becomes the mainspring of a reformative zeal bent on undoing social repression, and Rousseau returns often to the idea that we are originally sinless and free, honest, and capable of acting reasonably. Yet Rousseau (like Voltaire) was no facile optimist: in the *Discours sur l'inégalité* he does not present the primitive state as the sort of unfallen perfection we might associate with the Garden of Eden in the Augustinian tradition. Rather, Rousseau's primitives are dull and simple; yet they have the potential to develop a happy condition marked by morality, justice and community. The tragedy of history lies in the perversion and degeneration of this potential, and civilization must be reformed to enable us to recover ourselves as responsible, free citizens. The point is that we do not simply return to the original state, but develop its promise self-consciously, under the guidance of education.

Rousseau's arguments are mainly secular, and in this he inherits the full force of the Englightenment's critical spirit. Yet he, like Voltaire and Montesquieu, Lessing and Thomas Paine, retained a belief in God. The reason was partly polemical: the conviction of absolute goodness could serve all the more powerfully to show the moral depravity of humankind and the hypocrisies of the churches. Thus, Voltaire's favourite way of attacking the Bible was to show that it is morally objectionable and inconsistent with the idea of a good God. Following Tindal and Bolingbroke, Voltaire thought the story of the Fall not only absurd and degrading, but also an insult to the supreme being. In the *Philosophical Dictionary* he offers a strong moral objection in the manner of the Socinians and Unitarians: 'It is an insult to God, they say; It is accusing Him of the most absurd barbarity to have the hardihood to assert, that He formed all the successive generations of mankind to deliver them over to eternal tortures, under the pretext of their original ancestor having eaten of a particular fruit in a garden'. The institutional church with its childish mythology seemed to Voltaire first and last a means of entrapping and enslaving the credulous, and our conviction of radical guilt especially plays into the hands of rapacious and exploitative ecclesiastical institutions.

Rather, the new Enlightenment emphasis is on independent judgement ('My own mind is my own church', as Paine says) and moral responsibility. 'We lie under no necessary Fate of sinning', says John Toland: 'There is no Defect in our Understandings but those of our own Creation, that is to say, *vicious Habits easily contracted, but difficultly reformed. Tis just with us as with the Drunkard'.* The general Deist principle that revealed theology should be conformable to reason contributed to the same 'neo-Pelagianism' as the *philosophes* promoted. Not surprisingly, Methodism reacted as vigorously against the Deists as Luther did against Erasmus, and Augustine against Pelagius.

Although the developments outlined here are complex, it remains the case, as Peter Gay says, that during the eighteenth century 'both Christians and *philosophes* recognised that the Enlightenment's anthropology was revolutionary', and that the new general 'insistence on man's original innocence was a decisive break' with the participatory, guilt culture view of the human person that we have described earlier.

PV, 42–3

The widespread attacks on metaphysics as the main regulative science for understanding natural causes were so compelling that there was to be no turning back from Hobbes and Bacon or from the Humanist contempt for the abstract quibblings of scholastic debate. What then was to become of the sophisticated apparatus of metaphysical speculation and precise argument developed so painstakingly in the West since Plato and Aristotle? One answer is that metaphysical language could be re-interpreted imaginatively, as a means of self-consciously re-enchanting a cosmos increasingly emptied of mystery under the influence of the 'reign of quantity'. Jacob Boehme is a key figure here, as Hegel points out, and Boehme can helpfully be approached by way of his English disciple, William Law.

23.

According to Boehme, the Abyss or *Ungrund* underlies all manifestation, and the unknowable will of this divine *Ungrund* is the Father, whose fiery energy is manifested through the tempering principle of light, namely the Son, mediated and perfected by Spirit. These three principles are complexly inter-involved and they give birth to eternal nature, the first stage of God's self-manifestation. By a process involving the energy of seven properties, the creatures come into being, each recapitulating according to its capacity the triune Godhead. Three of the seven properties are dark (suggesting individual, self-centred identity, or nature without God), and three are light (God made manifest in the creatures). The mediating fourth, the 'lightning flash', turns the dark ternary towards light.

The fall of angels and humans is to be understood through Boehme's seven-fold scheme. Lucifer's jealousy of the Son and his desire to know the source of God's will caused the egocentric fire-principle in himself to burn up as wrath. Lucifer's apostasy then precipitated a catastrophic chain-reaction through the creation under his control, as the dark principle was expressed in isolation from the light. We learn then of a second creation and of Adam's fall from the androgynous state of his paradisal body into the divisions and separations to which flesh is heir. God subsequently defined the material world in its present form to impose a limit on the fall. Since then, the energies of good and evil have remained at war within the material world as we know it. Christ, the cosmic redeemer whose seed is in each of us, was born as a man to conquer the principle of fiery self-will in humankind and nature alike. He took on the condition of our material nature, and after death reassumed a spiritual body. We are asked to imitate this act by surrendering our own self-will and releasing the seeds of light and good that are striving to find God, even while held captive within the material world.

Boehme lived too early to have a strong sense of the deontologising of space that reached full expression with Newton, but he did realise that the old Ptolemaic explanation no longer saved the appearances. Also, as a Lutheran who had witnessed the proliferation of sects and the damage caused by widespread religious war, he was aware of how fragmented the old idea of Christendom had become. Some new way of configurating the whole picture, both cosmic and personal, needed to be found, and Boehme's response to this challenge – visionary and syncretistic – is the first major formulation of a structural dynamic within which a distinctively modern sense of the personal has continued to develop. To understand this, we need to look briefly again at the legacy of the Florentine Hermeticists and the cult of the magus.

One consequence of the Humanist and Reformation revisions of the idea of a unified Christendom was to bring to the light of day not just the *Corpus Hermeticum*, but the occult (that is, occluded) vocabularies of alchemy and Kabbalah. To varying degrees, alchemists and Kabbalists shared with Hermetic philosophers a concern for the will's transforming power and the instrumental energies of human intelligence seeking to control nature's hidden forces. Boehme borrowed heavily from this tradition (or variety of traditions), and his aim was to recast the ancient myths of the fall and redemption in a more fundamental way, focusing on the transformation of the will (which he referred to as 'magic'). By so doing, he hoped to render obsolete the narrow differences that had produced widespread violence and persecution among Christians.

The will, then, is central for Boehme, and just as in the seven properties the lightning flash turns the dark, fiery ternary back towards light and love, so in the individual person an analogous process occurs when we allow Christ into the soul to overcome the dark urges of self-will that have beset us since the Fall. The love-light of Christ then tempers the fires of selfish desire, and our personal joy and peace become part of the process of restoring the paradisal radiance of our original material bodies. Through the continued exercise of our beneficent will, this process can extend into the whole creation. Boehme thus sees the relationship between human will and nature as a dialectical exchange of energies, and then posits this dialectic within God: there is a dark side to the *Ungrund*, and God's fiery element also has a compulsion to self-manifestation. God creates in order to know himself, and because some of his creations are made free, he in a sense depends on them to co-operate in restoring the cosmos after the serial catastrophes of the fallen angels, the original Adam, and then Adam and Eve. In all this is a strong suggestion of God being constrained by the conditions of his own creation, and of humankind as a co-creator who will help to heal the self-division and tragedy suffered in God's own nature by the abuse of freedom among his creatures. As with the human relation to nature, so God and all he has made can be understood as a dialectical exchange of energies driven by the force of will either towards darkness, wrath and violence, or towards light, love and reconciliation. Moreover, this dialectic is construed as a process that develops through time.

Hegel described Boehme as the first true German philosopher, and praised him for his insights into the development of self-consciousness. Hegel's own theory of a dialectically unfolding reality in process towards self-realisation as an Absolute Subject has itself strong affinities with Boehme. As is well known, by inverting Hegel's emphasis, Marx dispensed with the Absolute and called upon the human subject alone to transform the natural world. Human action now defines human nature, and historical change takes place through a dialectic between necessity and human freedom. For Marx, the end term is a classless society where appropriative self-will is replaced by co-operation and willingness to live for the good of others. In short, as David Walsh says, in Boehme we find 'the genesis of one of the most influential symbolic complexes of the modern age', namely, the idea that reality is a movement towards fulfilment in time through a set of dialectical oppositions, through which human persons are also shaped.

DM, 119–22

24.

In *Some Animadversions on Dr Trapp's Late Reply*, William Law makes clear that Boehme was 'no Messenger from God of any Thing *new* in Religion'; his theories are not '*necessary* to be received, or as a Rule of Faith and Manners'. At the same time, Boehme experienced genuine insight into 'the grounds and Reasons' of Religion and Nature, and, as we learn in *The Way to Divine Knowledge*, his intuitions are not just '*notional*', but constitute a truth that can be seen only when 'you stand where he stood'. Boehme is true, that is, because of his power to move the heart (spiritually) and save the appearances (scientifically). Law thus complements his interest in Malebranche by introducing a metaphysical vision of the cosmic origins of sin, suffering, and redemption. He offers this vision as a personal achievement, neither 'notional' nor 'necessary', but none the less compelling. He realised that, in a world filled with suffering, natural science must seek to improve the human lot by gaining control of nature and by understanding nature's laws. But, so long as the scientific method cannot explain the fact of suffering, the gap between reason and mystery needs to be bridged by imagination, from which the heart finds direction and which must, with increasingly self-conscious explicitness, be deployed to protect the scientific method from its own potentially anti-human excesses.

DM, 140–41

In conclusion, it is again helpful to consider how a non-Western culture encountering the challenges of modernization reproduces the conflicts between reformation and tradition, anti-mythical rationality and the persistence of older ways of behaving and thinking that we see in the European phase of 'Disenchantment and Discovery'. In the first half of the twentieth century, the impact of science and technology on Sri Lankan Buddhism brought about a series of tensions between tradition and innovation that are interestingly analogous to what we see in Europe.

25.

By coining the label 'Protestant Buddhism', Obeyesekere attempts to describe some main characteristics of the reform movement in Sri Lanka that I have now briefly outlined. Yet there are some obvious differences between the Protestant Reformation in Europe and the Sri Lankan Buddhist revival. For instance, unlike European Protestants, Sri Lankan Buddhist laypeople had little access to scriptures in Sinhala, and Buddhists by and large maintained respect for the *bhikkhus* and the *Sangha*, unlike European Protestants who repudiated monkhood and the institutional Roman Catholic Church. But the strong emphasis on lay participation and the development of meditation (hitherto reserved for the virtuosi *bhikkhus*) among laypeople were innovations analogous to the European Reformation. Also, revivalist *bhikkhus* adopted the Christian missionaries' preaching style, exhorting people to moral virtue, social engagement, industriousness, sobriety, and punctuality – in short, to virtuous behaviour appropriate for the daily activities of laypeople interested in getting ahead in a modern, industrialized world. Thus, Anagarika Dharmapala drew up a detailed code of conduct consisting of two hundred rules for the guidance of laypeople, pertaining to such matters as dress, eating, cleanliness, and the like. He also insisted that a true Buddhism should reject as superstitious many popular devotional observances, including drumming, fire-walking, and various kinds of magic. Such things were corruptions of Buddhism, and Obeyesekere's parallel to the Protestant Reformation is helpful here, insofar as it draws attention to a new, lay moral emphasis and to a repudiation of superstition in the interests of a purer form of observance, which, in turn, was seen to promote the Sinhala national cause.

However, despite denunciations delivered in the name of a pure Buddhism, popular religious practices did not die out. Indeed, they increased, and it is likely that to some degree the idealizing moral insistence of the revivalists precipitated a carnivalesque return of the repressed. Certainly, traditional and modernist types of Buddhism co-existed, often with complex crossovers.

SL, 57–8

26.

In an important analysis, Richard Gombrich makes a distinction between two main types of Sri Lankan Buddhism, which he labels 'modern' and 'traditional'. He is especially interested in the traditional, which, he argues, has scarcely changed in 1,500 years – that is, since the period of the fifth-century commentaries in which Sri Lankan Theravada Buddhism was consolidated. Although the polar opposition between Gombrich's two types is less clear-cut in experience than in theory, the distinction nonetheless effectively describes a broad, historically significant development within Buddhism in twentieth-century Sri Lanka.

To clarify this distinction, Gombrich points out that Sri Lankan Buddhists by and large subscribe to the basic teachings of the Pali Canon about *anatta* and *nibbana*, but in practice most do not aspire to *nibbana* in their lifetimes, but to a good rebirth. In short, ordinary people tend to go on thinking of themselves as persons who will survive their death, and the austere canonical teachings about *anatta* and *nibbana* are frequently interpreted in ways that allow an accommodating engagement with the complexities, hopes, fears and circumstances of everyday life and culture.

In this context, Gombrich describes a range of 'traditional' lay practices aimed at acquiring merit for a good rebirth. These include making pilgrimages, participating in festivals and other rituals, giving donations to support the *Sangha*, believing in and propitiating various minor and local deities (many of them Hindu), and so on. The intricacies of abstract doctrine and the rigors of meditation are left largely to the *bhikkhus* who also provide ritual services for the laity, from whom otherwise they remain apart. Traditional Buddhism, then, is culturally conservative and ritually based, and it accommodates a wide range of local beliefs and practices. By contrast, Gombrich describes modernist Buddhism as impatient of ritual divorced from socially responsible action. It emphasizes the role of the laity, thereby blurring the distinction between the people and the *Sangha*. It is practical and embraces the idea that education is the key to technological and industrial progress. As we have seen, Dharmapala spearheaded this modernist movement, and Gombrich rightly points out how radically it departs from older practices and assumptions.

SL, 82–3

2(d) Secularism and Modernity

The last of my three cultural phases in the development of the idea of the person extends from the seventeenth century to the twentieth. To provide continuity with the previous section, I begin with Ernest Gellner, who describes how the rise of science effected a transition to secularism and modernity and produced an exhilarating but volatile pluralism, within which the formation of personal identity faces unique challenges.

1.

Ernest Gellner argues that the extraordinary success of the scientific revolution brought with it the rationalism of the enlightenment that did much to diminish the prestige and authority of religion by allowing '*no* privileged facts, occasions, individuals, institutions or associations. In other words, no miracles, no divine interventions … no sacred churches or sacramental communities'. Instead, science 'disenchants everything substantive', and by so doing it transformed the world in which we live, especially through the application of technology to economics, warfare, and colonial expansion. One result is a marked asymmetry between countries in which science and technology have been central to development, and countries that realize they need the tools of science and technology even though they must abandon or modify many of their cultural traditions to acquire and use these tools.

Still, despite its extraordinary success, science works well only in certain areas and does not sustain human beings especially well through the personal crises of life with which religion and other analogous cultural institutions traditionally deal. Gellner sees the conflict and interpenetration between traditional beliefs and scientific method (with its attendant secularism) as central to the modern world. In this context, he interprets post-modernism mainly as a fad developed by Western (especially American) humanists and academics. But post-modernism is also a symptom of malaise in a culture so uncertain of its own values that it embraces a radical pluralism and relativism, which it pursues to the point of self-stultification and self-contradiction by endlessly examining 'the locked circles of meaning in which everyone is imprisoned, excruciatingly *and* pleasurably'. In short, post-modernism is a 'witch-hunt' against objectivity, and too easily ignores the epistemological foundations that have enabled its own critical practice to emerge and develop in the first place. Gellner argues that although such attitudes might do some good 'by encouraging political compromise', they too frequently discount the fact that most of the world wants science and technology. Also, Western pluralism, with its theoretical extension of toleration to cultures unlike itself, is easily confounded when challenged by a radical rejection of its own pluralist premises. How can one tolerate an intolerance that contradicts and condemns one's own toleration?

BE, 182–3

On the road towards secularism, John Locke is (once again) a central figure. As we have seen (I,1), for Locke personal identity is closely connected to consciousness, which, according to Locke, is dependent on sense impressions. He insists that we do not have access either to a higher metaphysical domain or to an underlying material substance. Human knowledge therefore operates laterally rather than vertically, and by insisting on this Locke lays the groundwork for similar, modern attitudes towards our self-understanding and the limits of what we can know, especially about ourselves.

2.

For Locke, who was duly observant of orthodox piety, God is the source and origin of everything, but Locke argues that God made us with a limited ability to shape our ideas. The *Essay* is largely devoted to demonstrating that these ideas (by 'idea' Locke means simply the object of understanding, whatever the mind can be employed about in thinking) are founded in sense impressions. He does not say that sense stimuli are all we know, for ideas are formed by sense plus reflection; yet our ideas are always based on sense. This is true even of our idea of God, a complex idea, says Locke, made up of other simple ideas, so that although we might be able to demonstrate with certainty that God exists, our idea of God will remain imperfect because it is derived from a mere laborious 'enlarging' of some basic simple components. The idea of God therefore is not innate and Locke criticises Descartes' ontological argument that claims to prove God from intuition alone. To shift, as Descartes does, from the idea of God to his existence, Locke argues, is to presuppose existence but not to prove it: no idea can prove existence, which can only be proved by existence itself. Such self-evidence Locke finds in the conscious self, which becomes conscious through the power of reflection upon sense impressions. Locke therefore has managed nicely to cut human beings off at both ends of the vertical axis – our idea of God is slight and by no means self-evident at the one end, and there is no idea of material substance at the other, from which we could argue to a realm of essences or divine ideas. Instead, all we have are the images and ideas within ourselves, and the notion that these put us in touch with anything like a Platonist world of essences or the Scholastic world of forms and *prima materia* is, for Locke, merely fanciful. It is one more example of the human readiness to mistake words, especially abstract words, for things, whereas the only significance of words lies in the fact that people have agreed on them to indicate a certain combination of ideas. Complex ideas thus have no reference outside themselves, and are their own essence. Certainly they do not refer to or figure forth, by some mystique of participation, a higher ontological realm, and belief that they do is erroneous.

Locke therefore takes the whole paraphernalia of transcendental Ideas and reduces it to images of sense engendered by bodies. The resultant 'ideas', as the psychological contents of our individual minds, are their own validation, and the conclusions we can draw with certainty from the fact that we have them, Locke warns, are very limited. But although Locke effectively de-emphasised the vertical axis, he greatly expanded the horizontal. That is, he focused especially on the contents of ideas with a shrewd eye to their humdrum earthbound origins and the means by which they can be most effectively and simply combined, especially in service of morality. The feeling that Locke everywhere gives of having his feet on the ground is confirmed by his refusal to allow images to mediate, on the old model, between the realm of matter and a transcendental world, and by his confident attitude towards his inferred material world, which he thinks of as solid, definite, and consisting of minute particles.

II, 194–5

3.

The primary object of Locke's attention is the *sensory* image, and here he states a kind of basic trust that is a precondition of any organised thinking about the ordinary world. Yet he insists repeatedly that we should not pry into whatever transcendent intimations seem to attend our image-making, for we can learn nothing real or useful from that kind of enquiry. The mind's powers, he acknowledges, are God-given, and insofar as Locke allows us on this basis the ability to relate and judge images, he is not expressing a radical hostility to the old picture, for the mind can indeed detect God's design in nature. Nonetheless, by concentrating so heavily on the sensory image grounded on material substance, Locke is able to condemn the fictive images of poetry because they are so uncritical in presuming to provide avenues to transcendent truths. My main point about Locke therefore does not deny his connectedness to the past, but suggests a powerful inclination in him against the habit of mind, which found in the effortless pursuit of analogies real evidence of divine Ideas.

II, 204–5

Locke's sceptical view of imagination was widely reproduced in the Enlightenment. By reaction, the Romantics virtually sacralized the imagination, but the problem of how, then, the individual, creative imagination might effectively engage with a triumphantly technological and increasingly secular society remained pressing. George Eliot wrestles, for example, with this set of issues in *Felix Holt*.

4.

The main problem in *Felix Holt* arises from whether or not Eliot's lovingly evoked Romantic organicism, rooted in imaginative sympathy for others and for nature, is convincing as a model for political reform in a society increasingly dependent on industrial technology. Despite his fine rhetoric calling for power for the working man, Felix argues against universal suffrage and ends up with a position confirming the traditional ruling class that the novel otherwise depicts as moribund and devitalised. At the end of the book, Felix settles for obscurity and even welcomes it as the best expression of his political opinions, so that we might after all think George Eliot's description of him as 'the Radical' is tinged with irony. In short, Felix's self-definition depends on his imaginative sympathy with others, which stands then in painful contradiction to the material determinants of the society in which he lives.

PV, 116

5.

There is a great deal throughout the novel reminding us that people's freedom of self-determination is limited because their choices are constrained by circumstances that impose their own design despite whatever personal feelings of imaginative sympathy we might have. Tragedy requires that we should experience the simultaneous grandeur and helplessness of human beings caught in the dense and imponderable meshes of such a predicament. But *Felix Holt* is less about tragedy than about social reform, and Eliot produces a strong sense that social destiny is determined, and individual psychology shaped, by that fact. The whole idea of effecting political reform by way of a mutual extension of personal sympathy and imaginative identification with others is therefore drastically limited, and, despite his fine rhetoric, Felix also capitulates to this inevitable consequence. As Cross says of Eliot:

> *Her roots were down in the pre-railroad, pre-telegraphic period – the days of fine old leisure – but the fruit was formed during an era of extraordinary activity in scientific and mechanical discovery. Her genius was the outcome of these conditions.*

Basically, that is, Eliot was strongly drawn to Romanticism and to educating what Wordsworth calls the 'primary imagination', but she needed to adapt this concern to a technological and urban society. And although in *Felix Holt* she presents a strongly imagined view of the conflict between the personal and political, she does not equally effectively imagine a synthesis whereby the laws governing society and personal creative freedom are mutually sustaining. As inheritors of the problem to which she gives such thoughtful consideration, we might better understand by reading her something of the necessary involvement of imagination with politics in the development of an adequate theory of the person, whose identity is irreducibly social, the facts of a limited creative autonomy notwithstanding.

PV, 116–17

The challenges posed to Romanticism by a society increasingly shaped by industrialization and the instrumentalizing of personal relationships can be exemplified also by the work of Richard Jefferies (1848–87). Jefferies had read Darwin and concluded that 'deity and the whole range of superstition' are 'invented because of misery' and 'there is not the least trace of directing intelligence in human affairs'. Consequently, there is 'no consolation'. And yet, Jefferies had deep intuitions of what he calls 'soul life' arising from his meditations on nature. As also in George Eliot, secular unbelief and Wordsworthian intuitions combine in Jefferies' literary explorations, especially *The Story of My Heart*, as a way of enquiring about the value of human experience and about the worth and status of the individual human person in a godless universe. The confrontation that we see in Jefferies between Romanticism and 'the reign of quantity' continues today, as an interest in Eastern religions and wisdom traditions helps to offset the widespread secular marginalising of Christianity – though not without giving rise to further problems.

6.

There is anguish in Jefferies' *Story*, and we can best assess it by looking at how he alludes repeatedly to circles interpreted in a negative sense, as suggested by the comparison of a watch-face to nature's blind mechanism. Jefferies everywhere insists that nature's laws, although consistent, show no evidence of guiding intelligence, and are in no way designed to assist or illuminate humanity but rather to confine it. Jefferies had read Darwin and was angrily opposed to the consolations of the world's Paleys, to the effect that nature's design entails a beneficent designer. Nature is 'a force without a mind', and 'no deity has anything to do with nature'. Nature is non-teleological, and is governed by chance and the economy of force. In short, it is indifferent, even 'anti-human'. In face of this, and of the sufferings to which flesh is heir, there is 'no consolation. There is no relief'. Jefferies is unyielding on the point, and his explicit refusal to find any 'traces' whatsoever of God in nature shows how far, in this respect, he differs from the medieval 'sacramental' view.

LM, 68

7.

Here is a passage from *Origin of Species* in which Darwin discusses natural selection:

> *In the literal sense of the word, no doubt, natural selection is a false term; but who ever objected to chemists speaking of the elective affinities of the various elements? – and yet an acid cannot strictly be said to elect the base with which it in preference combines. It has been said that I speak of natural selection as an active power or Deity; but who objects to an author speaking of the attraction of gravity as ruling the movements of the planets? Every one knows what is meant and is implied by such metaphorical expressions; and they are almost necessary for brevity. So again it is difficult to avoid personifying the word Nature; but I mean by Nature, only the aggregate action and product of many natural laws, and by laws the sequence of events as ascertained by us. With a little familiarity such superficial objections will be forgotten.*

'Metaphorical' and 'superficial' are telling words here, and they mark a main division between Darwin and Jefferies, who could not agree that the mind's contribution, through metaphor, was merely a matter of surfaces. Instead, Jefferies saw force as the superficial thing, and the mind's activity as the deep and worthwhile aspect of experience. Indeed, he uses the word 'deep' frequently throughout *The Story of My Heart*, and his sense of wonder is consistently associated with the idea of depth. Matter, by contrast, is a wheel, a clock-face, the shallow routine of those trapped by civilisation and convention. Interestingly, Jefferies on two occasions tells us he is no lover of painting because the flat surfaces seem dead to him: he prefers sculpture. A reason for this otherwise unexplained preference perhaps comes through his equation, elsewhere, of surfaces to mechanism, and the third dimension (shared by sculpture) with the 'depth' of inner life, the power of the psyche, which is the discoverer of form. Partly *because* of his Darwinian disenchantment, therefore, Jefferies is fascinated with the fact that within an alien, mindless material universe, psyche can realise its own personal 'interior' powers.

And yet the moral problem remains. God cannot be permitted into our universe because explanations that refer evil and suffering to divine purpose are 'a crime against the human race'. At one point, Jefferies begins to consider the suffering of children, but leaves off ('I can hardly write of it'), explaining how he could not enter a hospital lest his mind should be overcome. There is something here, again, close to Darwin, who turned away from medicine as a career because he could not bear to deal so directly with suffering. Throughout his life and writings, Darwin remained extraordinarily sensitive to, and grieved by, the fact of pain, both animal and human. Like Jefferies, he could not admit a 'trace' of God in the affairs of nature, and explanations that eliminated a morally unendurable deity were, in a way, liberating. Except, of course, that unlike

Darwin, Jefferies was afflicted by the exigency of his own 'soul life': without consolation, without relief, he allowed himself in the end to hope that beyond thought, beyond the circles of our present intuitions and dreams, there is something 'higher than deity'. This unspeakable God is described no further, but simply affirmed from the depths of the soul's experience, through each individual's personal demand for 'something better than a god'.

LM, 66–68

8.

I have treated *The Story of My Heart* as symptomatic because it raises questions central to literature in an age of science, in the context of Romanticism. But Jefferies' sensibility is also of our own times, and he sounds surprisingly like those modern radical theologians who also proclaim the death of a traditional God. 'I hope God will be forgiven', Jefferies writes, and calls to mind a similar 'protest atheism' widespread in this century. 'A person who is fully a man of our times', writes John A.T. Robinson, the so-called 'atheist bishop', '*must* – or, at any rate, *may* – be an atheist before he can be a Christian'. Robinson is echoed by William Hamilton ('the death of God must be affirmed') and Gabriel Vahanian ('God is man's failure') and by numerous others. Admittedly, these pronouncements often end by being less radical than they sound. God is needed after all, these writers seem to mean, though we must beware of the criminal follies that through the ages have been enacted in God's name. As Simone Weil says: 'There are two atheisms of which one is a purification of the notion of God'. This is not far removed from what Vahanian and Hamilton really mean, or from Jefferies' denunciation of God in the name of 'something higher than deity'.

If the idea of God has never been easy to manage, the present age clearly has not made it any more so, and in this context, Richard Jefferies is not just a 'nature mystic'. He struggles, rather, to open his vision to transcendence without surrendering the challenges posed to him by *deus otiosus*, by suffering, and the fragmentation of tradition so characteristic of the modern era.

LM, 68–9

9.

It can be a seductive idea, that non-action achieves more than action; that letting-it-be is more advantageous than always being-at-it; that going with the flow is the most effective way. The (apparent) quietism of these ideas was especially attractive to the counterculture of the 1960s, which did much to popularize Eastern thought in the West. But it is worth noticing also that a good many of the 1960s dropouts were happy to climb back on board as the reviled corporations marketed their music, turning rebellion into nostalgia. Reaganomics and Thatcherism then emerged in the ascendant, unperturbed by the flowers in the gun barrels, and revolution-lite did not, in the end, put much hurt on the military-industrial complex.

Yet, in a larger and more interesting sense, the 1960s interest in Eastern religions and religious philosophies can be seen also as an offshoot of that important earlier movement of protest and affirmation that we know as Romanticism. The heartbeat of the Romantic movement was the idea that nature should be trusted. A millennium and a half of Christian theology had promoted the contrary idea that, despite the original goodness of God's creation, nature is fallen. As the redoubtable Augustine says, each of us is a *massa damnata*, a 'damned lump', and only God's grace can restore us. Augustine's doctrine of original sin underlies the general Christian, specifically Puritan, subjection of the passions, but it also shaped the preconceptions and aspirations of early modern science, which sought to subject a hostile nature in the interests of improving the human lot.

By proclaiming the innocence of childhood and nature's nurturing beneficence, the Romantics of the early nineteenth century sought to let go of both Puritan self-hatred and the Faustian compulsion to dominate and control the natural world. The contest between a Romantic affirmation of nature and the scientific conquest of it continues to the present, even though religion no longer governs the debate from the centre. Modern secularism – itself an offshoot of the great prestige of modern science – has driven a wedge between religion and science, religion and politics. Today, original sin, hell, and damnation no longer pass muster as the dominant ideology, and one appeal of Eastern religions in the second half of the twentieth century has been to provide an alternative to these tired doctrines, but in a way that also addresses the Romantic critique of scientific instrumentalism. Taoism is a case in point. It does not posit a creator God and has no theory of original sin. Rather, we are asked to trust nature and to discover the Tao for ourselves by being in harmony with the great sustaining rhythms of the natural world. The values here are broadly Romantic – critical of conventional morality and vigorously individualistic.

Seen in this light, Taoism, for Westerners, enters into an already complex cultural debate. The 1960s counterculture preferred to opt out of this debate altogether and to start afresh, seeing in Eastern religions the possibility of a new beginning. But, ironically, the desire to opt out presupposes a prior immersion, and attempting to turn away and just let things be can soon be enervating rather than liberating.

TM, 123–5

As a key figure in the Modernist movement, T.S. Eliot addresses the same core questions as George Eliot and Richard Jefferies about imagination in relation to secularism, industrialization, and materialism. Again, these concerns bring us back to Locke and to the dislocation of human knowledge from traditional metaphysics and from belief in an inherently meaningful natural world. Following World War I, an already widespread sense of disenchantment deepened into a profound experience of cultural and personal fragmentation, in the face of which art was forced to make a radical new assessment of its significance and techniques.

In this context, a broad range of Modernist writers in addition to Eliot proposed a self-conscious deployment of the fragmented tradition itself in the shaping of personal meaning and identity. Aldous Huxley, David Jones, James Joyce, and Samuel Beckett provide examples, while D.H. Lawrence and Robert Graves show how technique can be used self-consciously to explore the limitations of technique in the pursuit of an authentic, personal means of expression – again a hallmark of Modernism.

10.

In a well-known essay, T.S. Eliot writes:

Our civilization comprehends great variety and complexity, and this variety and complexity, playing upon a refined sensibility, must produce various and complex results. The poet must become more and more comprehensive, more allusive, more indirect, in order to force, to dislocate if necessary, language into his meaning.

This is at once a diagnosis and a prescription. The artist is to select signs and discover in so doing how to infuse them, and the fragmented tradition from which they are drawn, with fresh meaning. Art then becomes self-consciously non-representational to show that it is neither naively imitative of the 'real' outside world or 'real' inside emotions, but aware of its status as a symbolic structure. It is to reflect a critical awareness that language conveys imperfectly and indirectly what it describes, for images and analogies no longer reveal a divinely ordained purpose for things, and the empirical tradition has insisted that transcendental ideas are not useful for scientific enquiry. Twentieth-century art therefore assumes its share of the burden of that broad divorce between empirical science and theology initiated by a revolution in thought three hundred years ago. In so doing, it faces a key difficulty in the classical empirical approach to knowledge. John Locke, we may recall, had proposed that we are ignorant both of transcendent Ideas and of the real material world, but then countered the potential excesses of this theory by confirming what common sense has always demanded: there is a concrete reality outside us, and ideals do in fact shape human lives. By and large, in the Enlightenment Locke's empirical psychology and plain man's philosophy managed to chieve an acceptable synthesis, until, that is, it became increasingly clear that the process which cuts us off from transcendent ideas in order to give us knowledge of the world cuts us off also from the world. In so far as art in the twentieth century continues to deal with this problem, it has been forced to become highly self-reflexive, as Eliot Says.

SA, 14–15

11.

Samuel Beckett's *Endgame* is full of fugitive allegories not quite distinct enough to elicit our full affirmation while also provoking us to follow the allegorical suggestions. Intimated significance (solipsism, chess game, playacting) combines with a frustrating randomness to create the unique perplexities that are Beckett's hallmark. As we grasp at meaning it peters out, comically, inconsequentially, inevitably. Perhaps the black toy dog with a leg missing is God; perhaps the small boy outside, detected (or so Clov says) through the telescope, is hope, but perhaps not, for not all children are figures of hope, and not all black toy dogs with a leg missing are theological symbols. Even our reaching to make something of these motifs has a touch of comic desperation about it. 'Mean something! You and I, mean something!' says Clov, in incredulous protest, again, as it were, catching the audience in the act. Rather, a remorseless, nihilistic litany comments on how futile such efforts are: 'Zero ... zero ... and zero', says Clov. There is 'no more' nature, or bicycle wheels, coffins, sugar plums, navigators, rugs, or pain killer: an improbable list, its very disconnectedness confirming the randomness of events in a meaningless world, leading us to the inevitable common denominator, 'nothing'. 'There is nothing to say', Clov pronounces at last.

It is tempting to link all this to a general twentieth-century preoccupation with alienation and absurdity, especially as formulated by the existentialist development of Heidegger's analysis of death, nothingness, and the unexplained 'thrownness', of our condition. Not surprisingly, scholars have suggested that Beckett and Heidegger share a number of basic concerns. For instance, both have a similar sense of contingency, of our simply 'being there' in a world, thrown into the midst without explanation. Thus Malone finds himself, absurdly, in his mother's room, which becomes his world, and *Act Without Words* begins with 'The man flung backwards on stage'. Likewise, Heidegger's account of action and choice in a world where we are confronted by the twin abysses of alienation and unrealized possibility might remind us of many situations described by Beckett. So, in *Endgame*, Hamm's name suggests that he is an inept actor, called to play a part like Heidegger's *Dasein* and also to be as he is not, like his near namesake, Hamlet. Clov's name is a version of cloven, suggesting our isolation from one another, and the incompleteness of our personal identities and projects despite our interdependency (as Hamm[er] to *clou*, or nail). All this is recognizably the world of Heidegger, Sartre and their followers.

Still, despite these affinities, Beckett cannot simply be labeled Heideggerean or existentialist. As T.W. Adorno says, Heideggerean ontology has a place in *Endgame* but only in so far as it is parodied. Heidegger uses the idea of 'thrownness' as Sartre does 'absurdity', to transform 'senselessness itself into sense'. But Beckett does not admit this redemptive move, and the meaning of *Endgame* is, precisely, that it does not have any such sense: 'Understanding it can mean nothing other than understanding its incomprehensibility, or concretely reconstructing its meaning structure – that it has none'. For Beckett, the identity of the subject remains illusory (a preoccupation that haunted him from his early essay on Proust), and 'the ontological tendency of every existentialism, even that of *Being and Time*', as Adorno says, is abandoned in *Endgame* 'like an obsolete bunker'.

Adorno's point about parody reminds us that *Endgame* is also wonderfully humorous. Indeed, Harold Bloom uses this fact to criticize Adorno's despairing assessment, and insists that an 'extraordinary gusto informs *Endgame*', however much 'indistinguishable from an acute anxiety attack'. It is but a short step from Bloom to Bakhtin's 'carnivalesque', which is invoked by Sylvie Debevec Henning to suggest that Beckett challenges both the modern sense of despair (which *Endgame* shows us) and also our lingering 'familiar teleological hermeneutics'. Beckett's comedy offers a resistance to philosophical interpreters, and this is a product of the play's marvelously perplexing and anguished tone as a whole, but it is caught also in flashes, as when Hamm remarks about God, 'The bastard! He doesn't exist!'; or when he asks if the black toy dog is white and Clov replies 'Nearly'; or when Clov turns the telescope on the audience ('I see ... a multitude ... in transports ... of joy'). 'Nothing is funnier than unhappiness, I grant you that' says Nell, voicing the paradox with a wry and dispassionate mournfulness, to which Beckett amazingly gives life.

PV, 26–8

12.

D.H. Lawrence, despite his dark gods, is driven by an acute awareness of the human struggle for consciousness, and it is a vexed question how we should relate this impulse in his work to his interest in the irrational. Although Paul Morel in *Sons and Lovers* trembles at the great orange moon, swaying in the womb-like fecundity of the cherry tree, both of which exclude the spiritual Miriam, it is she who brings out the artist in him. And at the opening of *The Rainbow* the church spire stands above the ploughed fields. Our true destiny, we deduce, lies with both together, just as the man who died (in Lawrence's story of the same name) discovers himself alive between the peasants and the shrill purity of his own past life.

It is therefore less than totally disarming to point out the paradox of Lawrence's deploring sex in the head and yet, in writing novels about it, putting it there. Such a predicament corresponds exactly to Graves deploring the Apollonian and yet using the results of recent anthropological and historical research. The problem in both cases is characteristically modern: the artist deploys his technique partly to explore the nature and limitations of the technique itself, much as we explore the idea of personal identity to discover that it cannot be described.

SA, 56

13.

In an article on Samuel Beckett, Northrop Frye suggests that in every age dominant theories of society and of personality mirror each other. For instance, Plato's view of the wise man's reason ruling his appetite is reflected in the idea of a state where the philosopher king rules the lower orders of society. In the twentieth century, Freud provides a theory of personality which is also 'the picture of Western Europe and America, hoping that its blocks and tensions and hysterical explosions will settle into some kind of precarious working agreement'. Frye goes on to suggest that much twentieth-century literature responds to and confirms this Freudian view by creating 'the atmosphere of an anxiety dream', where personality is unstable, carried along by the force of habit and conditioned reflex. In parallel, 'bureaucratic anonymity' makes the state a frightening, incalculable force, ordering and disposing human bodies without regard for their personal integrity or dignity.

PC, 76

So far, I have interpreted modernism in light of an evolution of the idea of the person through the phases of Sacramentalism, Disenchantment, and Romanticism. In writing about the letters of Vincent van Gogh, I suggested that the term 'post-Romantic figural' is helpful for describing the high degree of self-reflexiveness characteristic of our modern self-fashioning as a result of these developments.

14.

As we have seen throughout this chapter – and as Van Gogh clearly understood – the 'new thing without a name' in fact requires names in order to be sought after in the first place. Consequently, some of the core values of the religion of his youth continued to inform Van Gogh's search for the mysterious, the transcendent 'it', the 'white ray' that is the source of creativity and of life itself. As he kept insisting, the transcendent is immanent in our immediate relationships with other people and with nature, and I have tried to show that, at their best, Van Gogh's letters themselves express this inter-involvement. But I would like to end this chapter by noting how his insistence on the immanence of the transcendent relates also to his practice as a painter who is neither wholly expressionist nor wholly concerned with the faithful representation of appearances.

Erich Auerbach's term 'figural' is helpful here, even though Auerbach uses 'figural' mainly to describe medieval literature (especially Dante). In so doing, he distinguishes between *allegoria* and *figura*. That is, in *allegoria*, events and characters are invited to illustrate an abstract idea; in *figura*, a thing or person is felt to be the bearer of some further, mysteriously resonant but unconceptualized, significance. In an earlier study, I described the poetry of Seamus Heaney as figural in Auerbach's sense. In so doing,

I wanted to elucidate how Heaney holds the carefully observed phenomena of nature on the edge of some broader significance that does not harden out conceptually but that is felt as vital and emotionally charged rather than abstract. In Heaney's case, this broader significance is frequently self-reflexive, returning us to the craft and achievement of the poem itself. This self-reflexiveness results from the fact that a main difference between Heaney's figural mode and Dante's is that Heaney lacks Dante's medieval sacramentalism and trust in the objective, God-ordained hierarchies of the chain of being. Instead, like Wordsworth, Heaney turns to the ordering effect of the poem itself to express the resonance between the creative mind and the natural world. In this, he reflects a typically modernist self-consciousness, whereby art supplies the loss consequent upon the receding 'sea of faith', as Matthew Arnold says. We might describe the combined effect of these elements as 'post-Romantic figural'.

For Van Gogh, too, nature is figural. That is, in the absence of a traditional religious faith, he looks to the work of art to express the mysterious, life-enhancing resonance between the human mind and the undisclosed dimensions of nature. All of this helps to explain something of the special appeal and achievement of his paintings, as well as some of the most striking effects of his writing. For instance, in the following excerpt, he describes how he longs to paint landscapes, and how 'in all of nature, in trees for instance, I see expression and a soul, as it were':

> *A row of pollard willows sometimes resembles a procession of orphan men.*
>
> *Young corn can have something ineffably pure and gentle about it that evokes an emotion like that*

aroused by the expression of a sleeping child, for example.

The grass trodden down at the side of a road looks tired and dusty like the inhabitants of a poor quarter.

After it had snowed recently I saw a group of Savoy cabbages that were freezing, and that reminded me of a group of women I had seen early in the morning at a water and fire cellar in their thin skirts and old shawls.

In discovering 'expression and a soul' in natural objects, Van Gogh points to the interpenetration of the mind and nature as the means of disclosing some fresh understanding of nature and of human nature simultaneously. The point about the corn, trodden grass, and Savoy cabbages is not that they look like babies, slum dwellers, or poor women. While the pollard willows might possibly suggest a procession of dejected men, someone looking at a painting of the trees would not necessarily see represented there anything as specific as an actual group of 'orphan men'. Rather, these objects evoke a set of feelings that we might identify as resembling the feelings evoked by the human referents Van Gogh suggests. Again, he is not saying that a viewer of a painting of trodden grass should see that it resembles the 'inhabitants of a poor quarter'. Rather, the trodden grass is figural, which is to say that the meaning it suggests is not specified but is registered on our emotions nonetheless. We can well imagine a sensitive observer saying: 'How tired and dusty that grass appears; why, it reminds one of the plight of some poor people in our cities, of whom we really ought to take more care'. But another observer might just as well explain the feelings in other terms and still remain responsive to the trampled and dusty appearance of the grass. The significance here is not allegorical – that is, there is no governing idea or concept to which the trodden grass corresponds; rather, it is figural, causing the observer to experience a feeling-state in which personal emotion and a sense of compassionate concern are disclosed in and through nature.

LV, 203–5

15.

Van Gogh's letters contain many reflections of this sort on the power of art to disclose 'the concealed originality of the source of one's own being', as Heidegger says – that is, the depths of being from which manifestation and consciousness both emerge and to which Van Gogh attached a high value, which art expresses. Consequently, he explains how 'in life and in painting too, I can easily do without the dear Lord, but I can't, suffering as I do, do without something greater than myself, which is my life, the power to create'. In a frequently cited passage, he goes on:

> And in a painting I'd like to say something consoling, like a piece of music. I'd like to paint men or women with that je ne sais quoi of the eternal, of which the halo used to be the symbol, and which we try to achieve through the radiance itself, through the vibrancy of our colorations.

(673/4:253)

The language here is a mixture of clarity and vagueness. The repeated 'I'd like to', together with the insistence on the 'vibrancy' of the colours and on actual 'men or women', communicates Van Gogh's characteristically direct engagement with his practice. By contrast, 'that *je ne sais quoi* of the eternal' and the allusion to something of which 'the halo used to be the symbol' are deliberately indefinite, suggesting the mystery that conventional religious language no longer adequately describes. W.H. Auden points out that Van Gogh is 'the first painter, so far as I know, to have consciously attempted to produce a painting which should be religious and yet contain no traditional religious iconography'. Auden's claim is exemplified in the above passage, where the quality once represented by the halo is implicit not only in the painting Van Gogh wants to paint but also in his writing about it.

LV, 56–7

As Tsvetan Todorov points out, the rise of modern literary theory 'is born ... only with the twentieth century' and brings a new self-reflexiveness to bear on the meaning and significance not just of literary discourse but of discourse itself in a fragmented culture given over in large part to instrumental knowledge and the depersonalising of others. And so modern literary theory can be seen as a further development of the Modernist project as a whole.

16.

The well-tried methods of practical criticism and the so-called New Criticism of a generation ago taught readers to concentrate on the analysis of texts with a view to disclosing patterns of metaphor, tensions, paradoxes and ambiguities, which the work of art holds together in unity. Despite certain modifications, the broad influence of a Coleridgean theory of imagination is not hard to detect here. Coleridge had focused on the polar relationship between the whole and parts of a poem, and had proclaimed that a literary work carries within itself the reason why it is so and not otherwise. A similar emphasis on 'the text itself' among New Critics (and here I can include the followers of F.R. Leavis) produced much fruitful interpretation, but also effectively separated literary criticism from philosophy. The doorway to a new concern about the philosophical bases and implications of critical procedure and indeed of 'writing' itself, lay then through linguistics and anthropology.

The speculations of Ferdinand de Saussure on the structure of linguistic discourse as a system of differences combined in modern literary theory with Claude Levi-Strauss's investigations of the myths and social structures of so-called primitive cultures as complex relational systems expressed as metaphor and ritual. The joint influence of Saussurian linguistics and anthropology is further implicated with phenomenology, Russian Formalism, Semiotics, Marxism and psychoanalysis, in a creative ferment that has its share of smoke and mirrors, but also of brilliant illuminations and far-reaching challenges. The net result for the future of literary studies is not easy to predict. But the questions raised by the literary theorists are radical, concentrating on the fact that texts now seem less privileged and more a part of the network of other texts, dependent for meaning not only on the writer's culture and language, but also on those of the reader, who may be said partly to create the literary work in the act of reading it. Also, because writing is arbitrary it is a system of codes aiming to persuade.

Not surprisingly, the philosopher who has most energetically set about discovering the persuasive metaphors that give away key latent assumptions in the works of other philosophers has appealed most to literary critics. Jacques Derrida's 'deconstruction' of philosophical texts sets out to show that philosophy is more like literature than philosophers assume. Like all writing, philosophy is rhetorical, and because it uses language (an endless network of signifiers, the sense of which depends mainly on differences from other signifiers), it never manages to stabilize meaning, which is perpetually deferred. Derrida pushes his case to the very edge of (some think, beyond) self-defeating skepticism. How, we might ask, can he make such a case at all, if language is incapable of reliable meaning? The notion that philosophers (and other writers) always rely on metaphor understandably appeals to literary theorists because poets and critics usually have been quite open about the rhetorical nature of their discourse and the self-referencing element in imaginative writing. It is as if literary people have been onto the game all along, as the others are now coming to realize.

A great deal of discussion among literary humanists these days is therefore concerned with the nature and possibility of meaning itself. In short, modern literary theory is strongly drawn to hermeneutics, a discipline which had its origin in the study of Biblical texts. There, too, relationships between belief and meaning, texts and the spirit of interpretation, words and the stable transcendent Reality that they indicate, are the core issues. Indeed, the latest trends in literary theory seem to have led critics back to the kinds of questions about meaning and belief originally engendered by study of the New Testament itself, just as recent developments in Biblical criticism have led to a renewed interest in myth and imagination. Significantly, the literary critic Northrop Frye acknowledges that he approaches the Bible by way of the hermeneutic theory of Paul Ricoeur and H.G. Gadamer. Conversely, the New Testament scholar Daniel Patte's study of the Pauline Epistles draws on A.J. Greimas, and reads remarkably like a modern study of a literary text. These are typical examples of what seems to be a widespread rapprochement, still in the making, between Biblical scholarship and secular literary criticism.

NT, 5–7

17.

F.R. Leavis's influence on the development of literary criticism is difficult to overestimate, but it is usual also to notice the elitism of his general position. This is already evident in an early essay, 'Mass Civilisation and Minority Culture', where he argues that a 'discerning appreciation of art and literature' depends on 'a very small minority', and throughout his career, Leavis held that in the modern age this discerning minority fights a rearguard action against the dominant forces of mass production in a machine-run society that deracinates and effects a 'standardization of persons'. Leavis assures us that one consequence of modern culture is a loss of 'the organic community', by which he means a pre-industrial golden age when people were supposed to dwell in sustaining closeness to the environment, finding satisfaction in personal and social relations that grew out of a direct relationship to nature. This Romantic – and largely fictitious – notion of a lost culture and way of life remains basic to Leavis's claims for literature and the critical minority able to appreciate its value. Literature, we learn, restores the 'concreteness' and 'texture' of actual experience over and against the abstractions, empty trivialities and stock responses promoted by the machine age.

There is something Heideggerian in all this, though – as is well known, Leavis shied away from philosophy, linking it with the kinds of abstract language against which he felt poetry is ranged. Thus, in his 'Memories of Wittgenstein', Leavis is keen to acknowledge the philosopher's genius, but even keener to assure us that their relationship involved no discussion of philosophy ('I had better say at once that I didn't discuss philosophy with Wittgenstein'). Rather, Leavis describes walks they took in the country, and their discussions about people. Of Wittgenstein's reaction in a particular instance, Leavis pauses to comment:

> It was a spontaneity of recoil, uttering a judgement expressive of the whole Being. To know Wittgenstein was to recognize that tone, that force, again and again.

This is entirely characteristic. Leavis is interested in 'the whole being' rather than just ideas, and his personal interaction with Wittgenstein was more significant for him than was Wittgenstein's philosophy. Just so, Leavis looked to literature as the most compelling means of giving us a sense of personal wholeness in a society otherwise disposed to produce, among other things, 'standardised persons' as distinct from vital human beings. In short, although he did not develop any philosophical theory of the modern person, Leavis saw literature as a means of shaping personal values in an increasingly depersonalized society.

SD, 5–6

3   THE STATE APPARATUS AND THE RULE OF FORCE

Civil order and the rule of law are maintained by the threat of force, which is the prerogative of the state. René Girard describes how religious rituals, especially sacrifice rituals, are a means of concealing the fact that the origins of the social contract are violent. Preventing this fact from being openly acknowledged enables the transcendence of the law to be agreed upon, and violence then is all the more readily imagined as coming from outside, from enemies who are often projections of a repressed and unacknowledged violence within. In turn, this projection encourages the objectification and stereotyping of the enemy as alien and not like ourselves.

These complex dynamics are the focus of the following excerpts, which gather around the idea that violence is the most radical form of depersonalization – the means, that is, by which a person is turned into an object, an other who is not like us, who has no interiority or capacity for relationship.

In I, 2 (a), I cited a passage in which Girard describes the connections between violence, sacrifice rituals and scapegoating. In the present context, I will assume the relevance of that passage to the fact that we all too readily conceal from ourselves our complicity in violent acts of the kind that we overtly condemn. With this in mind, I turn to the hunger strikes in Northern Ireland in 1981, in which inmates who claimed to be political prisoners were officially designated criminals. To protest against the criminalization policy and the increasingly inhumane treatment by which it was enforced, they refused food. The confrontation, which lasted almost five years, culminated in a hunger strike in which ten men died. The strike and the conditions that precipitated it provide disturbingly explicit examples of the rule of force, and of the depersonalization, stereotyping, and demonizing that are often at play in social and political life, even if not openly declared.

1.

Complicity in violence is a condition of being civilized. As is generally agreed, order is maintained by observance of the law; in turn the law is maintained – as it was established – by force. When disagreements occur between states, diplomacy seeks to avoid the use of force and to settle things by words. But when the fence of words and the citadel of law are breached, the edifice of the civilized itself comes under threat.

Outside the halls of diplomacy, non-violent confrontation is sometimes efficacious. Mahatma Gandhi and Martin Luther King are the best known modern examples of how non-violent protest might throw into confusion the state's confidence in its right to use force. Something comparable occurred in the decisive civil rights marches of 1968 in Northern Ireland, when the RUC battered peaceful demonstrators, including the present Lord Fitt, then West Belfast MP at Westminster. Yet much depended, on that occasion, on television crews and journalists who made the facts known to an audience sufficiently conscionable to be concerned. As we might safely guess, had Gandhi, say, been a Kurd conducting a protest against Saddam Hussein, or had Martin Luther King been a Cambodian taking to the streets to challenge Pol Pot, both would have vanished without trace. In short, non-violent confrontation works only in special circumstances, within which it may also assume various forms.

For instance, non-violent non-cooperation and non-violent protest are strategically different and will have different effects. Again, a non-violent group might find itself in uncomfortable allegiance with others who do not share the same principles though espousing the same cause. In a situation where supporters of this common cause mingle in large numbers, non-violence can be difficult to maintain, and its proponents are vulnerable to manipulation. Likewise, just as non-violent protest frequently depends on the conscience of those against whom it is directed, so it may also rely on the mobilizing of a wider jurisdictional power against some local form of oppression. Thus, federal troops were deployed in the southern US to implement desegregation; and in Northern Ireland in 1972, direct rule replaced the Stormont regime, which had assumed that local show of force would secure the *status quo*. Even the professedly non-violent are therefore not always free from complicity in the deployment of force that they theoretically oppose. With this in mind, I want to return to the idea that it is better to talk than fight, and also to suggest that the opposition between speech and violence is complicated in much the same way as is the opposition between non-violence and violence, personal communication and the objectification of others.

The philosopher Eric Weil argues that discourse – which he describes as the true end of philosophy – is always inherently opposed to violent action. In reply, Emmanuel Levinas suggests that the conceptual coherence at which philosophical discourse aims is itself suspect because it imposes a totality upon others and therefore does not escape the taint of violence altogether. Although Levinas might seem here to extend the meaning of violence too far, the point he makes is hard to ignore once it is raised. Indeed, the injuring and killing of human beings is incommensurate with the effects of threat, verbal abuse, or argument, and it is well not to lose sight of this difference. Yet, everyday uses of the word 'violence' commonly reproduce gradations of meaning of the kind to which Levinas points. Thus, we might talk about a violent disagreement, a violent rugby tackle, a violent storm, or a violent opinion. Also, the idea of violence is not far removed from the idea of violation, and we can talk of someone's privacy or integrity being violated, thereby invoking a notion of quasi-violence but not necessarily entailing physically violent action in the usual sense. It seems, then, that we readily attribute violence to nature's unconscious processes, human pastimes, opinions, intentions, and speech, as well as to physically abusive behavior.

I do not want to discuss these various usages in detail, but simply to notice that inter-relationships between violence and language are complex. Jacques Derrida even suggests – developing Levinas – that speech produced 'without the least violence' would 'determine nothing, would say nothing'. Consequently, we find ourselves constrained to oppose violence mainly by some lesser violence, and we should understand how deeply we are compromised by history itself, which forces such constraints upon us.

HD, 1–3

2.

I want now to suggest that among the many modes of discourse through which violence can be described and assessed, literature is distinctive because it personalises and complicates the conceptual descriptions by which we might contrive to define violence in order to keep it at a safe distance, more or less. This does not mean that we should eschew the conceptual; only that the quest for rational clarity ought to remain alert to the gaps and fissures between ideas and experience.

Broadly, violence occurs whenever another human being is treated as an object or thing, rather than as a person able to give or refuse consent to enter into discourse or relationship. Any attempt to deface or absorb another person without regard for that person's willing co-operation is therefore violent. As Simone Weil eloquently says, violence congeals, hardening and turning the other to stone. Its supreme expression is making a corpse of the other – that is, something wholly inert. But violence also can congeal life before abolishing it, and this is the condition of the enslaved and oppressed.

Clearly, the most explicit violence is physical, producing corpses and effecting the abjection and silencing of its victims. But violence takes many forms, and finds a principal aider and abettor in lies and propaganda. As we shall see, propaganda simplifies the truth about violence in much the same way as violence simplifies the truth about personal relationships. By contrast, the fictive dimension of imaginative literature (itself, paradoxically, a kind of lie) can discover in new ways the deceptions on which propaganda depends – the lies, that is, at the heart of violence. But although literature and propaganda are opposites, this does not mean that there is, somehow, a single literary vision of violence. Rather, each writer's achievement remains distinctive, and the singularity of a personal voice – the individual's personal experience taking the form of words – is itself a value that the impersonal mechanisms of violence would destroy. Still, in unmasking the over-simplifications by which violence is perpetrated, the fictive imagination can help us also to discern and describe certain mechanisms characteristically at work in violent behavior, operating often beneath the threshold of the perpetrators' consciousness, and frequently as seductive and compelling as they are dangerous.

HD, 3–4

3.

As Feldman says, within the H-Blocks (a prison in Northern Ireland) we see the body as a 'stage where the state is made to appear as an effective material force'. That is, the individual is depersonalized, and in a Foucauldian manner, as Feldman goes on to say, the state produces political subjects conformed to its own image. In the process, the body is objectified, its innermost privacies invaded by mirror searches and by surgical instruments. It is decontaminated by chemical disinfectants, and repeatedly abased, reduced to a thing with no interior, no personal dignity.

The prisoners responded in two main ways, both of which confirmed the irreducible value of the human person. The first was to show that whatever hardships were imposed on them they would transcend by being even more severe on themselves. Thus, they refused to cooperate with orders to wash, to bend over, to do as they were told on simple matters, even though knowing that such refusals were a licence for violence against them. The blanket and dirty protests were self-inflicted, and the words of the 1917 hunger striker, Terence MacSwiney, came to define a whole way of life: 'it is not they who can inflict most, but they who can suffer most, will conquer'. The second way was to find support from the mythology of traditional Irish Republicanism, which was closely involved with the Irish language and the Catholic religious heritage. Although Bobby Sands often speaks like a modern socialist revolutionary, he just as easily invokes the Catholicism of his early upbringing as, for instance, when he tells how he and his fellow prisoners recited the rosary in unison from within their cells. As we shall see, this mixture of religion, violence, resistance, criminalization and nationalism is highly volatile and ambivalent.

PP, 148–9

4.

Throughout, Sands makes clear how the abjection of the prisoners is directed at having them conform; in short, their bodies become an arena in which war is waged against their determination not to yield. On one side, Sands feels himself pitted against the sheer material force of a state apparatus bent on criminalizing him – for instance, by the deployment of 'heavy gear' (hoses and disinfectant), and the manhandling where he is 'thrown like a side of bacon' and spread 'like a pelt of leather'. On the other side he feels a determination, which he describes in terms of spirit: his captors 'had destroyed my body but had failed to break my spirit'; 'they have nothing in their entire imperial arsenal to break the spirit'; 'they cannot nor ever will break our spirit'. Consequently, the more insistent spirit is on its freedom and integrity, the more mechanical and impersonal is the material force used against it.

This violent opposition between matter and spirit is represented by Sands' frequent allusions to birds, in which he draws a contrast between their natural song and flight, and the fact that they are imprisoned in cages. The symbol of a lark singing on a strand of barbed wire soon became a popular icon representing the plight of the H-Block prisoners and of the 'national liberation struggle' in general. The symbol originates with a story Sands learned from his grandfather, and which he published in an essay entitled *The Lark and the Freedom Fighter*. The story tells of a man who captured a lark and kept it in a cage to hear it sing. However cruel the man became, the lark refused to comply, and eventually it died. The song is the lark's freedom: 'as my grandfather rightly stated, the lark had spirit – the spirit of freedom and resistance', and Sands now feels he has 'something in common with that bird'. Also, the cage does not just represent confinement; it is an assault on the prisoner's 'humanity', as a result of which he becomes 'a type of machine', a thing produced by the material force used against him to destroy his spirit. Eventually, in the story, the man who captured the lark gets caught and dies in a trap of his own making. Then, 'the birds came and extracted [sic] their revenge by picking [sic] his eyes out, and the larks sang as they never sang before'.

PP, 150–51

5.

Population shifts in Northern Ireland in the early 1970s resulted in extensive geographical segregation, especially in Belfast, and the main boundaries were marked by so-called 'peace lines' – that is, the high walls and palisades that still criss-cross much of the urban landscape, and which effectively keep the ghettoized communities locked in and intruders locked out. In 1972, the city centre itself was barricaded and supplied with checkpoints and extensive surveillance to monitor anyone entering or leaving. Emergency powers allowed the authorities to arrest people on suspicion, and despite the fact that a very small number of those arrested were indicted, the vast majority were interrogated for periods exceeding three hours, even if they confessed straight away. Clearly, the security forces wanted as much information as possible about people's lives and habits in order to oversee and to control more effectively an already highly segregated population. Surveillance cameras, helicopters (heli-tellys), image-intensification night telescopes, radar, remote recording devices, checkpoints, road blocks, constant army patrols, arrests on suspicion and internment became common facts of life as the Troubles escalated. Also as the prison population soared and as the distinction between 'special category' (political) prisoners and ordinary criminals was hotly debated, the plight of the prisoners itself came to resemble in an intensified form the plight of the ghettoized elements of the community at large. Thus, in his prison memoir, *Cage Eleven*, Gerry Adams suggests that the internees' relatives – 'thousands of wives and mothers and fathers and husbands and children' – year after year 'do the real time'. A booklet, *The Outsiders*, produced by the Northern Ireland Association for the Care and Resettlement of Offenders (NIACRO), does much to confirm this point. Despite its cautious attempts to play down the political aspects of imprisonment since the start of the Troubles, *The Outsiders* makes clear how extensive and profound are the effects on families and communities of having one of their members arrested – in short, how imprisoned the outsiders often are by the plight of those held inside.

BE, 147–8

6.

With all this in mind, it should not be surprising to find the extreme factions in the Northern Irish conflict directing mirror-image accusations of genocide against one another. Thus, an *Orange Standard* headline announces 'Ethnic cleansing on our own doorstep', and goes on to describe Ulster Unionist leader James Molyneaux's message to Americans that the world press has swayed public opinion against the Serbs, but has ignored the plight of Ulster's Protestants, who, like the Bosnians, have also been subjected to 'ethnic cleansing'. By contrast, 'anything hinting at intimidation of Roman Catholics has received saturation coverage'.

Not surprisingly, *An Phoblacht/Republican News* carries a similar headline: 'Release of UDA genocide plan carefully timed'. The article goes on to describe a loyalist 'Doomsday' scenario designed to be put into operation should the British attempt to withdraw. Among other things, loyalist control will be consolidated by 'a process of ethnic cleansing', and, again, a parallel is drawn with Bosnia. We learn also that canvassers for some loyalist candidates in local elections wore badges inscribed 'Ulster Needs Ethnic Cleansing', and that the loyalists' preferred option 'has always been the mass murder of nationalists'. Here we notice a certain reluctance to align the 'nationalist community' directly with religion, but an earlier paragraph does clearly identify nationalists as Catholics who 'would be rounded up for mass execution'. In these examples the ethnic groups again mirror each other's rhetoric, locked into the same, depersonalizing routine of mimetic rivalry and recrimination.

Nicolai Berdyaev is a philosopher who especially insisted throughout his career on the opposition between true Christianity, which focuses on the person, and morality based on what he calls the 'herd instinct'. Freedom was Berdyaev's lifelong preoccupation, and he argues that tribal, ethnic, and national groups are driven by imperatives directed at their own survival, thereby diminishing individual freedom. By contrast, Jesus' core teaching aimed at breaking the impersonal, instinct-driven bondage of the tribal or ethnic unit, and such freedom can be experienced only by individuals who take the risk, as Jesus did, of transgressing creatively against the depersonalizing confinements of the prevailing group morality. Berdyaev's insight into the positive function of the law in protecting people from violence and exploitation often comes close to Girard's, but Berdyaev pushes the enquiry in a more philosophical direction, claiming that law is powerless to effect the kind of creativity – always an act of the Spirit – by which individuals emerge into personhood. Here, as everywhere in his work, Berdyaev holds that human beings do not properly exist apart from others in community, which is to say, persons meeting one another in freedom beyond the confines of the herd and its loyalties and rivalries. A community of persons is what is meant by God's kingdom, and the gospels consistently point to the limitations of the kinds of order forcibly produced and guaranteed by the law. Berdyaev goes on to argue that there can be no Christian state, and the tragic tension between personal freedom and society will remain until the Kingdom of God is realized and the state will pass away.

BE, 18–19

The violence inflicted on the hapless Northern Irish 'joyrider' Harry McCartan was met by official denials that sectarianism was a contributory factor, despite the perpetrators themselves saying the opposite. This disregard of the obvious was clearly an all-too typical means of affirming and maintaining the transcendent impartiality of the law without regard for the actual, personal experiences of those involved.

7.

In 2002, Harry McCartan, aged twenty-three, was apprehended in the loyalist Seymour Hill area of Dunmurray. Harry came from the nationalist Poleglass estate, and was a notorious joyrider. That is, he stole cars and drove them dangerously and at high speed, ditching them when he was done. One report claims that he had stolen more than two hundred cars, and for his trouble he spent time in jail.

By all accounts, Harry was a reckless customer, and recklessness is made up of bravery and stupidity mixed to varying degrees. Thus, he was brave enough to steal cars from within loyalist enclaves and stupid enough to be found drunk by a group of Seymour Hill vigilantes on their own turf.

There is some suggestion that Harry was set up by people who wanted to see him dealt with, but details of this sordid little subplot remain unclear. By contrast, the main outcome of Harry's reckless behavior is not unclear at all: he was beaten until he was unrecognizable, and was fastened to a wooden stile by six-inch nails driven through his hands. Locally and internationally, news reports described Harry's ordeal as a crucifixion, and I want to ask what is entailed by saying that.

Harry's hands nailed to a post might well evoke the

judicial torture favoured in ancient Rome and made famous by the execution of Jesus. If the resemblance seems at first not especially striking, we might reflect that some thought must have gone into providing a hammer and nails, so that even the dullest among the perpetrators would have registered – especially in the context of Northern Ireland's sectarian strife – a glimmer (at least) of recognition that here, however crudely, they were enacting the ritual made famous as Christianity's chief symbol.

Still, it does not matter so much what the vigilantes thought they were doing. The point is that they did in fact evoke the religious symbol in a disturbing way. News reports seized on the point, describing Harry as a 'crucified man', 'crucified by vigilantes', 'crucified by thugs', subjected to a 'crucifixion beating' by a 'crucifixion gang'.

By contrast, Superintendent Gerry Murray, who investigated the incident, is reported as having 'ruled out' a sectarian motive (*Telegraph*, 4 November 2002). This opinion is echoed by Chief Constable Hugh Orde, who advised caution: 'It's very easy to take short snapshots of this community – the lunatic fringe. It sells newspapers. But it's not capturing the reality' (*Boston Globe*, 9 November 2002). Yet, when it comes to evading 'reality', Orde and Murray seem at pains to avoid seeing the elephant in the drawing room, and in this they are followed by the imperturbable BBC (3 November 2002), which describes an 'impaling attack' but scrupulously avoids any mention of religion except to quote Superintendent Murray as ruling it out. The BBC even claims that Harry's father 'had no idea why his son was attacked'. As we shall see, other reports attribute quite different opinions to Harry's father and to other McCartan family members. In short, the BBC (like Murray and Orde) seems largely concerned to decontaminate Harry's ordeal, cleansing it of religious infection.

Responses in Poleglass and Seymour Hill were not so fastidious. Harry's mother is reported as saying that her son 'suffered like the Lord' (*Boston Globe*, 9 November 2002), and his father flatly condemned the attack as sectarian ('This is because he is a Catholic' (*Guardian*, 5 November 2002), as did Harry's brother, who points out that the loyalists 'knew that he was from Poleglass and they said "We have got a Catholic here"' (*Ireland On-Line*, 4 November 2002). For their part, astoundingly, some loyalists tuned right in, as ever unwilling to pass up an opportunity for bad publicity. Graffiti in and around Seymour Hill mocked at 'Harry ... also known as Jesus (Ha. Ha. Ha.)', while announcing to the world that 'Joyriders will be crucified' (*Boston Globe*, 9 November 2002; *Telegraph*, 5 November 2002). Although UDA boss Jackie McDonald assured the press that the attack was not approved beforehand, he added that if UDA approval were in place, Harry 'would have been nailed up in front of the estate as a warning to others' (*People*, 10 November 2002). The mixture of forced hilarity and menace in these loyalist responses, far from suppressing sectarianism, flaunts it.

The contrast between the official and local responses is all too clear: the authorities anxiously avoid the religious dimension, whereas the estate dwellers (on both sides) insist on it. We might now ask why this is so and what it might mean to say that Harry was crucified. On the one hand, he was not exactly a man of heroic virtue suffering for a high principle to which he dedicated his life, and we might hesitate to depict him too enthusiastically as Christlike. On the other hand, he was a victim, and Christ invited us to see the victimized as somehow like himself, enjoining us to treat them with compassion. Certainly the fact that Harry was nailed to a wooden stile suggests a parallel with Jesus as victim. And insofar as Christianity is concerned with the plight of victims, it calls attention to the depersonalizing mechanisms of victimization and scapegoating that operate everywhere in human societies. Knowing how this is so, people who get the message (not just committed Christians) might subsequently be better able to desist from such behavior. This is not a theological or faith-informed idea, but, rather, an aspect of Christianity that is too important to be left only to the churches and theologians. And so here I want to turn briefly to the French anthropologist and literary intellectual René Girard, who provides an account of the crucified Christ that focuses on the idea of the scapegoat victim.

Girard argues that human societies are founded on violence and are maintained by the threat of violence. This unpleasant fact is concealed as much as possible so that societies can run smoothly under a rule of law that presents itself as impartial and transcendent. Only by standing above group rivalries, feuds, and local animosities can the law quell the disruptive energies that swirl and eddy constantly through the social fabric. Yet some safe means have to be found to express and release the enmities, hatred, and rivalries which the rule of law causes people to repress, but which the law cannot fully control. Historically, religions have played a key part in helping to effect such a controlled release, and they do so through sacrifice and scapegoat rituals. That is, sacrificial victims and scapegoats become the focus of violent energies that might otherwise disrupt the social group, and these energies are allowed a cathartic release within controlled conditions. Emotional release and ritual are therefore often closely bound up together;

consequently, sacrifice rituals can give rise to powerful emotions, just as spontaneous violent impulses can find expression by taking a ritual, or quasi-ritual, form.

So, yes, Harry was maimed in an act not without religious significance, in which a spontaneous catharsis of pent-up fear and hatred was released in a quasi-ritual manner evoking a crucifixion, with an uncertain degree of self-consciousness among the perpetrators. Predictably, Superintendent Murray and Chief Constable Orde attempt to regulate the local rivalries by appealing to a decontaminated, transcendent law. Yet they do so without acknowledging how, in ethnic conflict zones everywhere, imagined representations of the other are the lifeblood of tribal hatreds and animosities ravenous for victims and fuelled always by a mixture of paranoia and resentment. In such situations, paranoia is a response to the supposition that the other group wants what you have (your job, land, assets), and resentment arises from a belief that members of the other group have access to pleasures and gratifications that you don't (a different kind of culture, sexual behavior, attitude to work, and so on).

Unfortunately, the reckless Harry triggered both responses simultaneously. First, he was an invader from the other estate, bent on stealing property; second, he was a joyrider motivated by an anarchic pleasure principle. Harry thus assumed (or had projected upon him) a representative rather than a personal identity, and the subsequent transfer to an objectified enemy of intensely imagined fears and resentments was expressed in an act of violence entailing extreme depersonalization.

IM, 110–14

As we see from the example of Harry McCartan, the differences between insiders and outsiders are central to the economy of violence, partly because the depersonalised and demonized outsiders are a means of ensuring group solidarity among the insiders and of smoothing over potentially violent internal divisions that might threaten the supremacy of the state. And so we often conceal our barbarity from ourselves by projecting it onto the barbarians outside the gates. But the hubristic consequences of this strategy need also to be reckoned with, as Virgil's story of the Trojan horse shows. In this context, I introduce the idea of 'regressive inversion' to provide some further clarification of the relationships between the depersonalizing agency of violent extremism and state power in modern ethnic conflict zones, such as Northern Ireland and Sri Lanka.

8.

In Virgil's account, as the Trojans break down their own walls to bring in the giant wooden horse, we are assured that they are 'forgetful, blind and mad', even to the point of ignoring the clanking armour of the Greek soldiers concealed inside. Later, when the city lies 'buried in sleep and wine', the Greeks let themselves out of the horse, kill the watch, and open the gates. Soon Troy is ablaze. Ironically, the Trojans are complicitous in their own destruction, as the outsiders are literally brought inside the city walls built to keep them out, and the poem stresses what an irrational act this was on the part of the insiders. Plainly, the horse is a stratagem, but it carries something also of its age-old association with irrational passion, here lurking unacknowledged among the Trojans themselves, as treacherously seditious in its own way as is the Greek ruse. It seems that one consequence of war against a depersonalized barbarian enemy is that it easily blinds us to our own barbarity, which then reappears as hubristic self-confidence or superstition redirecting our unacknowledged irrationality against ourselves, breaching our own walls. The paradox is that walls are necessary to repel violent invaders, but simultaneously they erect divisions that cultivate the very animosity they would repel.

PC 53–4

9.

People in the Middle Ages were inspired by high ideals (for example, the City of God), but were assured also of failing to realize them on earth because of Original Sin. Especially in the twentieth century, idealizing political movements contrived to keep, in secular form, the old desire for moral perfection, combining it with a secular pursuit of material progress and widespread skepticism about the idea of Original Sin. However, the combination of moral passion and skepticism has led to the disastrous vicious circles that Michael Polanyi calls 'moral inversion'. For instance, a person who desires the well-being of everyone soon encounters the recalcitrance of society as it actually is, and then confirms the purity of the moral passion for reform by denouncing the complacency and hypocrisy in those who have compromised with the current imperfections by accepting traditional social values. One way to preserve integrity is therefore to react violently against morality itself in its traditional forms. Nihilism is one result, and with it a ruthless purism enforced by a pitiless, impersonal machinery of violence that paradoxically is held to be a vindication of moral honesty in the pursuit of material progress.

SM, 133–4

10.

Primordial ties to kin-groups, cultural institutions and the like remain important because they provide stability for the development of a well-adjusted human ego. However, such ties also readily impart an exclusionary sense of identity that can be a source of prejudice. The Buddha's universalizing vision, like that of Jesus, directly challenges this kind of prejudice even while acknowledging the formative influence of the enculturation process. Yet, as the Discourses show, it is treacherously easy – despite repeated warnings and caveats – for the Buddha's teachings about absolute freedom to be re-deployed by a fatal misprision to supercharge the primordial passions informing the exclusionary sense of identity entailed by group membership. This process is *regressive* insofar as it reaffirms the depersonalizing mechanism of prejudice based on exclusion (the very thing that the universal religious vision was designed to transcend). Also, it entails an *inversion* of value insofar as it draws power and conviction from the languages and vision of transcendence.

SL, 114

Propaganda, lies, and disinformation have perennially been deployed in the exercise of state power and in legitimizing the use of force. The main antidote is supplied by personal encounter and dialogue, of which I take literature to be both a symbol and efficacious means. In the following excerpts, Homer's story about the Cyclops, in the *Odyssey* depicts how a failure of dialogue precipitates violence, and the disturbing example from Peter Conradi reminds us that in resisting the rule of force, dialogue and the invitation to personal relationship are often tragically ineffectual. In turn, the fragility of the interpersonal and the pervasiveness of anxiety caused by our mutual alienation leave the way open for propaganda to thrive, as Brigadier Kitson makes clear.

11.

Odysseus visits the cave of the Cyclops, Polyphemos, and makes an introductory speech, but Polyphemos does not answer. Instead, he picks up two of Odysseus's twelve companions by the heels and smashes their brains out on the floor, 'like killing puppies'. He then devours the dead men and rolls a giant boulder across the mouth of the cave to prevent the others from escaping. Later, he devours two more men and gets drunk on the wine Odysseus had brought as a gift.

As the Cyclops lies deeply asleep, Odysseus and his remaining crew prepare a wooden stake, hardening the sharpened point in the fire and then ramming it into the Cyclops's eye. The blinded Polyphemos rolls back the boulder to seek help, and Odysseus and his men escape. As he sets sail, Odysseus tauntingly reveals his name (he had concealed it earlier) and mocks at his distressed and raging enemy. But the elated Odysseus has not fully considered that the Cyclops's father is Poseidon, god of the seas on which Odysseus must sail. The vengeful Poseidon – able now to identify his son's enemy by name – ensures that Odysseus's journey is filled with misfortune.

Clearly, there is no talking to Polyphemos, bent on violence: no appeal could be made that would not merely confirm the terrifying gap between the personal appeal made by language and the sudden, shocking deaths of the men. Yet, equally clearly, Polyphemos does not imagine the consequences of his actions for himself. He is blinded physically, not least because he is already blind to the fact that violence begets violence unpredictably.

For his part, the altogether-too-smart Odysseus, whose desperate resourcefulness has saved the day, cannot contain himself, and his triumphalist bragging ends up eventually costing the lives of his entire crew at the hands of Poseidon. Like the primitive weapon he used in the cave, Odysseus's mockery is crude, turning the Cyclops into an object of contempt, just as the crewmen were nothing more than puppies to the Cyclops. In short, violence on both sides – whether we condone it or not – depersonalizes, and when it occurs, language either fails or is debased. Moreover, in response to the invasion of archaic terror and disorientation that violence brings with it, Polyphemos and Odysseus, not surprisingly, appeal to the gods – to Poseideon (for vengeance) and Athene (for deliverance).

Homer's ancient story is not just an engaging fiction; it is exigent, telling us that we cannot talk to the Cyclops who has decided on violence, and if we do it won't matter. This is because speech involves relationship, requiring mutual understanding, but violence depersonalizes and silences its victims. Today, paramilitaries wear masks and their victims are blindfolded or otherwise 'disappeared'. In Northern Ireland, the Shankill Butcher, Lenny Murphy, finished off one of his victims with a spade, smashing in his face after having first removed his teeth with pliers. The killers of ex-IRA member Eamon Collins mutilated him and seem to have run a car over his head to finish the job. The effect in both cases was to render the victim faceless and voiceless – not a person – by an extreme objectification, the ferocity of which betrays how desperate the anxiety is to conceal or obliterate the fact that your victim is your fellow creature, a person like yourself.

IP, 116–7

12.

In his remarkable autobiographical reflection, *Going Buddhist*, Peter Conradi relates a story he heard in Poland about the deportation of Jews to the gas chambers at Treblinka. The families who had been rounded up in the city square knew that they would not return from the place to which the cattle trucks would take them:

> In the square the terrified, ill-nourished women from the ghetto passed their babies over their heads from one to another set of upraised hands – I saw it in my mind's eye, with care, though presumably also with haste – towards a high wall enclosing them. They were thrown over to the other side, where pious Catholic Polish women waited and caught, collected and brought them up as gentiles.

The core of this horrifying narrative is the plight of the mothers passing their babies over the wall, by way of the other pairs of hands conveying them there. As Conradi says, thinking about it 'stops my mind'. But in what sense might a Buddhist describe the mothers' action as an example of 'non-attachment'? Could we imagine the mothers saying, yes, personal attachment brings pain and it is better for us not to feel our loss? Clearly not. The mothers' loss is lacerating, and the literal non-attachment between mother and child causes barely imaginable anguish.

Yet the story does not just horrify, because courage and compassion manage also to register their own kind of protest. Just as the agents of state power depersonalize their victims, herding them like cattle, so, by contrast, the mothers and their helpers become for a brief time, as it were, transpersonal, reaching beyond self-preservation, beyond their individual concerns, in order to save the babies. Sorrow indeed persists, tragic grief and loss prevail – almost, but not quite.

In another, very different narrative about letting go, *Flight to Arras* (New York, 1942), Antoine de Saint-Exupéry describes a dangerous mission that he flew as an aviator during World War II. When his plane was struck by anti-aircraft fire, he felt he would not survive. The enemy shells, he tells us, 'drummed upon the hull of the plane as upon a drum. They pierced my fuel tanks. They might have drummed upon our bellies ... But who cares what happens to his body? Extraordinary how little the body matters'. He goes on to describe an exhilarating non-attachment, a lack of concern for his personal safety or survival:

> *Your son is in a burning house. Nobody can hold you back. You may burn up but do you think of that? You are ready to bequeath the rags of your body to any man who will take them.*

The body doesn't matter because 'Man is a knot, a web, a mesh into which relationships are tied. Only those relationships matter. The body is an old crock that nobody will miss'.

As first glance, Saint-Exupéry's account seems to have little in common with the story about the Polish mothers. The pilot experiences an elated self-abandonment, rushing headlong, like the boy's father, careless of consequences, vigorously active. By contrast, the mothers are victims, powerless and with no chance of escape. He survives to tell his story; the mothers do not. His voice speaks with authority; their voices are silenced. We know his name; they are anonymous. He loses nothing; they lose everything. The man rushes into the fire to bring back his son; the mothers attempting to save their children have them taken away.

Yet these opposites do not entirely exclude one another.

Saint-Exupéry is vulnerable before the high-powered weapons, as he realizes, and the mothers take action despite their powerlessness. In both cases separation is accompanied by intuitions of interrelationship, and in both, self-surrender does not preclude personal engagement but transforms it through love and courage.

And yet, any suggestion that there is a comforting moral lesson in either of these stories should make us hesitate. The bravado of the fighter pilot is too close to cliché – the self-immolating ecstasy of a warrior bound for glory and the 'ultimate sacrifice'. And the mothers' horror is somehow cheapened by the suggestion that their story has a palliative dimension. We need to be careful, if only because there is no way to calculate or map the interplay, here, among non-attachment, suffering, compassion, liberation, and tragedy – in short, the actual, personal entanglements that encompass and humiliate the theories by which we attempt to explain them. And so, although a moral teaching might well be clear, how it applies to the quick sands of our ordinary human confusions is another matter, calling for compassionate understanding rather than principle alone.

IP, 59–61

13.

In his book *Gangs and Counter-Gangs* (1960), Brigadier Frank Kitson describes how his anti-Mau Mau strategies in Kenya depended on undermining the enemy by infiltration and by creating a crisis of confidence focused on doubts about who exactly the enemy was. Thus, counter-gangs were deployed both to win the confidence of and to terrorize the real gangs. In 1971, a year after Kitson was appointed to command the 39 Brigade in Belfast, he published another book, *Low Intensity Operations*. Basically, he argues that the limitations imposed on modern warfare by nuclear weapons will result in a global increase in low-intensity conflict. The army must learn to deal with this new face of modern warfare, and Kitson stresses that effective intelligence networks are the key to doing so successfully. To this end, he recommends (among other things) the use of the same kinds of 'pseudo gangs' as in Kenya, as well as 'psychological operations', propaganda, informers, and captured insurgents who can be persuaded to switch sides. In this context, he takes to task conventional commanders who insist on making 'rousing speeches' while indulging in 'activities designed to create the illusion of battle'. By such behavior, these old-fashioned soldiers merely lead their men 'away from the real battlefield onto a fictitious one of their own imagining'. By contrast, for Kitson the real war against insurgency is a battle of minds, and he presents the world of 'psy ops', disinformation, and organized treachery as less 'fictitious' than the old-fashioned rhetoric of martial heroism indulged in by those who have not yet caught up with the new reality. In a sense, Kitson is right – the rhetoric of martial heroism is indeed frequently self-deluding, naïve and dangerous. But the 'reality' to which he directs us is hardly reassuring, if only because lies, deceit and manipulation are basic to it, so that the 'fictitious' now itself becomes the 'real' thing. The usual depersonalizing strategies of those bent on violence now combine with a cynicism that willfully undermines the basic structures of human trust and relationship.

HD, 55–6

14.

Further covert aspects of army operations, in so far as these have been documented, open upon an even more disturbing, shadowy world of undercover operatives, shoot-to-kill ambushes, murders that were covered up (as in the so-called 'pitchfork killings'), disinformation and black propaganda (via the 'Lisburn lie machine'), the treatment of prisoners in a manner condemned by the European Court of Human Rights as 'inhumane and degrading', and the out-of-control killings of unarmed civilians by the paras in the events of Bloody Sunday (1972). In short, even under the fairly close scrutiny permitted by the accessibility of Northern Ireland to journalists and news media, violence conducted by the state all too readily spirals out of control and is consequently masked by undercover operations, concealed by disinformation, and confused by internal rivalries. This is not to deny that there is a real difference in degree between the worst violence – exemplified, say, by the Shankill Butchers and the Omagh bombers – and the violence of the army and police putatively attempting to secure civil order while observing legal guidelines. By and large, this difference in degree is significant and has done much to prevent Northern Ireland from descending into the chaos of civil war, but I am keen to stress that difference in degree is not difference in kind, and the lesser and the greater violence are violence just the same, binding its practitioners into the same frightening strategies of depersonalization that can best fuel blind hatred. What, then, might literature add to this already compelling body of information?

HD, 28

In response to the question about literature and violence raised in the previous excerpt, my main suggestion is that literature is well-ordered to reveal how ambiguities, ironies, lies and confusions can combine to legitimize force and to conceal its dehumanizing consequences. In the following excerpts, John Millington Synge's

The Playboy of the Western World is partly about the transgressive, personalising power of literature in relation to the over-riding hegemony of the state. Thomas More's astonishing portrait of Richard III shows how a climate of lies, half-lies, fear and uncertainty undermines personal relationships and is a breeding ground for tyranny. Graham Greene's interview between the pious woman and the prison guard in *The Power and the Glory* depicts a conflict between personal loyalty and the law – a conflict that remains as unresolved as it is moving and revealing. Dostoevsky's episode of the Grand Inquisitor in *The Brothers Karamazov* is a searching enquiry into the perplexing relationships between state power and personal freedom. Samuel Beckett's *Catastrophe* deals with the interplay between violence, depersonalization, and how readily we might normalize our own submission to social regulation under the concealed threat of violence. Beckett dedicated this short play to Vaclav Havel, who at the time was imprisoned for insurrection in Soviet-ruled Czechoslovakia. In this context, *Catastrophe* addresses the relationships between state force and depersonalization, and how we construct differences between insiders and outsiders.

15.

As Christy Mahon says in *The Playboy of the Western World*, 'the blow of a loy' taught him about the difference between the 'gallous story' and the 'dirty deed'. In dialect speech 'lie' is pronounced almost exactly like 'loy'. Thus the loy with which Christy delivers the blow to his father is also the lie by which he contrives to escape the consequence of his action. In this context, the depiction of Christy as a parody of Christ ('Christy Son of Mahon', says Hugh Kenner) takes on an added dimension, for the law here also is transcended by the power of the word, namely Christy's tall story. Synge then goes on to show us how people can co-operate with their oppressors, as do Pegeen and the others who first indulge Christy's romantic fantasy as an escapist distraction, and then shut out its transforming potential in order to return to the impersonal edicts of the Western World ruled by Father Reilly and the peelers. Paradoxically, Christy re-shapes himself personally through imagination, though he is forced also to adjust his 'lie' to a disenchanting reality before he leaves, in charge of himself and at last (relatively) independent.

PV, 10

16.

The History of King Richard III, as Alistair Fox says, is full of people who know or suspect tyranny but who are too burdened by circumstances, or too half-hearted, or too much in complicity, or afraid, or compromised, or who think it is not their business, to do anything about it. There is thus a sheer empirical tyranny of circumstances, which, in neutralizing the will of individuals, indirectly feeds the blatant tyranny of a singular will to power. The fascination of Richard is not, after all, that of Iago, whom everyone thinks honest. Richard does not care to be thought honest, only sufficiently credible, or interesting, to take advantage of ordinary moral ambivalence. He knows the immense gulf between rhetorical structures and moral intent, between words and action, and he knows that action alone counts. It is not so much that he is increasingly a poor performer; rather that he cares less about appearances (or words) as his power is increasingly assured. Appropriately, the terms 'colour' and 'frame' are used throughout to describe his devisings: he presents 'colorable proofe' that Rivers and the dukes are guilty, he puts 'some colour' on the matter of Hastings's arrest, he accuses Shore's wife when he cannot 'colour' matters otherwise, and the Queen is worried because the princes are put 'in duress without colour' and may likewise be killed without cause. Shaa undertakes to 'frame' the city to accommodate Richard's plan, things are 'oute of al frame' when the sermon goes wrong. Buckingham expects a response from an audience that 'the Mayer had framed before' and Hastings advises the lords not to raise objections that might put things out of joint so that they 'shold never be brought in frame agayne'. All this suggests painterly illusion and perspective, which Richard knows how to manipulate, not so much in order to simulate a real world as to raise questions – as in the various experiments in curious perspective among Humanist painters – about the peculiarities of our own point of view. Richard provides just sufficient colour, a just sufficiently oblique angle to confuse his interlocutors, to undermine their personal trust in one another and even in themselves. He disturbs their equilibrium just sufficiently to make their day-to-day passivity seem positively tempting.

DM, 31–2

17.

Not many writers have a keener sense than Graham Greene of how complex and ambiguous we are as moral creatures. His novel, *The Power and the Glory*, is about a priest who is hunted by the military in revolutionary Mexico as part of a repression of organized religion. The soldiers will shoot the priest if they find him, and he is trying to reach the border in order to escape. As a priest, he is a bit of a disaster. He drinks heavily and he has a child. He travels rough, as a peasant, one of the people (which he is). By and by, he is picked up for vagrancy, but he is not identified by the police and he has to spend a night in jail because he can't pay the fine. He is so exhausted and dis-spirited that he wishes only to be caught so that his ordeal will be over. And so, during the night, in the crowded jail cell, in the darkness, he confesses to the other prisoners that he is a priest and also that he is a bad priest – a whiskey priest who has a child. He makes these admissions, hoping that one of his cellmates will inform on him. In the darkness, he is scolded by a pious woman who has been locked up for the night because she was caught with a religious object on her person. She is disgusted by what she sees as the priest's betrayal of his office, and she says, angrily, that she will report him to the bishop.

The next morning, when it is time for the prisoners to leave, the woman passes by the priest, and he whispers, 'Pray for me'. A guard overhears and asks, 'What did you say?'. The woman replies, 'He was begging. I have nothing for him'.

And so, although the pious woman despises the priest, she won't turn him in. Some deeper loyalty prevails. Still, she wants him to know that she holds him in contempt, and so she insults him: he is a wretched creature, a beggar, and she wants nothing to do with him ('I've nothing for him'). The reader alone recognizes here that the woman unwittingly condemns herself out of her own mouth. 'I've nothing for him' means that her world, her values, are quite separate from the priest's. And indeed her conventional piety knows nothing of the way of the cross that the priest will embrace by and by.

Think of the interplay of awareness through the several points of view – of the guard, the woman, the priest, then extending further to include the reader. Each level carries a moral judgement marked by a conviction of objectivity, but they are all in fact compromised and partial. And is this not true to how we are as complex persons who are often conflicted, caught, as is the pious woman, between the impersonal prescriptions of the law and other, more personal kinds of loyalty and relationship?

BH, 108–110

18.

Ivan [in *The Brothers Karamazov*] is an intellectual who finds himself in a state of emotional confusion. He wants to get to know his younger brother Alyosha, a novice monk attached to the elder, Zossima, who has told him to leave the monastery and go out into the world to marry. Alyosha is impressed by Zossima's sanctity, but is confused and upset at the prospect of the old man's imminent death, and by being ordered to return to the secular world.

In order to meet Alyosha in private, Ivan invites him to an inn, claiming to have a private room so that Alyosha need not be discomfited at appearing there in his cassock. But Ivan tells less than the truth, for he has merely reserved a table separated from the rest of the room by a screen. He then orders Alyosha fish soup, tea and jam, which the ascetic young man enjoys, and in this context Ivan explains his objections to religion. Critics sometimes assume that Ivan is an atheist, but it is not clear that he is. Earlier, he had flatly denied God ('No, there's no God'), but now he tells Alyosha he did that to tease him: 'Well, this may surprise you, but perhaps I accept God'. He goes on to explain that 'it is not God I do not accept, but the world he has created'. Yet even this is carefully hedged, and, as with his article on ecclesiastical reform, which puzzled readers because they could not determine Ivan's position, here again his stance is elusive and provisional. His admission, 'it is not God I do not accept' does not entail that he does accept God, and so he remains equivocal.

Ivan begins with the problem of suffering, and especially the suffering of children. It is incomprehensible to him that a good God should allow it, and it is repugnant to condone it as God's way. Ivan illustrates his case with descriptions of cruel acts inflicted on children, and, with Alyosha, we indeed feel pinned to the wall. Then, after telling an anecdote about a General who has a small boy torn to pieces in front of his mother by hunting dogs, Ivan asks what should be done to the General. "'Shoot him!" Alyosha said softly, raising his eyes to his brother with a pale, twisted sort of smile.' Ivan goes on to conclude that even if God offered him the benefits of some higher understanding, the price would be too great: 'I don't want it, out of the love I bear to mankind. I want to remain with my suffering unavenged. I'd rather remain with my suffering unavenged and my indignation unappeased, *even if I were wrong*'. For similar reasons, Ivan says he does not want to give Alyosha up to the influence of 'your Zossima' at the monastery.

In this context we come to the Legend of the Grand Inquisitor, an unwritten poem that Ivan summarises for his brother as a way of confirming the case set out in the anecdotes about cruelty to children. Ivan imagines that Christ returns to earth and performs miracles during the Spanish Inquisition. An old Inquisitor, who has just overseen the execution by burning of one hundred heretics, recognizes Christ and has him arrested. The Inquisitor promises to burn Christ the next day, but goes on to divulge, for the first time, 'what he has been thinking in silence for ninety years'. He begins by accusing Christ of valuing personal freedom too highly, instead of providing miracles at the right time and place so that his divine authority would be sufficiently evident that people would submit to it. After all, most people need to be ruled and guided, and the forces of 'miracle, mystery, and authority' alone can assure their happiness. But, says the Inquisitor, 'you rejected all three and yourself set the example for doing so'; instead of asserting his authority, that is, Christ 'chose everything that was exceptional, enigmatic, and vague' as a way of throwing people back upon their own freedom. This is especially evident in the temptations in the wilderness, which were themselves miraculous because so perfectly representing the human weaknesses that are best controlled by authority. But Christ 'did not want to deprive man of freedom' and so he refused all three. For the same reason, he refused to come down from the cross when the mockers challenged him to do so: 'you did not want to enslave man by a miracle', but, rather, 'you hungered for freely given love', even at the cost of great suffering.

In short, the Inquisitor accuses Christ of respecting human beings too much, and of making them unhappy by imposing the burdens of freedom upon them. If people are free to love, they must be free also to do evil, but most people are little better than 'children rioting in class', needing to be controlled for their own good. Consequently, the church has attempted to repair the damage done by Christ's high-mindedness, and under ecclesiastical regulation 'men rejoiced that they were once more led like sheep and that the terrible gift which had brought them so much suffering had at last been lifted from their hearts'. Because human happiness needs to be legislated, its burdens are shouldered by the few who, like the Inquisitor, understand and are willing to 'guard the mystery' by taking upon themselves the 'curse of knowledge of good and evil', so that thousands of millions of fortunate people can live harmoniously within a well-governed society. As for Christ, who has come again now to meddle dangerously – well, he will be burned alive like the other heretics.

Through all this, Christ says nothing, and at the end kisses the old man on the mouth: 'That was all his answer'. The Inquisitor starts back, but then opens the door and sets Christ free, and we are told that although 'the kiss glows in his heart', the old man 'sticks to his idea'. Thus ends Ivan's account of his unwritten poem, and immediately he laughs it off as nonsense. But Alyosha is saddened because such things weigh upon his brother's heart, and, 'without uttering a word', Alyosha rises and kisses him. Ivan recoils in delight, accusing Alyosha of plagiarism, of having stolen this gesture from the poem, and with that he sends Alyosha back to his *Pater Seraphicus*, Zossima, who, as Ivan and Alyosha both know, is dying. Ivan asks only for another kiss before they part, but Alyosha hastens away, forgetting the violence done by Dimitri to their father, Fyodor, which had given rise to the meeting with Ivan in the first place.

I have summarized the Legend with some attention to its context because Dostoevsky's genius is especially evident in how a character's ideas are made enthrallingly perplexing by the personal circumstances in and through which they are expressed. Consequently, as soon as we begin considering the case for and against the Inquisitor's attitude to freedom, we begin to spill from depth to depth of indeterminancy as we consider the different perspectives, strategies, motivations, and vulnerabilities of the characters and their situation. Dostoevsky drives us into a luminous obscurity that confounds the clarity that it simultaneously elicits, and Dostoevsky's extraordinary power lies in his ability to lead us into the depths of the human personality, and to provoke us to these kinds of complex reactions.

PC, 119–21

19.

Samuel Beckett's play, *Catastrophe*, depicts a rehearsal, involving a character called the Director, aided by a Female Assistant, and a lighting technician called Luke (who is offstage). These three work on a fourth character, the Protagonist, arranging and fixing his position and gesture. They remove his hat and dressing-gown, roll up his pyjama sleeves and trousers, and whiten his arms, legs and face. The light then fades, illuminating only the Protagonist's bowed head, and the Assistant 'timidly' asks, 'What if he were to … were to … raise his head … an instant … show his face … just an instant?'. The Director then replies angrily: 'For God's sake! What next? Raise his head! Where do you think we are? In Patagonia? Raise his head! For God's sake!' Having rejected the suggestion, the Director looks again at the Protagonist and makes a swift conclusion: 'Good. There's our catastrophe. In the bag. Once more and I'm off'. The lights routine then is repeated, leaving the head illuminated, and there is a storm of applause. The action seems concluded, but, as the stage direction indicates, 'P [the Protagonist] raises his head, fixes the audience. The applause falters, dies'. There is another pause, and the light fades. That is all.

The Director's production of a satisfactory catastrophe, the high point in his play, depends on controlling the Protagonist's passive body. The Director talks in cliché throughout, and, as one critic suggests, comes across as a kind of 'invincible institution'. The Protagonist's limbs and head are whitened, maximizing their visibility and suggesting the control exerted on these moving parts of his body. The Protagonist is thus depersonalized, turned into a spectacle, an object to be viewed, and his eyes are kept lowered. Though he is not female, his condition resembles that described in Laura Mulvey's analysis of the typical depiction of women in Hollywood films, and something of the same political point is being made. But when the Protagonist looks back, fixing the audience at last with his own gaze, another catastrophe occurs – an upset of the Director's production, and one which silences the spectators. It is as if an indolent Belacqua at last lifts his head from his Dantesque torpor and now looks back, demanding acknowledgement of his own personal presence. Yet the audience is too discomfited to give such an acknowledgement, and is so habituated to the spectacle of passivity to which it is conditioned by the directors of its own political condition, that it now pays to come and see the same routine confirmed in the theatre.

Still, the audience I am now discussing is the fictional audience within the play, and a moment's reflection reminds us that the Protagonist's raised head is itself a gesture approved by yet another Director – the invisible one of the play we ourselves are watching. The Protagonist's subjectivity is therefore, after all, produced, and our own applause at the end will confirm our comfortable relapse into the conventional habit of letting ourselves be controlled, the Belacqua-like torpor we imagine we can avoid. The produced gesture does not threaten us because it is just another part of the process of manipulating the Protagonist's body. The suggestion that the Protagonist's response is subjective is therefore conjured away, as the Protagonist takes his place in the play we are watching, which is distinct from the play performed for the imaginary audience within the play. Nonetheless, we do not entirely succeed in conjuring away the return gaze, even though our desire to acknowledge it is frustrated by our spectator's role. This complex frustration is an entirely Beckettian effect, and depends on his keen sense of the conundrums and duplicities inherent in the mind-body problem.

A considerable, further poignancy is added to all this when we consider the dedication of *Catastrophe* to the imprisoned Vàclav Havel. On his release in 1983, Havel wrote to Beckett to say how moved and sustained he had been to learn of the play and its production at Avignon in 1982. 'For a long time afterwards', he wrote, 'there accompanied me in prison a great joy and emotion which helped me to live on amidst all the dirt and baseness'. It is unclear what exactly Havel's reaction was to a play he had not seen, and news of which was relayed to him indirectly, to avoid censorship. But we can take his remark at face value: across the divide of the Iron Curtain, Beckett's play sustained the prisoner. For audiences who actually saw the play, knowing the dedication to Havel, the Protagonist's challenging gaze must have seemed – as it still does – a personal gesture of defiance against the oppressive state. Yet the audience simultaneously is made aware, as we have seen, that theatregoers place themselves in the passive role they like to think they repudiate. Materially, that is, they remain conformists, even while, as private individuals, they might think otherwise.

PC, 97–99

The legitimizing of oppression with a view to shaping an apparently 'normal' or 'natural' social order is nowhere clearer than in the concerns highlighted by feminism. As Ashis Nandi points out, post-colonial societies and ethnic conflict zones provide especially good examples of this problem. In light of Nandi's description of how women are arbitrarily cast in prescribed roles, questions arise about how to describe the differences between men and women in the first place, as the following excerpts point out by describing a variety of feminist approaches to the personal.

20.

Nandi suggests that colonialism is based on patriarchal rule, ensuring subservience and representing the colonized people as feminine. But when the colonizers depart, the rulers of the new state all too frequently mimic the authoritarianism of their erstwhile masters, from whom they often received an education in the Enlightenment ideals encouraging them to rebel against colonialism in the first place. Consequently, the new rulers tend to reproduce the old patriarchal stereotypes, to the disadvantage of women, who continue to be made subservient. In short, the 'colonised men colonise the women', inflicting the same oppression that they themselves had endured, unable to break the entail of scapegoating and violence. All too frequently, women's contributions during the early phase of rebellion and national liberation are neutralized by the new state that goes on ruling in the only way it knows how. Elsewhere, Geraldine Meaney also cites this analysis, arguing that the process is especially evident in 'the sexual conservatism and political stagnation of post-independence Ireland', and that women are 'the scapegoats of national identity', symbols of the nation over which men exercise power, and are therefore not recognized as persons in their own right.

BE, 110

21.

It is important to notice that diversity and difference cannot in and of themselves produce equality. Indeed, as Mark Ryan points out, cultural pluralism can strengthen the established state apparatus because many interest groups in contention with one another are forced to appeal to the centralized state power to enforce their individual claims. In short, some other common values must be brought into play if pluralism is not to become a mere confusion, confirming the status quo. And so the question arises: if some progressive elements of feminism in Ireland are pluralist, and if pluralism itself might well leave state power too much unaffected, how then are we to describe the contribution of feminism?

Even a brief look at a recent collection of essays, *Revaluing French Feminism*, shows how complex debate is among feminists on this topic. Yet, one particular conceptual challenge keeps emerging and can be summarized as follows. Some feminists argue that women are different from men in ways that men cannot know; yet these differences should not prevent men from treating women equally. But how, then, are we to name this equal factor? Whatever words we supply to describe equality (human nature, personhood, universal human subject, and even the word 'equality' itself) will open us to a charge of essentialism that ignores women's different experience. It is surprising with what insistence the old medieval 'nominalist' and 'realist' (here referred to as 'essentialist') conundrum reappears in this collection of essays. Indeed, Fraser is explicit about this, arguing that women need 'to navigate safely between the twin shoals of essentialism and nominalism, between reifying women's social identities under stereotypes of femininity, on the one hand, and dissolving them into sheer nullity and oblivion, on the other'. 'Gynocentric' feminists such as Luce Irigaray and Hélène Cixous, who insist on a distinctive female experience, are sometimes accused both of essentialism and biologism. But Linda Alcott warns also against the opposite problem, which, like Fraser, she calls nominalism, and which is exemplified by Julia Kristeva's rejection of claims for any kind of stable identity as metaphysical and repressive. Kristeva calls in question the very meaning of the word 'woman'; instead, she associates 'heterogeneity' with the desired decentering of identity, linking it also to the feminine because it deconstructs the patriarchal or 'symbolic' social contract. Judith Butler in turn argues that Kristeva's theories end up supporting the hegemony of the 'symbolic' (the domain of paternal law, which is the culturally intelligible and rule-governed) rather than effectively contesting it. That is, by linking the feminine to an unnameable heterogeneity, Kristeva deprives women of a shared critical stance challenging to patriarchal structures on matters of principle. Clearly, there is an analogy between Ryan's view that pluralism consolidates state power, and Butler's that heterogeneity consolidates the Law of the Father. It seems important, therefore, as Fraser says, to avoid the determinisms lurking on both sides of the binary opposition, avoiding the Scylla of nominalistic heterogeneity and the Charybdis of essentialist biologism in assessing the idea of the person in a feminist context.

BE, 113–14

22.

For the moment I want to consider what positive values Daphne Hampson attaches to the kind of emancipation from biblical religion she recommends, while remaining within her Western heritage. The main answer is that she proclaims the importance of personal equality. For instance, she accuses men who accept stereotypical views of women as having 'failed to see me for the person who I am, or to envisage what equality might mean'; under the influence of patriarchal religion, a woman is not allowed to be 'another human person'; an 'explicit recognition and value' should be 'accorded to each person'; feminists in theology are especially interested 'in the understanding of the human person and in human relationships'; feminist themes such as 'the mutual empowerment of persons' are too often missing from Christian exegesis. She argues that men must join women 'on a basis of equality', and for this to happen, men must give up the desire to dominate, because their own personal 'dignity and self-esteem' depend on them doing so.

BE, 117

23.

Let us briefly consider Maria Pilar Aquino's *Our Cry for Life. Feminist Theology from Latin America*. Aquino is a liberation theologian interested in the social relevance of the gospel in a Latin American culture oppressed by 'imperialist capitalism' as well as racism and sexism, all under the aegis of a particularly virulent '*machista structure*'. In this culture, *machismo* reinforces capitalism, and women are doubly oppressed, 'both because they are poor, and because they are women'. But Aquino also calls liberation theology to task for ignoring women's experience. This is a contradiction, she says, if only 'because liberation theology assumed the principle of total liberation and fullness of life for the poor and oppressed, among whom women stand out for their neediness'. In part, Aquino repairs this omission and in so doing she appeals repeatedly to the equality of persons. Thus, she recommends that in exploring their identities, women will be 'rediscovering ourselves as human persons'. This means that particular differences will be brought into play, that dialogue will be a means of exploration, and individual women will recover 'the elements of our own originality'. Persons here are agents whose dignity and originality require respect; they are unique individuals and yet are fulfilled through dialogue and insertion into society. In some such manner, women must seek 'to construct equal models of interhuman relationships', and one chief problem about gender stereotypes is that both men and women 'are amputated in their personalities'.

Aquino comments frequently on how women are depersonalized, and she hopes for 'the creation of an egalitarian alternative society' which would be fully 'interpersonal'. She describes the subordination of women also as 'the most prolonged, scandalous and hidden of existing inequalities', and then looks to a 'multidimensional', bodily rooted, and flexible set of approaches to anthropology as the best means of moving forward in this 'open, plural, ongoing task'.

Like Hampson, then, Aquino resorts repeatedly to the idea of the person as a foundational concept, as do various other feminist theologians. For instance, Anne Loades calls for 'a Christian understanding of the whole person' and indicates that the 'possibility for women as well as men' becoming a 'whole person' will require 'real change in the nature of the community'. Monika K. Hellwig likewise insists on our equality as 'persons in the divine image', and Rosemary Radford Reuther's telling analysis of patristic and medieval interpretations of the *imago dei* (wherein women were thought to be ontologically unfit to bear the divine image) stresses equality of personhood as the main criterion for asserting other kinds of equality, wherein 'we open our hearts to all persons as bearers of God's image'.

Again, Beverley Wildung Harrison argues that the way forward is 'to build up and deepen personhood itself', and she condemns the misogyny of the dominant forms of historical Christianity – the 'hatred and fear of the real, full, lived-world power of female persons!'.

The condemnation of misogyny among these theologians is no less heartfelt and vigorous than that expressed by Hampson, though in Hampson's case the critique entails a break with Christianity, but not with the idea of the person. In short, there is a wide range of views in theological feminism, from a 'post Christian' position that remains within Western liberal tradition, to the Latin American liberationist view that criticizes Western liberalism, and then to historically and theologically based critiques of various kinds, reproducing the complexity of feminist debates elsewhere.

BE, 118–19

4   LANGUAGE, DESIRE, AND SUFFERING

Because we have language we have the future tense, and so we can imagine ways to improve our lives and make them more meaningful. But the gap between imagining what might be and our immediate experience of what actually is can never fully be bridged, and desire therefore is accompanied by feelings of separation and longing. Tragedy focuses especially on this perennial un-fulfillment of desire in an imperfect world where standards of fairness and justice are discovered to be imaginary and scandalously incommensurate with the sheer enormity of unjustified suffering. The first excerpt, below, deals with *Romeo and Juliet,* a play in which the fatal interconnections between the central characters and their circumstances lead to the tragic conclusion in which, ironically, the life-affirming energy of the young people – the very thing that we admire – is their undoing in the situation in which they find themselves. Reason supplies no sufficient consolation, and yet we keep looking for reasons because, as persons, we are shaped by desire and committed through language to meaning, even as we recognize that we cannot fully attain it.

1.

Near the end of the play, when Romeo and Juliet are already dead in the tomb, a watchman arrives and asks for directions. A frightened pageboy points ahead: 'There, where the torch doth burn' (V.3.172). A torch has been placed outside the tomb because Romeo needed to find his way there at night, and so the watchman should now go in that direction. Yet, the pageboy says more than he knows, as audiences and readers quickly understand. Insofar as the torch is a beacon indicating the way ahead, it belongs within a series of references throughout the play to navigation, linked in turn to Romeo and Juliet as 'star-crossed' lovers. Whether or not they are fated to disaster (their destiny written in the stars) or have navigated badly (their choices caused them to founder) is kept in a carefully unresolved suspension, which contributes greatly to the disturbing poignancy of their story. The torch burning bright against a somber background reminds us that the young people had shone out against the troubled world of their feuding families, and just as the torch brings illumination to the dark place of the ancestors in the tomb, so Romeo and Juliet's marriage promised to bring new understanding to the feuding houses. But these meanings are now painfully inverted because Romeo and Juliet are in fact dead and their light is extinguished. We are left wondering if they are dead because they were young and foolish (compelled by eros) or because the world of the grown-ups crushed them with its enmity and greed (civilization taking its toll).

Shakespeare's tragic vision invariably returns us to the core predicament that we see here, yet again. That is, we are asked to consider that the qualities for which we most admire a person will, in certain circumstances, bring about that person's destruction. For instance, Hamlet is so thrillingly intelligent that he captivates and dazzles any audience or reader who cares to listen. The bravura performance is of course Shakespeare's, as he offers to explore the tragic potential of a highly gifted mind and then creates a poetry that really does express great intellectual distinction. But also, Shakespeare creates a set of circumstances in which Hamlet's high intelligence and powers of analysis are a liability, virtually guaranteeing his demise. The very gifts we admire render him fatally vulnerable in his particular situation.

Another tragic figure, Othello, offers an exact counter-case, as A.C. Bradley pointed out long ago. Othello is an accomplished military leader with a passionate, romantic sensibility that is expressed in glorious poetry. Provoked by the scheming Iago, he becomes pathologically jealous and murders his innocent wife. Everything depends on Iago preventing Othello from pausing to analyze the situation, and if Othello and Hamlet were to change places, each finding himself in the other's situation, there would be no tragic endings. Othello – decisive and effective, a man of action – would not hesitate but would confront the murderous Claudius. Hamlet – introverted, analytical – would take his time and easily see through the monstrous Iago. In short, Othello's tragedy is that he does not hesitate, and Hamlet's is that he does, and Shakespeare imagines a set of circumstances in which hesitation on the one hand and precipitate action on the other are irreparably destructive.

Yet, within each play, circumstance and character also remain so interwoven that we cannot simply moralize (the tragedy is caused by personal weakness) or simply resort to fatalism (circumstances alone are to blame). The tragic fact is that gifted and admirable human beings can be destroyed because of their gifts, and where is the justice in that? Shakespeare doesn't say, but if we cannot admire and have compassion for the heroes for being the remarkable people they are, then Shakespeare's poetry fails; if we do not feel defiant about the cruelties of fate, mediated by society and its impersonal constraints, then we do not grasp how vulnerable even the most gifted people really are.

IM, 157–9

2.

Elvira Madigan is a Swedish film made in 1967. It is based on the story of Sixten Sparre and Elvira Madigan, who ran away together and then committed suicide. Sixten Sparre was a lieutenant in the Swedish army, and Elvira Madigan was a tightrope walker in a travelling circus. Elvira Madigan was her stage name. Her actual name was Hedvig Jensen. Their story is famous in Sweden – their version of 'Romeo and Juliet' – and several films have been made about it. Pure liebestod, not to everyone's taste. But the photography is so rendingly beautiful, and the music (Mozart's piano concerto 21, now popularly known as the 'Elvira Madigan Theme') so perfect, and the girl so overwhelmingly lovely, that I can't help but look beyond the 'Aren't they self-indulgent' criticisms to something deeper and more touching and permanently real about human experience and about love 'as strong as death'. Unamuno writes of fated lovers such as these that the 'supreme longing for life, for more life, the longing to prolong and perpetuate life urges them to death'. The problem they force on us then is 'tragic and eternal, and the more we seek to escape from it, the more it thrusts itself upon us'. Without a tragic view of life, says Unamuno, we don't really experience what is most vital in our own personal lives at all. With complete cheerfulness, I have to confess that actually I don't trust anybody who doesn't have a tragic sense of life – though I don't much advertise that.

BH, 98–9

Aldous Huxley's novel, *Island*, explores how a small society's successful attainment of co-operation and freedom comes into conflict with the greed, hatred, and delusion of the world at large. Ironically, the interpersonal co-operation characteristic of advanced social groups such as Huxley's island community is precisely what leaves them vulnerable and open to exploitation. This is a different emphasis from the one we find in tragedy, but Huxley understands very well how enduring the conflict is between a personal commitment to the shaping of a common good, and the impersonal, predatory mechanisms that seek to exploit the benefits that are thereby achieved.

Vincent van Gogh was well aware of this same broad state of affairs. In a world that often harshly rejected him he looked to art in order to affirm the ideals to which he aspired and which were a means for him to keep desire alive despite his own tragic suffering. As Van Gogh understood – and as Hans Georg Gadamer explains – art engages desire in order to further understanding, but this process is never finished and remains as open-ended as desire itself.

3.

In Aldous Huxley's *Island*, the descriptive, novelistic passages are carefully paralleled by discursive sections wherein the complementarity of image and idea is probed and tested. The inside of the ideas is, as it were, scrutinized in terms of outside criteria brought to bear on them. And so, the inner sanctuary of the island stands symbolically against the outside world of hard facts that threaten to destroy it. ('And meanwhile the outside world has been closing in on

225

this little island of freedom and happiness'; "Are you that man from Outside?" she asked. "Almost infinitely from the outside", he assured her. ... "We're all very sorry for you", she said'). Likewise, the main character's personal inner experience is challenged by the world of other people and objects in which he is to find either divine enlightenment or demonic isolation. ('By what sinister miracle had the mind's natural state been transformed into all these Devil's Islands of wretchedness and delinquency?'; 'William Asquith Farnaby – ultimately and essentially there was no such person. Ultimately and essentially there was only a luminous bliss, only a knowledgeless understanding, only union with unity in a limitless, undifferentiated awareness. This, self-evidently, was the mind's natural state'). The opposites are carefully balanced, and Huxley's concern is not to allow advantage to the side of eternity or to the personal desire for wholeness and completion without presenting the counter-case which checks our enthusiasm. And so, positive utopian ideals are forced repeatedly to make concession to an anomalous, alien reality that seems to refute them, and the most compelling effect of *Island* is the sense of how Huxley absorbedly and painfully wrestles with himself to be honest in assessing his own theories. His personal vision emerges from within this tension itself.

SA, 33

4.

Farnaby reads in the *Notes on What's What* that 'one third, more or less, of all the sorrow that the person I think I am must endure is unavoidable. ... The remaining two-thirds of all sorrow is home-made and, so far as the universe is concerned, unnecessary'. Yet the irreducible one-third emerges more and more clearly as Huxley's central preoccupation, and the 'Essential Horror' persistently haunts Farnaby and afflicts even the most saintly of the Palanese: "'How can anyone take yes for an answer?" he countered. "Yes is just pretending, just positive thinking. The facts, the basic and ultimate facts, are always no."' You are always alone, Farnaby observes. 'Alone in your suffering and your dying', and 'what about the presence of cancer, the presence of slow degradation? What about hunger and overbreeding and Colonel Dipa? Are *they* Pure Suchness?'.

These passionate arguments are resolutely dramatized because Huxley sees that to validate in human terms his belief in the imageless transcendent, he must force himself to return again and again to the facts of suffering and so to the horizontal time-dimension where suffering belongs. In so doing, he makes of his ideas – literature. Near the beginning of *Island*, for example, we listen to Nurse Appu's encouraging lecture to her patient, Farnaby, on preventative medicine: "'So whether it's prevention or whether it's cure, we attack on all the fronts at once. *All* the fronts," she insisted, "from diet to auto-suggestion, from negative ions to meditation."' But Nurse Appu's idealism is offset by the account of how she could not prevent her own irrational infatuation for the nasty Murugan. Likewise, the elevated teachings of the Raja's *Notes on What's What* are countered by the bookmark happening to be a poem of Susila's that reveals her recent bereavement. So the extended account of the idyllic and scientifically advanced Pala is qualified by the 'senselessly evil' facts of death. Farnaby recounts his memory of Molly's cancer, while Dr. Robert's wife dies from the same disease. 'Only God', says Farnaby, 'can make a microcephalous idiot', and even the 'occasional islands of decency', such as Pala, are 'always totally surrounded by the Essential Horror'. Again, for Huxley, the human predicament is constituted by the contradictions themselves.

SA, 34–5

5.

The troubles that persistently destabilized Van Gogh's life help to explain why he repeatedly sought anchorage in an all-but-undauntable utopianism, despite the fact that his idealistic aspirations kept running aground upon the shoals of a predictably recalcitrant actuality. Still, his many disappointments notwithstanding, he sought to go on affirming the 'everlasting *yes*', as he says (borrowing from Carlyle). Throughout the letters, we find ourselves everywhere engaged by a remarkable conversation between these strongly contending aspects of Van Gogh's personal experience – a dialogue, as it were, between his unusually unstable ego and the self-identical utopian ideals to which he aspired. In turn, the poles that constitute this dialogue also define the parameters within which imagination operates as it infuses (general) ideas with (particular) sensuous immediacy. Moreover, as with the adventure of self-fashioning itself, imagination is fraught with uncertainty and peril, and in committing himself to imagination as the foremost means of his own self-fashioning, Van Gogh encountered these difficulties head-on. Consequently, I want to consider how, throughout the letters, Van Gogh's many reflections on imagination mirror and intensify the challenges, as well as the gratifications, that lie at the heart not only of his own self-fashioning but of the self-fashioning process in general.

PW, 146

6.

As Hans Georg Gadamer says, imagination seizes our whole being and opens us to new integrations and unforeseen possibilities by showing us the limits of our cultural horizons and unconscious prejudices. That is, we all inherit the biases implicit in our language and social mores which enable us to take hold of the world and engage it in a personal manner. And so Gadamer argues that tradition enables understanding, but he goes on also to point out that a work of art surprises us, taking us out of the habitual patterns that shape our understanding. We are thereby able to come into a more open and more personal relationship with others who likewise allow their prejudices to be tested and unsettled. Works of art perennially provoke surprise and illumination, inflaming our desire for understanding.

NT, 34

By focusing on the crucifixion of Jesus, the gospel narratives of the New Testament put the problem of innocent suffering starkly before us. Jesus experienced the bitterness of abandonment and failure, and the resurrection effectively makes its protest against tragedy only when tragedy has been encountered in its full, unspeakable extremity.

In this context it is worth mentioning the influence on Western Christianity of the *Song of Songs*, a love poem that has stood as a figure for spiritual desire from its origins in the Hebrew scriptures to its virtual ubiquity in medieval Christian monasteries. Whereas the cross takes us into the abyss of abjection, the *Song of Songs* insists on keeping desire alive, affirming that there are moments of illumination along the way, touches of bliss, visits of the bridegroom. As Karl Jaspers says, tragedy should return us to the ordinary world and to an enhanced sense of communion – of being more personally in touch with others through the deeper, shared knowledge that reflection on tragedy allows. As long as we are not silenced by suffering, our not giving up on desire is therefore a means for expressing a life-affirming defiance against the scandal of suffering with which tragedy confronts us.

7.

Mark's narrative reminds us, then, that faith is not formal or aesthetic, and the special test of faith is the cross, the problem of suffering innocence. It is worth noticing that the gospels provide a strikingly consistent account of the cross, which occupies a commanding role in all four narratives. The event threw the disciples into disarray in an embarrassing fashion that is unlikely to be invented. The Roman procurator who ordered the execution is named, and the events are described to emphasise that they actually occurred, even though, admittedly, the gospel narratives are also theological through and through and were written in light of the resurrection kerygma. But it seems that if we doubt the historicity of the crucifixion, we must doubt even more radically the historicity of everything else that the gospels tell us.

Here, then, the gospel as literature, concerned with signs and the interpretation of signs, pushes us, as it were, to the very edge of its own universe of discourse. In Mark, especially, the cross is the sign which stands for the failure of signs to provide solace or certainty. This is not just another strategy within the text; it is the record of an event, the place of abandonment where the Son of God cries out, 'My God, my God, why hast thou forsaken me' (15:34). The confounding reality of what actually happened is confirmed by the rhetorical pattern of *katabasis* and *anabasis* being turned inside out, as Jesus' mockers call on him to provide a sign to come down from the cross, on which, in his vulnerability, he has been raised up. Here, the usual pattern of raising up to significance what has fallen down into suffering and emptiness is inverted. The story of the cross confounds the paradigm of the narrative which presents it, and in showing us this, the narrative once more lurches at the brink between sign and event. And we are asked to assess what this means. We might, for instance, read Jesus' cry of abandonment as a quotation from Psalm 22, and thus through further exegesis of that text see him calling on God even in forsakenness. Yet such a reading might be sentimental, a desire, still, to read significance into a situation where there is none. The cry could just as well mean – as it has no doubt for many subjected to extreme suffering – that 'God' at last is an empty word. How are we to know? How are we to read such an event, such a narrative describing the significance of such an event, and derive knowledge from it that faith will sustain us in *extremis*? The striking achievement of Mark's treatment of this, and of the other signs in his gospel, lies in the way he presents how difficult our personal experience of such questions is.

NT, 20–21

8.

In the face of these facts, the claim that Jesus is God is either wishful thinking (the merest fiction), or a compelling truth about the human condition, which we accept on faith. Such faith is, then, like a two-pronged pincer. It demands on the one hand that we take an affirmative attitude to the world, and, on the other that we accept that God's way in the world is to crucify the innocent. This paradox can produce considerable existential anguish, which, as a literary document, the New Testament brings vividly to life. It does so, in part, by making us acutely conscious of how suffering innocence challenges any belief at all in a good God. The startling conclusion that the transcendent, unapproachable deity comes among us to die and to be raised up is therefore either a mere story expressing imaginatively our all-too human desire for an encompassing meaning, or a revelation compelling our assent because it alone permits us to reconcile God and the world.

NT, 8–9

9.

In the Song of Songs the poems for the most part are in direct speech, as the Lover and the Beloved address one another, expressing their mutually felt intensity or lamenting the anguish and longing caused by separation. The individual poems perhaps describe a narrative sequence, as when the Beloved seeks the Lover through the streets, questioning the watchman and eventually taking the Lover back to her mother's house. Yet the narrative does not make complete sense, and the dialogue is not fully coherent, despite strenuous exegetical attempts to make it so. Moreover, the richly contrived metaphors and similes counteract the narrative progression, turning it into a kind of splendid blazon. 'Thy teeth are like a flock of sheep that are even shorn'; 'Thy two breasts are like two young roes that are twins, which feed among the lilies'; 'thy nose is as the tower of Lebanon which looketh toward Damascus': the extravagance of these comparisons is arresting, and it is as if the narrative is frozen while the comparisons move laterally, appropriating to the body various aspects of the world in which the body dwells. Thus, as Francis Landy says, a whole series of interconnections and fusions takes place between the lovers and the world, which is thereby drawn into the relationship they celebrate even though the very arbitrariness and wildness of the metaphors also simultaneously signal a division or incongruity. Yet in the interruption of the narrative by these emblazoned and paradoxical similitudes, allegory finds its opportunity, reaching for the encompassing and unifying idea (or higher narrative). Still – as with the eroticism and sensuality – the dramatic elements will not simply be absorbed into allegory and the Song of Songs continues to strike us as a series of celebratory love poems, a discontinuous and polymorphous interpenetration of elevated possibilities and imaginative immediacy.

At every point in his *Commentary*, Origen asks us to acknowledge that the Song of Songs is both narrative and dramatic. In the prologue, he explains each of these in terms of the other: 'For we call a thing a drama, such as the enaction of a story on the stage, when different characters are introduced and the whole structure of the narrative consists in their comings and goings among themselves'. Throughout the *Commentary*, Origen tells us who the characters are, and how they interact. In the first *Homily*, he admits that the issue is confusing, and is not sure about precisely how many *dramatis personae* there are, but there seem to be four main elements: 'the Husband and the Bride; along with the Bride, her maidens; and with the Bridegroom, a band of intimate companions'. Yet noticing Origen's broad emphasis here can help us also to see how thoroughly it is overwhelmed by his actual exegesis. His attention to narrative and drama is supplanted by what really interests him, which is to say, not the actual story but a transcendent meaning which is spiritual or allegorical. Thus, he proceeds from the 'superficial meaning of the story' to the 'mystical exposition', and his originality as a biblical scholar lies in his insistent seeking of a 'spiritual' sense, the highest fulfillment of desire, which becomes for him the way to perfection. The manner in which desire, here, opens upon the transcendent even as it remains entangled in a confusing material world describes very well the perennial tensions inherent in the human condition.

SD, 49–51

As I have suggested, imagination is central to the tragic sense of life because imagination identifies the goals to which desire aspires, thereby enabling us to feel all the more strongly the painful dislocation between the ideal and the actual. In this context, George MacDonald provides a link between the previous excerpts on Christ's crucifixion and the uses and functions of imagination in fantasy as a way of describing our human situation. MacDonald's central insights are reproduced in a different mode by Lewis Carroll, and with his usual uncanny insight, Shakespeare in *The Winter's Tale* challenges us also to interpret the claims of reason, desire, and imagination in the context of a difficult experience of personal self-fashioning and self-understanding in the light of loss and suffering.

10.

Fantasy, MacDonald thought, takes its life from the conflict between an actual world of adult responsibilities and an imaginary, dream-like one to which we cannot altogether escape, except, perhaps, through death. In raising the problem of mortality through the opposition between real and imagined worlds, fantasy presents us with the problem itself of belief. 'We live by faith, and not by sight', MacDonald writes in his essay, 'The Imagination', and in a world where many things are not clear, imagination moves as 'the presence of the spirit of God', directing and enticing us to a vision of happiness beyond. But faith cannot turn away from the world in which we live, and 'What can be known must be known severely'. Such knowledge – especially the unavoidable facts of suffering and death – is mitigated by the solace imagination offers.

It is no great step from here for the Christian MacDonald to conclude that Christ's cross is the most important example of suffering, and that the cross shows faith opening up to imagination the perspective of hope: 'Sorrow the Pledge of Joy'. Also, because the cross puts so clearly the difficulty of accepting what imagination seeks to reveal, Christ's cry of abandonment is 'the deepest practical lesson the human heart has to learn'. MacDonald consequently maintains that great art, and especially fantasy, shows us something of this lesson by re-enacting how a person 'gazing about him in pain ... suddenly beholds the material form of his immaterial condition'. In our own lives, then, we should strive to imitate the cross, but not, MacDonald insists, by relying on 'formula or creed'; rather by attempting, like Christ, to do God's will.

MacDonald's argument shows how he looks to the cross and resurrection as the supreme factual example of what imagination attempts to effect in a different mode. But we ought not to impose our religious beliefs, and the point is ruined, MacDonald implies, as soon as fantasy becomes allegory, for then the pain is not well enough represented and the problem of faith does not challenge the reader directly. The cross, it seems, must remain implicit if fantasy is effectively to delineate a fulfillment beyond death. In that case, the status of the resultant work as specifically Christian becomes questionable, but the means by which it deploys imagination to evoke the personal struggle of each of us for belief or unbelief remains compelling.

SA, 94

11.

When Lewis Carroll's Alice awakens with a new knowledge of death, we see that although she has overcome her childish fears, she does not outgrow the physical anxieties on which they are based. These instead are deflected into the adult world, and in one sense the *Alices*, simply, are about the arbitrariness of adult reason in an environment where, inexplicably and often terrifyingly, we live, knowing ourselves mortal. What we take for civilized order is therefore often the imposition of shared prejudice, the bizarreness of which is plain if we analyze its conventions imaginatively. The Gryphon and Mock Turtle are absurdly composite beasts, but they are recognizable social types as well as fantastic inventions, and their literary effectiveness depends on our seeing both elements. The Gryphon is heraldic and noble; the Mock Turtle ungainly and comically awkward. High-minded social pretensions are 'mocked' truly enough by the nonsensical combination of turtle and calf, as also by the Gryphon's inability to reproduce in his own (ignoble) speech the high symbolism of his nature. Although the Mock Turtle has had an impressive education, the result is a babble of ludicrous puns upon which he erects the twin self-indulgences of rudeness ('Really you are so dull!') and sentimentality concerning his own last end ('Soo-oop of the e-e-evening, / Beautiful, beautiful soup!').

But although the episode makes fun of Victorian adults, Carroll does not underestimate how oppressive their world is, and the Mock Turtle and Gryphon also represent the social prejudices and conditions to which Alice must adjust. She may not offend by raising the subject of death (she keeps checking herself from saying she has had fish for dinner), and yet must not be intimidated. Everywhere, instead, she measures the claims of passions that are ungovernable and rude (the Red Queen), against those of the disembodied symbol-making intellect (the White Queen), and the ensuing conflict raises questions about language itself. Humpty Dumpty's disquisition on words, like the white sheep's myopic attention to the particular sense, opens upon an entire panorama of riddles, puns and parodies. These give delight, but help also to show us, with Alice, something of the discontinuity between language and things, and how the identity of each of us is formed within that gap.

SA, 95

12.

England's greatest poet shows us how intriguing and uncanny the threshold between imagination and the sense of an encompassing mystery is. At the end of A Winter's Tale, Hermione, abused wife of the tyrannical King Leontes, is restored to him after sixteen years. Contrite and repentant, Leontes is invited by his wife's loyal servant, Paulina, to view a life-size statue of Hermione, whom he believes dead, and who, indeed, seems also to us to have died of grief sixteen years previously. As the characters stand in silence, the statue, astoundingly, comes alive.

This sublime conclusion to the play strikes us in a number of ways. When we first see the statue, we experience an agonizing hope that, somehow, the man and his wife will be re-united, and then indeed they are. Paulina promises explanations afterwards, but we begin immediately on our own account to ponder what such explanations could be. Hermione, we surmise, had not died, but lived in seclusion for sixteen years until this moment when reconciliation with Leontes would be most perfect. But this reasonable explanation makes a peculiar story out of the play's action, and especially the part Paulina plays in it. Perhaps, it occurs to us momentarily, Hermione did die, and, with Leontes, we witness a miracle. That, of course, offends reason because we do not rush at the miraculous when there is evidence for an alternative solution. Yet the miraculous makes a claim if only because of our desire that Hermione *should* be restored. Even if a statue must be brought alive to do it, the rightness of the conclusion would answer our profound wish, beyond reason.

We misread the poetry if we do not feel *both* that the play shows us it contains its own reasons, and yet that beauty arises also from how the images awaken in us a desire, a poignancy, that the literature itself does not undertake to explain, and which both opens out upon the encompassing mystery (by way of Apollo's oracle), and in upon the mystery of ourselves. In showing us the awakening of desire together with the finally unexplainable dissatisfactions that accompany it, imagination reveals the core tensions at the heart of the personal itself.

LM, 37

Religious promises of an imagined afterlife in which desire is fulfilled and there is no more suffering have all too often had harmful consequences for those alive here and now in an imperfect world. Secularism has done much to curtail the excesses of religious zeal in compelling assent and enforcing religious belief, and yet secularism has also promoted utopian ideals in ways that have caused a great deal of suffering.

In the broad interplay between utopian aspirations and critical reason, discernment is necessary, as, for instance, the Buddha's discourses remind us. A serious engagement with literature also requires the exercise of analogous kinds of tact and critical perception, as examples from Samuel Beckett and Brian Friel show. That is, a tension between the counter-factuals that we imagine and the actual state of affairs that we can describe needs to be kept in balance, and our personal decisions repeatedly negotiate these tricky currents between 'is and not-yet'.

13.

Promises carry a liability, and by failing to acknowledge the relationship between the promises of perfection and the imperfections of history, the world's religions have contributed greatly to suffering. Tyrannical devotees have too readily worshipped their own desire for power projected onto powerful deities whose imagined will becomes their own. How sublime a submission. Voltaire's écrasez *l'infame* rang out in protest against the manipulations of fear and ignorance by the special interests of the religious, and a century later Nietzsche lamented caustically that there was not even enough religion left in the world to destroy the world's religions. This secular critique promoting modern skepticism and secularism must either help to bring religion home to itself in the task of redeeming humanity and humanizing nature, or help us to dispense with religion altogether.

My main comments here are directed from this broad perspective towards the Judaeo-Christian tradition, not only because it expresses the main religious aspirations of Western literature and culture and in so doing contributes to the idea of the person developed by that culture, but also because the Judaeo-Christian tradition received the full attention of the Enlightenment critique which, in a way, it produced from within itself. Christianity is therefore especially pertinent to a discussion of how religious and secular languages might act co-operatively in negotiating the way towards a renewed understanding of the personal in a transformed world, the omega-point of eschatological promise in which there is no division between secular and religious.

LP, 144–5

14.

In these examples, the Buddha engages us imaginatively in order to dissuade us from foolish attachments to transitory pleasures which are a source of suffering. Yet we might also notice a further dimension to the Buddha's repeated meditations on death and disease. These meditations do not just cause us to recoil in horror; they also familiarize us with unpleasant facts that, for the most part, we prefer to ignore. Frequently repeated, vividly imagined evocations of sickness, disease and death do indeed contain a warning about the futility of sensual indulgence, even as they also offer an invitation to embrace with equanimity these perennial facts of our human condition with equanimity. A *bhikkhu* should feel at home among the corpses, unafraid because fear itself is part of the suffering from which he seeks liberation. Likewise, the world-hating ferocity of the extreme ascetics is a manifestation of fear and loathing, and imagination helps us to understand that such behavior is harmful. After all, the aforementioned meditation on the beautiful girl would not be effective if we did not appreciate and value beauty, just as we appreciate and value life and health. As always, the middle way requires discernment, and we need to be educated not only to understand this fundamental principle, but also to negotiate the felt complexities of our emotional lives, shaped as they are by forces, cultural and otherwise, beyond our conscious control.

So far, I have noticed how frequently the Discourses draw attention to language, and how there is a real analogy between a life conducted according to the *Dhamma* and a conversation that promotes understanding and insight. As we see, craving, desire, and attachment need to be convincingly, even sympathetically, evoked if the unenlightened are to be instructed effectively about them. And so the Discourses teach us the art of the detached agonist who engages with the sufferings of others out of compassion, whose detachment is not indifference, and whose engagement is not indulgence.

SL, 38

15.

In Samuel Beckett's novel *Murphy*, the title character early on compares himself to Belacqua, the inhabitant of Dante's *Purgatorio*, Canto 4, who is being punished for indolence by having to wait out a period as long as his earthly life before being allowed to climb the mountain of purgatory. As he waits, Belacqua's awareness that it would be better not to be indolent is cancelled by his knowledge that it is fruitless even to think of not being indolent until his waiting period is served. To be merely indolent, as in his earthly life, would be to lapse into a kind of torpor, but to be condemned to indolence removes whatever solace is provided by stupefaction, even while perpetuating the indolent condition. The poignant, agonizing fruitlessness of Belacqua's enervate but painfully aware condition appealed to Beckett, who makes use of it several times.

The Belacqua-like Murphy lives in London, and through connivance with his landlady he fraudulently sponges off a rich uncle in Holland. Eventually, the prostitute Celia gets him to propose to her, but they need more money in order to live together, and so Murphy looks for work. After consulting an astrologer, and as a result of further chance encounters, he ends up as a male nurse in a mental hospital where he is given a small room with a gas fire fed by a tap in the toilet. Soon he feels entirely at home among the insane, and so he stays there, abandoning Celia. He also strikes up a special relationship with a Mr. Endon, but at last gets blown up in an accident with the gas fire so confusingly linked to the toilet.

At the beginning of the novel, we find Murphy tied to a chair and attempting to put himself into a trance, a spiritual condition which would divorce him from his body and where he could be protected from outward events. He goes on seeking this condition throughout the novel, and thinks he comes closest to it in the insane asylum. Yet he also needs some further, personal relationship with others, as is evident in his regard for Celia and in his concern for Mr. Endon. With this in mind, at one point he looks into Mr. Endon's eyes, holding the man's face so close to his own that their foreheads almost touch. And this is what he sees:

> *Approaching his eyes still nearer Murphy could see the red frills of mucus, a large point of suppuration at the root of an upper lash, the filigree of veins like the Lord's Prayer on a toenail and in the cornea, horribly reduced, obscured and distorted, his own image. They were all set, Murphy and Mr. Endon, for a butterfly kiss, if that is still the correct expression.*

And so Murphy sees his own image reflected, but Mr. Endon does not recognize Murphy at all, and when they part, we are told, 'The last Mr. Murphy saw of Mr. Endon was Mr. Murphy unseen by Mr. Endon'. Also, the close-up reveals in detail the anatomy of Mr. Endon's eye, with its mucus, suppuration, and so on, and Murphy notices how the cornea distorts and reduces the reflection. All this has something in it of a scientist's objective view, but with a touch of rebuke to Murphy himself, who appears 'horribly reduced, obscured and distorted'. The sentence on the butterfly kiss then is whimsical, drawing our attention to the highly unromantic reality of the romantic motif of the mutual gaze. The comically painful close-up gives Murphy only a disenchanted view of himself and of Mr. Endon, and leaves Murphy with the deflating recognition that he is utterly unrecognized. Clearly, this account of looking at another person for whom you care is quite different from the full Dantesque vision where the other person is most fully recognized as a mirror of God's perfection.

PC, 85–7

16.

As Brian Friel's play, *Translations*, suggests, translation omits something, misrepresenting or distorting the original, and here commentators point to George Steiner's *After Babel*, on which Friel draws for this idea, as is acknowledged in a programme note.

In the play, Maire is indeed foolish to let her ambition to speak English blind her to the danger in which she places Yolland by her affection for him. And yet, the relationship between them, symbolized by the desire of each to learn the other's language, qualifies our reservations about their self-deluding romanticism and imprudence. In a remarkable courtship scene, they declare their love by reciting a litany of place names to one another. Their attempts to use each other's language become then a means of special intimacy rather than of public reference, and also an intimation of the mutual relationship between public and private that might obtain in a happier society. This scene shows us also how transgression can liberate, and the love relationship here is exogamous in the way language itself is exogamous, reaching for communication across differences... Yet the play is equally concerned about privacy, the mysteriously vulnerable and irreducible personal centre wherein the dignity of persons resides. Here and elsewhere, Friel is fascinated by the failure of language to contain the personal centre, even while enabling us to intuit its significance, as the languages of art are especially ordered to do. 'The private core will always be ... hermetic, won't it?' asks Yolland at the conclusion of his remarks on how difficult it will be for him to learn the 'language of the tribe'. Again he speaks more than he knows, because the private relationship he comes to share with Maire seals both of them off from the community at large.

Towards the end of the play, when Jimmy Jack gives us his reflection on exogamy, it is important to see his speech in the context of Hugh's new educational enterprise (the 'exogamous' teaching of English). Throughout the play, the aging bachelor and 'Infant Prodigy', Jimmy Jack, takes refuge in the classics, struggling against his own loneliness and substituting his fantasies about mythological goddesses for his failure to find any actual woman. At the end, he announces that he is going to be married to Pallas Athene. Then, in a moment of pathetic confusion he admits to Hugh his desperate need of companionship, while making 'absurd gestures of secrecy and intimacy' to cover up his pitiful confession. Again, the play points to that private dimension which is part of each human person, but Jimmy has lost the capacity to adjust this private, interior world to the world of fact in a way that would make ordinary life manageable. Although his case is more extreme that that of the others, it is not unlike theirs. Thus, he asks:

> *Do you know the Greek word endogamein? It means to marry within the tribe. And the word exogamein means to marry outside the tribe. And you don't cross those borders casually – both sides get very angry. Now, the problem is this: Is Athene sufficiently mortal or am I sufficiently godlike for the marriage to be acceptable to her people and to my people? You think about that.*

On one level, the speech confirms Jimmy Jack's derangement, for he seems to be seriously pondering the propriety of his marriage to a Greek goddess. Yet the broader tension in this speech, which assumes familiarity with the goddess and yet does not communicate any sense of being out of the ordinary, points us to the question raised by the play as a whole about relationships between the powerful colonizers and the local inhabitants. It is easy to see also how the speech applies to Maire and Yolland, and to the fact that both sides have indeed become 'very angry'. Jimmy Jack therefore tells us about the dangers of crossing cultural borders in general, even while he illustrates a fatal disconnection between the private and the social in the shaping of a personal relationship, and how painful the consequences of that disconnection are.

BE, 90–92

In so far as beauty awakens desire we are reminded that desire remains unfulfilled, with the further consequence that beauty is also always to some degree poignant, even painful. By contrast, the glamorized images by which today we are on all sides bombarded by a meretricious, commercialized culture are better described as empty than as unfulfilled. That is, nothing in them engages us personally, because there is no opening to further discourse with those self-contained displays that are designed for no end other than commercial gain. By contrast, one characteristic of the truly beautiful is that it offers an opening, a vulnerability that invites us in, as it were, and it does this especially by thematising its own imperfection.

In this context, John Donne's difficult, extravagant *Anniversarie* poems are interesting because of how they draw attention so impressively to their own inadequacy. The death of the young girl, Elizabeth Drury, was the occasion for these extraordinary, elegiac performances commissioned by her parents. In attempting then to make sense of her death, the poet pushes language to its limits, as his hyperbolic praise of the girl compels us to see how hard he is working to accord her a transcendent significance, even as he remains aware of the fact that such significance fails to answer the core problem – the scandal itself of her death. Readers remain divided about whether or not the poems succeed, but it is clear that the poet deliberately thematizes the connection here between art and imperfection.

There is less doubt about the success of another poem by Donne, *The Extasie*, which also draws attention strategically to its own failure. *The Extasie* is about a trance experienced by two lovers lying on a bank covered with spring flowers. The description of the lovers' spiritual communion becomes so complex and tangled that it is no longer the welcome escape from the ordinary world, such as they imagined, and it is a relief for them to return to the physical here and now. The effectiveness of the poem therefore depends on its failure to describe the desired spiritual state adequately, so that the entanglements of the body will appear more gratifying after all. The reader might then wonder if the speaker's deliberately confounded praise of the ecstasy is not a seductive ploy, a ruse to allow this hypnotizing lover to get his lady back to the more pleasant entrapment of the physical body. The fascination of the poem as a whole arises therefore from its depiction of a perpetually unresolved desire, registered through the brilliantly self-thematising incapacity of the poem to describe its own subject adequately.

Rudyard Kipling's Mowgli, in *The Jungle Book*, is also insightful about the relationship between beauty and imperfection. Mowgli is a child who was lost and then was raised by wolves, but by and by he realizes that he must leave his animal friends in the jungle and return to human civilization. He finds then that the language of nature and the languages of humans are different, and, for Mowgli, entering human society involves pain and loss. Kipling makes a rich and poignant poetry out of the different kinds of failures in the languages Mowgli learns, and in which desire, nostalgia, and imperfection combine to create the distinctive, strange beauty of *The Jungle Book* stories.

17.

The *Anniversaries* are significant less because of their obvious failure to make, as it were, a viable metaphysical symbol out of Elizabeth Drury's death than for a kind of covert success that comes from the sense they convey of why they cannot succeed, conveyed partly by a self-protective bravado and display of extravagance for its own sake. 'Nor could incomprehensiblenesse deterre / Mee, from thus trying to emprison her', Donne writes. This remarkable statement partly acknowledges the poem's limits, but it is no mere gesture of respect for the mystery; it is an insistence also that the poem has attempted a task beyond its scope and has taken its life from that trial. 'Incomprehensiblenesse' in this case offers a kind of release, a licence for wit to fill the gap between heaven and earth, even though Donne's inordinate, gratuitous wittiness itself calls attention to the absence at the centre, which allows that wittiness free rein.

DM, 99

18.

> *She, shee is dead; shee's dead: when thou knowst this,*
> *Thou knowst how lame a cripple this world is.*
> *And learnst thus much by our Anatomy,*
> *That this worlds generall sicknesse doth not lie*
> *In any humour, or one certaine part;*
> *But as thou saw'st it rotten at the hart...*

This could very well seem to say that the girl's death calls into question the meaning of creation itself, 'rotten at the hart'. Protest atheism of course is not Donne's explicit intent; none the less, he was attracted to forbidden lines of thought and sentiment, letting us be touched by them, just as in the *Songs and Sonnets* and *Elegies* we are made to feel the morbid, obsessive, vindictive and gloating divagations of those thwarted male egos the poetry dramatizes, and which are in some sense also Donne, but with which we cannot identify him *tout court*. William Empson draws attention to Donne's 'secret largeness of outlook', which consists, partly, of the poet's willingness (and ability) to communicate the weight of opinions he does not fully endorse. *Biathanatos*, written just before the *Anniversarie* poems, is an example, and the 'largeness of outlook' is much less guarded there than usual.

In *Biathanatos*, Donne tells us straight out that he has often felt a 'sickely inclination' to suicide, and believes that insufficient charity and compassion are shown to those who kill themselves. The question, he argues, is complex, but there can be no healthy thinking about it until it is made provocative, just as the pool at Bethesda brought no health until its waters were troubled. The author's deliberate pursuit of 'compassion' therefore depends on his ability to vex the question, as he does by providing some alarming insight into the ambivalence of human motivation and the fine points of distinction between commendation and condemnation. And so he imparts to *Biathanatos* a frisson of hypnotizing doubt and existential terror.

Something of this effect is present also in the *Anniversaries*. It comes, partly, from the way the hyperbole itself vexes us, communicating by its excess how difficult it is to detect a providential order based on the facts as we know them, the main fact being the death of a child. On the question, for instance, of whether Elizabeth Drury is restored to heaven, the poet replies, 'Heaven may say this, and joy in't, but can wee / Who live, and lacke her, here this vantage see?' ('A Funerall Elegie', 11. 47–8). To our chagrin, we face here yet a further question, a further uncertainty, for the world has grown mute trying to explain God's higher purposes in the teeth of the darkly perplexing evidence. Such are the facts, and *The First Anniversarie*, with all its protracted analysis of the body's suffering and the soul's anguish, is a lament, but a lament touched with protest, and protest then crossed in turn by fear lest it tip too far into unseemliness. Jonson was right, after all, to detect blasphemy, but not because Donne praises Elizabeth Drury unduly; rather because the hyperbole itself carries the flavour of a rebuke to the powers that be for providing no better evidence of their benign purposes. And yet the hyperbole itself goes some distance towards neutralizing its own protest because, simply, it so often strikes us as an extravagant game, a huge, witty display which can veer off, for instance, into odd moments of inappropriate satire: 'One woman at one blow, then kill'd us all, / And singly, one by one, they kill us now' (FA, 11. 107–8). John Carey thinks that the main point about the *Anniversaries* is their venal exaggeration, not their serious grappling with conceptual difficulties that Donne was trying to solve. Although I find the poems more sincere than Carey, he is correct to point out that the complex tone has a way of deflecting us from a uniform high seriousness as distinct from a kind of unprincipled, reckless indulgence in exaggeration. The catalogue of the girl's perfections is preposterous, a witty effort to make her more than we know her to be. But the witty excess none the less calls attention covertly to a kind of failure, to the fact that the poet here has his wheels spinning off the ground, as it were, because he cannot find purchase on a symbol adequate for teaching us about the girl's death: a symbol such as a poet could grasp and write about with confidence.

DM, 90–91

19.

The Extasie then turns to the ecstatic condition itself, describing the union of souls and their identity in the disembodied state. But problems soon arise. If the souls do indeed interpenetrate perfectly, what is the difference between them, and how should this difference be described without reference to a body? Here is what the speaker says:

> *This Extasie doth unperplex*
> *(We said) and tell us what we love,*
> *We see by this, it was not sexe,*
> *We see, we saw not what did move:*

But as all severall soules containe
Mixture of things, they know not what,
Love, these mixt soules, doth mixe againe,
And makes both one, each this and that.

The promise of the first line, that the ecstasy clarifies ('doth unperplex'), is undermined by what follows as the argument swerves ingeniously through a perilous, complex course which is captivating but can hardly be said to 'unperplex'. 'We see, we saw not what did move' sets the tone, as we find ourselves caught in a momentary hesitation, grasping for the sense. The souls are apparently mixed of 'things', but 'they know not what', and the mixed souls are then mixed again, so that the 'this' and 'that' are made one. Perhaps the speaker means that the highest (rational) soul contains the lower (animal and vegetable) souls, and by a process of refinement, or remixing, the spiritual part emerges and is able to enter into communion with another spirit, far superior to the mere physical union of ordinary lovers.

The speaker's sophistication and intelligence are clearly on show here, as he praises the transcendent value of spiritual communion. But a current of ironic humour also runs through these lines, as the slick, bewitching complexity ends up demonstrating that the ecstasy is, in its own way, just as problematic as the experience of being tangled and trapped in a material body. Consequently, as the poem moves to a conclusion, the speaker, with some relief, turns away from the ecstasy and back to the material world:

But O alas, so long, so farre
Our bodies why do we forbeare?

But having spoken so highly of the ecstasy, the narrator must now make a commensurate case for the body, and there follows another dazzling passage on why we should be grateful to have our bodies, and to return to them.

IM, 92–3

20.

The lyrical range of Kipling's style, embellished with exotic artifice, provides a strangeness at once fresh and heightened towards the poetic. His writing evokes the preconceptual, fearless and wild world which Mowgli enjoys, but which cannot be described by the conventions of prose realism. Kipling therefore intersperses his narrative with songs and poems, for refrain and incantation suggest the rhythm of the primordial energies underpinning self-conscious human thought.

This technique of mixing genres in puzzling, often provocative ways enables Kipling to create the sense, comparable to the effects we find in Carroll, of exploring the limits of language for conveying the un-self-conscious quality of Mowgli's innocent childhood. When the wolf pack howls to confuse the vain hunter, Buldeo, it does so in verse, and we are told, 'This is a rough rendering of the song, but you must imagine what it sounds like when it breaks the afternoon hush of the Jungle'. And then, 'no translation can give the effect of it'. The problem of language therefore becomes the key to Mowgli's encounter with adults. 'What is the good of a man', he said to himself at last, 'if he does not understand man's talk? Now I am as silly and dumb as a man would be with us in the Jungle. I must learn their talk'.

As his name implies, Mowgli, the frog, is amphibious,

and Kipling's achievement is to make us feel his predicament, which is also that of the child poised on the edge of words. Likewise, the stories themselves are poised, elegantly and strangely, between the songs and poems and the archaic lyrical speech of the boy to the animals ('but, oh, they have handled ye grievously, my Brothers! Ye bleed'), and the claim of human language upon him ('I know not what I know! I would not go; but I am drawn by both feet'). To heighten the contrast, Kipling turns to mythology as well as verse. The elephant Hathai recounts, within a narrative frame which describes the jungle in severe drought, the myth of creation and fall among animals. He tells how the once golden tiger was marked with the killer's stripe because the destroyed paradise by hunting. In so doing he also introduced to the animals a hairless creature going upon its hinder legs, the harbinger of fear: the human animal.

SA, 101–2

Vincent van Gogh is especially insightful about the relationship between beauty and imperfection described in the preceding excerpts, and he is highly self-conscious in expressing that interconnection in his painting. Throughout his life, Van Gogh was sensitive to the plight of the poor, and at the beginning of his career as an artist his work had a strong moral focus as he depicted the condition of abject and marginalized people. In that context, he came to see that the beauty arising from an artistic representation of abjection was often more authentic and poignant than the conventional beauty favoured by the salons and art dealers. As his technique and understanding developed, Van Gogh concluded that imperfection could itself have an aesthetic effect, and that a painting might be made more beautiful by being deliberately imperfect, and even 'ugly'.

21.

'Oh, how much sadness and sorrow and suffering there is in the world, both in the open and in secret', writes Van Gogh from Amsterdam in 1877. Earlier, in 1876, he had wanted to serve as a missionary to the poor in the London suburbs, and in 1878 he wrote to Theo about the 'misery' of people's lives in Montmartre, which seemed so appalling as to be 'among the things that have no name in any language' (144/1:224). The hardships of the miners in the Borinage are also recorded with indignation and compassion, and Van Gogh objects to the dismissive and callous stereotyping of miners and weavers as merely 'a race of criminals and brigands'. He also has a special sympathy for streetwalkers: 'I felt as though those poor girls were my sisters, as far as our circumstances and experiences of life were concerned' (193/1:340). As he says, his compassion for Sien Hoornik arose partly from the fact that she, too, was a social outcast whose suffering and deprivation were evident to him also in her smallpox scars and ugly speech. 'I see so many weak people downtrodden', Van Gogh says, and is it wrong that 'my sorrow indeed aroused a need for compassion with others???'. In a poignant passage, he recalls a scene in the Borinage: 'There was a girl there, at night in that stable – in the Borinage – a brown peasant face with a white night-cap among other things, she had tears in her eyes of compassion for the poor cow when the animal went into labour and was having great difficulty'. The pain of the animal in labour goes straight to the child's heart, and in recalling the scene so simply and economically, Van Gogh allows us to grasp something of the immediacy of the compassion called forth by pain, beyond reflection or explanation – much like his response to the horses in the earlier examples. He never surrendered this kind of sensitivity, which drew him to seek subjects for painting in locations where he could focus on the everyday lives of the poor – for instance, soup kitchens, places of refuge for the elderly, and the homes of wood gatherers, peasants, and weavers. 'I've spent so many evenings sitting pondering by the fire with the miners and the peat-cutters and the weavers and peasants here', he writes, convinced that his work lay 'in the heart of the people', especially the deprived and overburdened. Later, when he himself was confined in an asylum, he experienced '*much* true friendship' among the afflicted inmates, and he never lost sight of the principle that had guided him since his early years: 'blessed are the poor in spirit'.

In the letters written before he dedicated himself to art, Van Gogh favoured authors and painters who felt as strongly as he did about the plight of the poor. He was much impressed by *Uncle Tom's Cabin* and by Multatuli (the Dutch writer Eduard Douwes Dekker), as well as by Ary Scheffer's *Christus Consolator* and the illustrations in *The Graphic,* which, he says, writing from The Hague in November 1882, would 'keep alive sympathy for the poor'. His admiration for Zola and other French Naturalist writers reflects the fact that they also shared his feelings about such matters, which continued to underpin Van Gogh's thinking after he abandoned the religious convictions that had driven him to his first, passionate expressions of concern about the plight of the poor.

LV, 117–18

22.

Thus, Vincent reports to Theo that he told his (no doubt bemused) art dealer Uncle Cor that instead of a conventionally beautiful woman, he would prefer 'one who was ugly or old or impoverished or in some way unhappy, who had acquired understanding and a soul through experience of life and trial and error, or sorrow'. Likewise, in Antwerp, he admires a group of girls, 'the best-looking of whom was ugly'. He explains that she had 'an ugly and irregular face, but with vivacity and piquancy, 'a la Frans Hals'. It is as if the girl's inner qualities, expressed as liveliness and piquancy, transfigure her plainness but without concealing it. The very irregularity of her features then becomes the vehicle for an especially affecting kind of beauty, making her more remarkable than her conventionally good-looking companions.

Van Gogh never lost sight of this idea, whether in observing people or in painting them or in responding to art. Thus, he describes girls dressed in pit rags as 'superb', and he admires Gavarni's drawings of London drunkards and beggars, as well the 'toothless laughter' in a Rembrandt self-portrait. Of course, there is nothing exceptional in the notion that art can transfigure unpleasant aspects of reality (as in tragic drama, for example), and on the face of it, there is nothing exceptional in Van Gogh's claim that painting can discover beauty in suffering. Still, his position is distinctive because he uses this idea about art in such a confrontational way, as a consciousness-raising strategy to promote actual solidarity with the poor. Then, he takes a further, typically disconcerting step: good painting does not just transfigure ugliness; sometimes good painting can itself *be* ugly, so that its very crudeness and imperfection are part of its aesthetic effect. This is a risky argument because it opens the way for incompetent pseudo-artists to claim that their lack of talent in fact expresses profound insight: all we have to do is to appreciate the irony that incompetence is really a higher form of authenticity.

When Van Gogh discusses the 'ugliness' of his own paintings, he can be uncomfortably indecisive about this set of issues. For instance, in September 1888, he describes his painting *The Night Café* as 'one of the ugliest I've done', going on to discuss the lurid colours in detail. He then explains how he tried to capture 'the terrible human passions', and he compares this painting to his *Potato Eaters*. Earlier, in June 1888, he describes his drawing of a Zouave as 'very ugly', and 'harsh and, well, *ugly* and badly done'. In discussing another painting of a Zouave, he tells Theo, 'it's a coarse combination of disparate tones that isn't easy to handle', and yet 'I'd always like to work on portraits that are vulgar, even garish like that one'. In describing *The Potato Eaters* to Bernard, he pauses to reflect on 'how ugly they'll find it'. On the one hand, he laments that 'I'm unable to render' the external beauty of things 'because I make it ugly in my painting, and coarse, whereas nature seems perfect to me'. On the other hand, he explains how studies such as *The Night Café* '*usually* seem to me atrociously ugly and bad', yet 'they're the only ones that seem to me to have a more important meaning'.

In these examples, Van Gogh seems sometimes to be criticizing his own failures. Thus, he is 'unable to render' nature's beauty because his technique is limited. When he says that the drawing of the Zouave is 'ugly and badly done', he is making much the same point, as he does again in his admission to Theo that he didn't find it 'easy to handle' the colours in the painting of the Zouave, so that the result is a 'coarse combination of disparate tones'. Yet he goes on to tell Theo that he wants always to work on portraits that are 'vulgar, even garish like that one', and we are invited to make a distinction here between an expressive vulgarity and a mere clumsiness resulting from Van Gogh's limitations as a painter. The ugliness of *The Night Café* might seem at first to indicate an artistic failure, but the rest of the quotation suggests that the ugliness is a deliberate means of expressing 'the terrible human passions'. A similar ambivalence is evident in Van Gogh's linking (by way of Dostoevsky) the 'atrociously ugly and bad' *Night Café* with a deeper, 'more important meaning'.

In none of these passages does Van Gogh discuss the difference between the kind of 'ugly and badly done' that an artist might deploy as a strategy and the kind that is just plain ugly and bad. Rather, he floats uncertainly, even perilously, between these alternatives, making his riskiest – if also most characteristic – case for finding beauty in ugliness, rejoicing in the midst of sorrow, experiencing joy in the heart of life's tragedy. By such means, throughout the letters he attempts to counter the harsh realities of abjection and suffering – the cab-horse predicament, as it were – and to rescue beauty from ugliness, joy from sorrow, life from all that oppresses it.

LV, 121–3

Van Gogh's paintings of a sower and a reaper return us to the over-arching conundrum of our mortality, and also to the affirmation offered by art as it stimulates desire while also bringing home to us our imperfection. For Van Gogh, art therefore is a privileged means of representing our need to shape our lives meaningfully, even as we realize that, in our personal quest for fulfillment, we remain incomplete.

23.

In a letter, Van Gogh discusses the sower, explaining how 'the night café is a continuation of the sower' and emphasizing that the colour 'isn't locally true from the realist point of view of *trompe l'oeil*, but a colour suggesting some emotion, an ardent temperament' (676/4:260). And in a letter in which he admits that the sower 'still continues to haunt me', he says that paintings like *The Night Café* and *The Sower* are deliberately 'exaggerated', so that the effectiveness of the painting depends on a heightening of juxtaposed colours, even in defiance of what is conventionally 'realistic'.

After Van Gogh entered the asylum at St. Rémy, he described his painting of a reaper, which he saw as complementary to *The Sower* so that they make a pair: 'The canvas of the reaper will become something like the sower of the other year', he writes, and in a further letter he describes the reaper painting in more detail:

> *I'm struggling with a canvas begun a few days before my indisposition. A reaper, the study is all yellow, terribly thickly impasted, but the subject is beautiful and simple. I then saw in this reaper – a vague figure struggling like a devil in the full heat of the day to reach the end of his toil – I then saw the image of death in it, in the sense that humanity would be the wheat being reaped. So if you like it's the opposite of that Sower I tried before. But in this death nothing sad, it takes place in broad daylight with a sun that floods everything with a light of fine gold.*

Although this passage begins by drawing attention to the colours of the painting, it quickly veers in another direction as Van Gogh describes the reaper's hard labour, which in turn prompts an almost allegorical observation: 'I then saw the image of death in it', just as he also sees 'humanity' in the wheat. By means of this contrast, the life cycle is itself represented – from sowing to reaping, planting to harvesting, life to death. But the sower and the reaper are not just opposites. They also complement each other, and, as a result, death is made to seem less frightening. The last lines of the excerpt can then be read almost as a welcoming gesture – an attempt to make friends with the grim reaper who is now paradoxically associated with the life-affirming 'sun that floods everything with a light of fine gold'. The reaper struggling to get his work done in the field is an ordinary worker, and yet he is also a 'vague' figure and the passing comparison to a devil ('struggling like a devil in the full heat of the day') suggests that he has a shadowy, almost allegorical aspect as well. Yet the insistence on 'broad daylight' and 'nothing sad' returns us to a positive interpretation of this figure who is both like us and unlike us, and whose significance seems at first opposite to that of the sower, to whom he is in fact complementary. 'Phew – the reaper is finished', Vincent writes at the end of the letter. 'It's an image of death as the great book of nature speaks to us about it – but what I sought is the "almost smiling"'. Death here is interpreted within the context of an encompassing natural process in which the opposites coalesce, so that death is (almost) benign rather than something to be feared.

As his health became more precarious and a series of devastating epileptic attacks left him debilitated for days afterwards, Van Gogh quite understandably became increasingly aware of the proximity to himself of the grim reaper. Also, he began to think about how the natural cycle of sowing and harvesting might be arbitrarily interrupted, as, for instance, when wheat is ground by millstones instead of being sown in the earth. 'I feel so strongly that the story of people is like the story of wheat, if one isn't sown in the earth to germinate there, what does it matter, one is milled in order to become bread'. He repeats this point in a letter to Willemien:

> Not every grain of wheat, once it has ripened, ends up in the earth again to germinate there and become a stalk – but far and away the most grains do not develop but go to the mill – don't they?
>
> Now comparing people with grains of wheat – in every person who's healthy and natural there's the power to germinate as in a grain of wheat. And so natural life is germinating.
>
> What the power to germinate is in wheat, so love is in us.

If the natural process of germination is thwarted, he goes on to say, we find ourselves 'placed in circumstances as hopeless as they must be for the wheat between the millstones'.

In these passages, Van Gogh is uncomfortably aware that the natural cycle, in which life and death are in complementary opposition, can be violently interrupted. That is, the process of germination – which, as he says, is a figure for love – can be thwarted by unexpected trauma, which he compares to being ground by millstones. And so the sowing and reaping metaphors give rise to a further concern about the scandal of unjust suffering, and this concern in turn reflects a renewed spiritual (rather than conventionally religious) interest that developed in the closing years of Van Gogh's life. For instance, he tells Emile Bernard about 'yearnings for that infinite of which the Sower, the sheaf, are the symbols'. In a following letter, he admires Christ 'as an artist greater than all artists', going on to praise the parables: 'What a sower, what a harvest, what a fig tree, etc.'. In admiring Christ as primarily an artist, Van Gogh avoids returning to conventional religion but instead points to how art itself is spiritually edifying. In this context, the sower, the wheat field, and the harvest become invested with a spiritual significance of which art is both embodiment and the expression.

PW, 73–5

PART 2

IMPULSE

5   DIALOGUE

Martin Buber describes dialogue as real talking that takes place in response to real listening, and as indispensable to personal communication and relationship. Dmitri Nikulin goes further, describing dialogue as the art itself of being human, in so far as the goal of dialogue is to be for another and then through the other for oneself, as Mikhail Bakhtin also says. For these thinkers, the ability to set aside selfishness and to be for another is what makes us distinctively human.

At the beginning of Western philosophy, Plato wrote about the centrality of dialogue both to the development of personal knowledge and to the shaping of a good society. The value that he attached to dialogue some 2,500 years ago is more than ever relevant today, especially in modern societies dominated by marketplace impersonality and the unprecedented instrumentalising of human relationships.

Well aware of these modern challenges, Bakhtin wrote insightfully about dialogue in relation to the idea of personal self-fashioning, focusing on Dostoevsky as the pre-eminent literary example of the dialogical process and the personalism that it entails. The following excerpts from Bakhtin are complemented by Maurice Merleau-Ponty, who describes art itself as fundamentally dialogical, a position held also by Hans Georg Gadamer. This point is further explored by Wolfgang Iser, who deals with the dialogical structure of the literary text as well as with the reader's dialogical response.

1.

In his study of Dostoevsky's poetics, Bakhtin argues that to be a human person is to be in communication, and thus 'to be for another, and through the other, for one's self'. That is, as Holquist explains, for Bakhtin every 'self' needs an 'other' even to begin to chart a course in the world. This is so because the person emerges only through relationships within specific historical situations. This is what Bakhtin means when he says that 'through the other' one comes to a sense of 'one's self'.

But, as Holquist points out, the relationship between 'I' and 'other' is asymmetrical because the self is perpetually 'open' and 'unfinished', a work in progress, vulnerable to uncertainties and insecurities and yet called to shape itself meaningfully. By contrast, the space and time of the other are accorded a degree of stability and identity. That is, by encountering what I see as a stable value represented by the other, I am able to accord my own 'open' and 'unfinished' self-fashioning a sufficient degree of structure to shape a meaningful engagement with the world and with my historical situation within it.

Yet when the other is a person (rather than, say, an idea), the values that I see as relatively stable are in fact experienced subjectively by that other, who is also a project-in-the making, likewise called to a self-fashioning that is perpetually in process. My encounters with the world thus confront me with a wide range of values in contention with one another, values that are often beset by insecurities even though called to objectivity and among which I must choose my allegiances.

Bakhtin's word for the endlessly complex and unobjectifiable multiplicity of dialogues that constitute the human quest for stability and meaning is 'heteroglossia'. In every individual case of self-fashioning, this multiplicity of dialogues affords the opportunities and constraints in terms of which each person is 'through the other, for one's self'. Personal identity is thus shaped by a process that is multi-directional rather than linear, entailing an array of dialogical relationships, within some of which, for instance, I might well shift my persona, aims, and allegiances. But if my persona (the face that I present to the world, for practical purposes) becomes merely a kaleidoscope of expedient manoeuvres, my personal identity will volatilize accordingly, and instead of 'making something of myself' (as the saying goes), I will 'come to nothing'. By contrast, a person's self-fashioning, amidst the all-but-infinite range of potential dialogues on offer, entails specific engagements, patterns of response, ways of imagining and thinking, which in turn can take on the shape of a narrative – 'the story of my life'. Still, this narrative is never complete, nor is it without discontinuities and contradictions, because the self is a provisional synthesis rather than a self-identical essence. The Buddha and David Hume were right about this – and so is Bakhtin.

In his book on Dostoevsky, Bakhtin develops these ideas about self-fashioning specifically in relation to literature, his main claim being that Dostoevsky's characters are given the status of 'authentic' persons independent of the author's own subjectivity. That is, Dostoevsky renders the 'unfinalizability' of the people whom he depicts, and, in so doing, his art 'liberates and de-reifies the human being'.

Dostoevsky's novels thus provide special insight into the process whereby the self is shaped dialogically, and, in his writing, 'referential meaning' is 'indissolubly fused with the position of a personality'.

PW, 9–11

2.

In *Problems of Dostoevsky's Poetics*, Bakhtin does not mention Berdyaev but insists nonetheless on many of the same themes and ideas. For instance, Bakhtin assures us of how 'profoundly personalised' is Dostoevsky's vision, how freedom is his special preoccupation and how his polyphonic structures create endless, fascinatingly refracted contradictions, within which something always escapes us. The main point at issue, according to Bakhtin, is a *'new integral view of the person* – the discovery of "personality"', and this *'internally unfinalizable something in man'* is the source of freedom and dignity, as Dostoevsky shows with unparalleled intensity and insight. Bakhtin never tires of insisting on how, for Dostoevsky, personality is rooted in free self-disclosure as distinct from the 'objectified analysis of a materialized person' – all of which remains close to Berdyaev's equally strong insistence on the same ideas.

Still, the points at which Bakhtin's study adds a dimension to Berdyaev's are also instructive. By showing how characters speak out of divided minds and voices, how hidden polemics can inhabit a discourse seemingly innocent of polemical intent, how borders are everywhere unpredictable as people enter into dialogue wherein everything is spoken with a sideways glance at others, Bakhtin produces a sense of the 'inescapable open-endedness' of persons, which he claims is the great triumph of Dostoevsky's polyphonic novel. Bakhtin especially evokes Dostoevsky's vitality – famously described as 'carnivalesque' – and the analysis, for example, of Dostoevsky's use of thresholds (doors, staircases, corridors, entrance ways) as the context of crises, and of public places (squares, dining rooms, halls) as the context of scandal, shows the extraordinary pains expended by Dostoevsky to represent consciousness as always complexly embodied.

As Bakhtin demonstrates, the main achievement of the polyphonic novel is to show how personality cannot be made into an object, and Dostoevsky 'cannot finalize' his characters 'for he has discovered what distinguishes personality from all that is not personality'.

PC, 117–18

3.

When Merleau-Ponty applies these ideas to language, he sounds very much like Bakhtin. For instance, in *Signs*, we learn that speech is 'always only a fold in the immense fabric of language', with which we are taken up in a perpetual dialogical relationship that does not 'leave a place for pure meaning'. Within this dialogue, 'at the moment of expression the other to whom I address myself and I who express myself are incontestably linked together'. Elsewhere, Merleau-Ponty goes on to explain that in such an 'exchange', 'there are never quite two of us and yet one is never alone'.

All of this is very much in harmony with Bakhtin's thinking on the same issues, but when Merleau-Ponty turns to literature, he has further points to make, especially about the relationship between dialogue and intent. Thus, in 'Studies in the Literary Use of Language', he describes literature as something that 'lives through an imposture' insofar as the sum total of the countless 'accidents' that influence the production of a text are taken to reflect 'the author's intention'. It is a cliché of literary criticism that the 'intentional fallacy' should be avoided: in other words, that readers should realize that the effects of the artifact outreach what the author thought he or she was doing at the time. In *Signs*, Merleau-Ponty extends this principle to painting, arguing that a painter 'is no more capable of seeing his paintings than the writer is capable of reading his work'. Rather, 'it is in others that expression takes on its relief and really becomes signification' – which is to say, the significance of the work is opened up by way of a dialogical relationship with the reader or viewer, thereby extending the significance of the work beyond the artist's specific intent, or 'personal vibration' and 'inner monologue'.

This is not to say that readers or viewers grasp the whole significance either. As we have seen, language does not give us 'transparent significations' and meaning is 'never completed'. As Greenblatt observes throughout *Renaissance Self-Fashioning*, the individual reader's codes and the cultural codes of the text interpenetrate in endlessly complex ways. Consequently, in matters of value, what we take to be truth comes to us dialogically and by way of a continuing exploration. As Merleau-Ponty says, sounding much like Heidegger, art presents us with 'a way of seeing' and of 'inhabiting the world', offering 'a certain relationship to being'. Merleau-Ponty goes on to stress that the internal organization of the work of art achieves a certain 'equilibrium', as a result of which the text is, as it were, in dialogue with itself, holding its own internal contradictions in suspension. In turn, this internal dialogue expresses a distinctive way of inhabiting the world, with which we are also invited to engage. Here, a Heideggerian understanding of the truth of art as disclosure joins with a dialogical view of the artifacts as culturally situated and contested, reducible neither to the author's intent nor to a reader's interpretation.

PW, 12–13

4.

It follows that the text is in dialogue not just with the reader but also with itself insofar as it attains a distinctive 'equilibrium' in tune with 'the law of its own being'. For Terry Eagleton, this internal dialogue is a fundamental 'strategy' of the literary artifact, and here he is drawn to Fredric Jameson, who sees literature as raising from within itself the ideological issues and contexts to which it then also offers a response. As Eagleton says, 'paradoxically, the literary work of art projects out of its own innards the very historical and ideological subtext to which it is a strategic reply'. In conducting a dialogue with itself, the text therefore puts on offer a way of 'inhabiting the world' that engages with the reader, again dialogically: as with every personal relationship, 'there are never quite two of us and yet one is never alone'.

PW, 14

5.

In *The Act of Reading*, Wolfgang Iser, like Bakhtin, insists that interpretation is unfinalizable and that the text is, like a person, 'an open event'. He goes on to explain that 'total organization' would be the death of literature because there would be 'nothing left for the reader to do'. By contrast, literature works 'to stimulate the imagination', so that meaning emerges from the reader's imagination-infused, dialogical engagement with the possibilities of interpretation offered by a text. In turn, these possibilities are organized in two main ways. First, a text has a 'repertoire', comprising common knowledge that, it is assumed, readers share and recognize and that draws from 'material selected from social systems and literary traditions'. Second, the 'strategies' of a text are the means by which it organizes or works upon the repertoire in a way that discloses aspects of experience and understanding occluded by conventional knowledge and belief. Readers are thereby enabled to take a 'fresh look' at ideas that they 'may hitherto have accepted without question', and they can come to see things 'in a new light' while also acquiring a more discerning view of how provisional self-knowledge is. Iser refers to this process as a 'dialogue' and because different readers interact with the text in different ways and various interpretations invite comparison with one another, this dialogue is never finalized. Open-endedness, however, does not entail relativism, because the strategies of a text impose constraints that serve as common reference points. That is, although the strategies do not impose specific interpretations, they offer certain possibilities, which a reader then fills out.

Even this brief summary shows how strong are the similarities between Iser's thinking and the main ideas set out in my introduction. That is, like Bakhtin, Iser insists on the centrality of dialogue to interpretation and on the idea that interpretation is unfinalizable. Iser's theories about 'strategies' also directly influenced Eagleton's use of the same term. Eagleton even quotes Iser's claim that literature is 'a reaction to the thought systems which it has chosen and incorporated in its own repertoire', as a way of showing how 'strikingly close' Iser comes to Jameson's concept of the 'self-fashioning artifact', whereby literary texts raise problems and issues to which they also respond. And when

Iser points to how 'the ultimate function of the strategies is to *defamiliarize* the familiar', he echoes the Heideggerian idea that art discloses fresh aspects of ordinary things. He also cites Merleau-Ponty in describing this defamiliarizing as a 'coherent deformation' – a means, as Merleau-Ponty says, of expressing a 'way of seeing' that is an 'emblem' of a particular manner of interpreting the world that a reader takes up and fills out.

Yet if Iser offers such a convenient reprise of some of the main ideas described in the introduction, the question arises as to why I did not make him a central point of reference there, instead of Bakhtin. The answer is that Iser is mainly concerned about the interplay of textual codes and structures, and his hypothetical reader remains more a theoretical construct than an actual grappler with complex problems and ideas. As Eagleton says, with Iser, 'it is as though the true referent of the literary work is not so much the social reality as the conventions that regulate it'. Iser has little interest in the rough terrain covered by Bakhtin's brand of personal self-fashioning, which is not just about reading but also about the conflicted situation of the radically insecure 'I' and the ambivalently attractive and threatening 'other'. The felt sense of recalcitrant biographical facts and of contending ideologies is the very stuff also of Van Gogh's letters, but not of Iser's analysis of the reading process.

Still, a further question now presses from the opposite direction. If Bakhtin offers a more helpful way to approach Van Gogh, why, in conclusion, do I turn to Iser? The answer is that he is especially helpful in clarifying how, in retrospect, we might think about the specifically aesthetic dimension of literature conceived as dialogue. In my earlier book *The Letters of Vincent Van Gogh: A Critical Study*, I dealt with key patterns of metaphors and concepts. These standard topics of conventional literary criticism help to show how Van Gogh's writerly imagination offers new ways of seeing as he uses language in a heightened or figurative way, contending with matters of significant human value in a style that is often arresting and distinctive. But in the present study, I describe the aesthetic dimension of Van Gogh's writing by means that lie outside the range of the critical practice exemplified by my earlier book. And in the present context, Iser can help, in conclusion, to describe the aesthetic dimension of literature conceived as a set of self-referential strategies in fruitful but unfinalizable dialogue, such as I have been claiming – by way of Bakhtin – is a main aspect of Van Gogh's achievement as a writer. Although Iser is mainly interested in fiction, his analysis of the aesthetic has a strong explanatory power when brought to bear on what I have described as the literary structure of Van Gogh's letters and the analogous process of self-fashioning that they describe.

In brief, Iser is not so much interested in what a text means as in what it does, and he locates the aesthetic in the 'effect' a text has on a reader. Yet because different readers respond to texts in different ways, an aesthetic effect cannot be prescribed or seen as, somehow, inhering in the text alone. It is, instead, best thought of as a *potential* of the text – a possible effect, actualized by the reader's experience of the particular kind of 'coherent deformation' that a reading produces. Consequently, 'aesthetic value is something that cannot be grasped'; rather, it is manifest 'in the alteration of what is familiar', as a result of a particular reading. Literary value thus emerges in an indeterminate way as an effect of a dialogue between reader and text, actualizing the further interplay within the text, between strategies and repertoire.

The analyses I have offered of Van Gogh's letters fit well with this broad understanding of the aesthetic. As Clark and Holquist say, there is no final word, and, just so, my readings of Van Gogh are a means of describing some of the effects that Iser sets out. Still, in turn, these readings cannot be separated from their inter-involvement with the ideas I described earlier about the interdependence of personal identity and a dialogical engagement with others.

PW, 167–9

The following excerpts deal with four writers who explore the inter-relationships between dialogue and the personal. These are Plato, Boethius, Erasmus, and Hume.

The inexhaustible riches of Plato's dramatised philosophical speculations record the moment in ancient Greece when oral discourse found expression in writing. Throughout the *Dialogues*, oral arguments are made by a variety of speakers with Socrates at the centre, and although these arguments are stabilized in writing they are not fully systematized. As a result, we experience something of how conceptual thought emerges from the personal concerns of the speakers, so that ideas are not depersonalized or divorced from their roots in a particular, embodied human situation.

In Boethius, philosophical argument to a large extent replaces the exchange of voices and contending points of view that we find in Plato. Yet Boethius remains Plato's disciple, and in *The Consolation of Philosophy* the dialogue between the speaker and Lady Philosophy invites us to participate in the personal transformation that encompasses the speaker's thinking as well as his feelings and emotions.

Boethius is also significant in the present context because of his influential definition of the person as an 'individual substance of a rational nature'. In applying this definition to the Trinity, Boethius takes the bold step of defining God as a communion of persons in dialogue. Christianity has always placed a high value on personhood, and yet the abstractions of Trinitarian theology also threaten to separate the idea of the person from the complexities of actual human experience that are better grasped in light of the Incarnation. In this context, the dialogical structure of *The Consolation of Philosophy* helps to return Boethius' definition to a realm of discourse in which the perennial human struggle for meaning is foregrounded.

The recovery of Plato's *Dialogues* in the West during the Renaissance led to a renewed interest in dialogue in education. Erasmus was influential in promoting educational reform based on recovering the spirit of Plato's *Dialogues*, and in his best-known work, *The Praise of Folly*, Plato's dialogical spirit breathes new life into the standard philosophical terminology of the late Middle Ages.

In *Dialogues on Natural Religion*, David Hume uses dialogue to investigate the answers offered by religion to the problem of evil and suffering. Like Plato, Hume is ironic and complex, while also voicing a skepticism informed by the spirit of disenchantment that has shaped the modern era. As he explores the positions of his three speakers, Hume leads us to an open-ended conclusion in which, again, the interconnections between the dialogical and the personal are thematised.

6.

Plato's conclusions are often speculative, and we need to acquire an appreciation of how there is in the Dialogues a special amalgam of drama, sophisticated humour, challenging intellectual arbitrariness and mytho-poetic speculation, which requires a special tuning of our receivers, so to speak, and which then takes on a quality of life distinctively its own, arising from the personal exchanges and interactions of the characters through whom the dialogue takes place. Plato comes alive, that is, when we begin to feel what he is getting at, and how, through a variety of points of view in contention he attempts to marry a Socratic ethical individualism with the claims of metaphysics and Sophist rhetoric; to discover how Homer's representation of the gods bears upon the philosopher's abstract monotheism; how the perennial intuitions about the unity and diversity of the world as the pre-Socratic cosmologists had described it are to be stabilized and reconciled; in what sense the problem of justice calls for the exercise of individual reason, for an understanding of cosmic order, for a reliance on traditional mores and on eschatological hope. The pressing issues of philosophy are all here, somehow massively coherent and yet creatively tentative, in process of formulation, dramatically rendered, provocative, inconclusive, yet gathering together an extraordinary range of past knowledge and endeavor. There had been no synthesis like it before, and nothing after it – including the scientific revolution – was untouched by it. Clearly, there is much more to learn by trying to read Plato on such terms, appreciating the dialogical vitality with which he presents the personally expressed subjective life of ideas, than by concentrating alone on the logical coherence or deficiencies of the various arguments, considered in isolation.

DM, 3

7.

In *The Consolation of Philosophy*, Boethius describes the predicament of a man unjustly imprisoned and losing his freedom, good name and material goods. In a dream, the man is instructed by Lady Philosophy, who teaches him that bondage to time – to the chattles, that is, of Fortune

– debilitates and corrupts the spirit. Happiness does not reside in the treacherous favours to be found at the perimeter of Fortune's wheel, but at the centre, the still point of eternity. In the course of a series of conversations, the imprisoned man gradually re-evaluates his position and comes to understand the eternal nature of the human person, whose existence is temporal but whose essence transcends time. Throughout the *Consolation* the theme of journeying from a place of exile or imprisonment to one's true home is carefully developed. A series of contrasts between key images suggests alternative directions, either towards egotistical self-indulgence or towards the spiritual resources which enable the prisoner to develop as a person who is not merely a victim of circumstance. So, placed against Fortune's wheel, which is perpetually deceptive, is the image of an orb of light, the true source of knowledge and illumination. Also, the dialogue form itself enacts the conflict through which a way towards the centre is discovered, as does the frequent alternation of verse and prose. Throughout, allusions to sickness and health suggest the ordeal of body, soul and spirit striving for personal wholeness, which is holiness, as well as health and wellbeing.

We are, furthermore, led through an imagined density of 'external' circumstances, working our way as we read, as it were, from circumference to centre. Book I is heavily biographical, most full of complaint and concerned with the outward trappings of the prisoner's life and circumstances. Book II remains on the circumference, but, by discussing the fickleness of fortune, leads us towards the interior life, suggesting that happiness is within. In Book III the prisoner feels stronger and begins actively to contribute to Lady Philosophy's advice. In Book IV he is able to discuss evil and injustice, concluding that the moral sickness of evil men is more terrible than the suffering of their victims. In Book V, the debate opens out in a more leisurely manner on the question of eternity, ending with a discussion of the Judge whose vision encompasses the divisions of time.

As the argument progresses, understanding therefore develops in proportion to mortification of the merely 'external' man and the relinquishment of his ego-assertiveness. So also, Boethius' use of poetry, serving to introduce or conclude an argument, is suggestively varied. Book I begins and ends with verse; Books II, III and IV begin with prose and end with verse; Book V neither begins nor ends with verse. It is as if the prisoner interiorizes the power of poetry as he grows more active in the process of the personal transformation effected by what philosophy has to teach him.

LM, 84–5

8.

Trinitarian theology describes God's innermost nature is an exchange of persons in relationship, the subsistence of each person being the relationship itself. In this communitarian or dialogical model, each person is defined by self-giving. God the Father (the name is a metaphor suggesting the mystery of origins), is then not a separate observer of the death of the Son (the divine Word, *Logos*), but is present to the Son through the Spirit of divine love. Pathos is therefore introduced into the Godhead itself, and when Jesus dies, God suffers. Origen in the second century thought this, but it has not been an easy idea for Christian theologians to accept. Yet a number of modern voices are bent on recovering an appreciation of God's personal and interpersonal solidarity in suffering, with Jesus as a witness to the tragic violence within the creation itself.

PP, 41

9.

Studies, Erasmus says, must be 'transmuted into morals', for the philosophy of Christ is not learned like a formula; rather, it depends on a 'disposition of mind' communicated by a personal quality represented 'by the very expression and the eyes'. What is important is not something to be proved or defined, but an attitude of the whole being, a kind of personal tact. The true philosopher, Erasmus argues, can avoid discord and violence only by 'what I might call a holy artfulness', the kind of thing we find in dialogue, exemplified by *The Praise of Folly*.

Erasmus thus combines a radical faith in Humanist secular learning, especially philology, with an ideal 'plain man's' straightforwardness based on co-operation and the open, dialogical communication of knowledge, and opposed to monological elitism and the powerful interests it protects. His anti-scholasticism, his sense of progress directed at the betterment of human society, and his egalitarian open-mindedness are forward-looking, modern attitudes, and yet Erasmus (like Thomas More) was himself anything but the plain and straightforward man of his own prescription. The education of a Christian disposition, 'the holy artfulness' of true diplomacy and learning, as he well knew, was indirect and fundamentally personal, achieved through dialogue. Consequently, the Christian philosopher must monitor and carefully adjudicate the degree of truth and falsehood contained in 'venomous language' and 'poisonous defamation', because tyranny arises from just such 'false accusation' rooted in powerful interests given to the manipulation of words. In *The Praise of Folly* we encounter the argument of 'a grim old man whose arrogance made it clear he was a theologian' on whether heretics should be burned instead of being refuted in argument. The theologian cites St. Paul – 'A man who is a heretic, after the second admonition, reject (*devita*)' – and explains that Paul means the heretic to be removed from life (*devita*). Folly tells us that some laughed at his ignorant abuse of the Latin, but others found the argument acceptable. Besides being arrogant, however, the theologian is irascible, and angrily roars out the verse from Scripture. Such a combination of obscurantism with a depersonalizing vindictiveness constitutes, for Erasmus, the most dangerous kind of human behaviour.

Erasmus's thinking about morality is, therefore, deeply rooted in a dialogical understanding of language. On the one hand he calls for clarity and directness; on the other, for subtlety and learning. We need to be artful because the masks of language are deceptive, and because there is no simple correlation between a person's disposition and the language in which it is dressed up, or between language and the things it seems to describe.

DM, 38–9

10.

In Hume's *Dialogues on Natural Religion*, it is tempting to equate Philo with Hume, but it would be risky to insist on their identity, even though Philo does express Hume's main views and characteristic turn of mind. Yet Hume does not in the end claim victory for himself through Philo, and in conclusion he has the student narrator say that 'Philo's principles are more probable than Demea's; but that those of Cleanthes approach still nearer to the truth'. The narrator's reliability (his student opinions are not entirely dependable) requires cautious assessment, but Cleanthes, the reasonable man who maintains a sense of wonder at the beauty and order of creation together with a willingness to argue for his beliefs in an intelligent creator, and who puts an optimistic face on things, is not dismissed. It is as if Hume wants to acknowledge the potentially debilitating effects of systematic skepticism. 'My sentiments', says Philo at one point, 'are not worth being made a mystery of', and in certain circumstances such a statement could be reassuring. But it is a cold and banal rationalism that is no more responsive to the wonder of human intelligence than that. The same trustworthy but lackluster reassurance recurs soon after when Philo warns against hypotheses: 'All that belongs to human understanding, in this deep ignorance and obscurity, is to be skeptical, or at least cautious; and not to admit of any hypothesis, whatever'. This is especially the case, says Philo, with regard to the causes of evil: 'None of them appear to human reason, in the last degree, necessary or unavoidable; nor can we suppose them such, without the utmost licence of imagination'. Hume, we conclude, is more complex than Philo, if only because the *Dialogues* are dialogical, and to leave no place for the personal interactions of the characters would be, in the end, diminishing.

DM, 135

Although dialogue requires co-operation, it is also transgressive in so far as it crosses boundaries and challenges habitual ways of thinking. Indeed, disagreement with an interlocutor is a standard component of dialogue – as long as it does not pre-empt listening and a willingness to keep the conversation open in the expectation of discovering some new, more adequate ways of thinking and understanding. By contrast, if a person refuses to listen or silences the other – by violence, for example, which is the most extreme form of depersonalization – dialogue cannot take place.

In writing about Northern Ireland, I suggested that two types of transgression correspond to these open and closed attitudes to dialogue. 'Negative transgression' is exemplified by violent attacks on an enemy that end up hardening boundaries, thereby confirming exclusion and preventing dialogue. By contrast, 'liberative transgression' takes a risk in crossing traditional boundaries, as a result of which stereotyping and alienation can be replaced by a productive merging of horizons.

Already in *The Republic*, Plato describes these two kinds of transgression through Socrates's encounter with the bullying Thrasymachus, and then with the more co-operative Glaucon and Adeimantus. Plato's point is that language can be used as an instrument to silence others, as we see with the overbearing Thrasymachus in contrast to the dialogical spirit exemplified by Glaucon and Adeimantus. We find a variation of the same point in Shakespeare's Hamlet, who so aggressively outwits his interlocutors as to undermine any common ground on which to base productive discussion. With Hamlet, we also have a foretaste of the extreme, post-modern relativism that likewise ingeniously undermines any and all personal affirmations of value by calling in question the assumptions underpinning them, thereby shutting down dialogue before it begins.

11.

Consequently, we can make a distinction between two kinds of transgression. On the one hand, negative transgression crosses borders in order to confirm them, declaring its own separateness and vested interests by defining and reviling the contaminated other through attacks across the segregating boundary. On the other hand, liberating transgression discovers its own anxieties and projections in the contaminated other, and by so doing escapes, through solidarity, from imprisoning ideological boundaries, though often not without suffering. ... Northern Ireland's poets of the past generation are sometimes criticized for paying too little attention to the political upheavals within which they live and work. Yet, I want to suggest that the poets in their own way show us the means of liberative transgression, and how difficult, necessary and complex it is. Poetry by its nature is transgressive, deconstructing ideological differences while showing everywhere the knotted contradictions and subtle interconnectedness of our personal lives.

PC, 144

12.

Throughout the *Republic*, Plato struggles to discover and acknowledge the limitations of reason even as he does his utmost to promote reason's cause. In this context, Thrasymachus is a centrally important character, even though he leaves the conversation early. Plato introduces Thrasymachus after some brief opening exchanges between Socrates, the old man Cephalus and his son Polymarchus. Socrates has an easy time, and these two characters are readily manipulated. We might even feel some relief when Thrasymachus declares that he is having no more of Socrates's sleights of hand. Thrasymachus then breaks in rudely and attacks Socrates for being a sham, and offers his own view of justice, which he defines as 'what is in the interest of the stronger party'. There is no appeal to ideals here, just an assertion, a full-frontal embrace of 'tyranny', which Thrasymachus defines as 'wholesale plunder, sacred or profane, private or public'.

The exchange with the angry, forceful Thrasymachus continues at some length, and when Socrates at last begins to gain an advantage, Thrasymachus responds by bluntly refusing to accept the conclusions. And here Socrates encounters one important limitation of philosophy's power to persuade: you cannot reason with people who are convinced that reasoning itself is futile, because, when all the talk is done, the depersonalizing use of force determines what is right. Terrorists, psychopaths, tyrants, and common or garden bullies everywhere at some point simply cancel the philosopher's guiding principle: let's talk about it. Thrasymachus is their exemplar, and if philosophical discussion is to continue, he must leave, as he does.

Then a remarkable thing happens. Two other characters, Glaucon and Adeimantus, take up where Thrasymachus left off. Glaucon provides a summary of Thrasymachus's main argument, offering to continue with it even though assuring Socrates, 'I don't believe all this myself'. Although Thrasymachus leaves the discussion (later, it is indicated that he continues to hang around, observing), the force of his objections remains. Throughout the *Republic*, discussions about tyranny and the rule of force keep bringing us back to the 'Thrasymachus factor', and Thrasymachus remains as a sort of philosophical Cyclops, a menacing reminder that reason itself can be used to argue for the futility of reason. One name for this position is nihilism, which, in the end, Socrates realizes he can't defeat. And so Plato concludes with a myth about perfect justice, hoping to keep alive, at least, our aspiration to the ideal.

But why do Claucon and Adeimantus insist on putting a case in which they say they don't believe? As we see, it isn't possible to enter into dialogue with just anyone, and the argument with Thrasymachus breaks down because he won't seriously consider positions other than those he already holds. When pressed, he resorts to a disagreeable, deliberately depersonalising attitude in order to short-circuit further discussion. But when Glaucon and Adeimantus continue to make Thrasymachus's case, they bring a different attitude to bear, sharing with Socrates a willingness to discover where the argument leads. The ability to enter into a personal, dialogical exchange in such a spirit is the central skill on which philosophy itself depends.

IM, 14–15

13.

I discovered that he was an excellent listener. Maybe I realized this because I had come, myself, to place a greater value on listening as a result of what the Art [of Kung-Fu] had taught me. Listening, after all, is a form of attention that decentres the ego by affirming the value of the other person. Without listening, nothing is learned. Without listening, there is no adequate response. Yet listening has to be learned as Kung-Fu is learned, and, in the end, the only way really to disarm violence is by dialogue. Violence occurs because dialogue fails, and dialogue fails because someone isn't listening. Like sparring, dialogue is an exchange between expert players, transcending egotism, transcending competition. High-ranking practitioners of the Art – I have seen this – can spar with extraordinary speed and power without doing one another the least physical harm. It is thrilling to watch. They make it look natural, spontaneous. By contrast, in a violent, physical confrontation, force is directed against an opponent in order to do harm. In Kung-Fu, we learn to deflect and return destructive energy to its source, so that the opponent might get the message: harm done rebounds upon the one who intends the harm.

He knew these things, and because I was coming to recognize them myself, I was able to see that he knew. Perhaps this is why we talked more easily than before.

KF, 49

14.

Hamlet of course sees through Claudius in a flash, and detests him for assuming such a veneer of trite sententiousness. Consequently, when Gertrude comes in on Claudius' side and asks her son reprovingly, 'Why seems it so particular with thee?', Hamlet turns on her:

> *Seems, madam? Nay, it is. I know not 'seems'.*
> *Tis not alone my inky cloak, good mother,*
> *Nor customary suits of solemn black,*
> *Nor windy suspiration of forced breath,*
> *No, nor the fruitful river in the eye,*
> *Nor the dejected havior of the visage,*
> *Together with all forms, moods, shapes of grief,*
> *That can denote me truly. These indeed seem,*
> *For they are actions that a man might play,*
> *But I have that within which passes show;*
> *These but the trappings and the suits of woe.*

(I,ii,76–86)

Hamlet picks almost manically on the word 'seems', for 'seeming' and reality are incommensurate, and he is especially intolerant of the hypocrisy that settles for a 'seemly' show of rehearsed ideas, such as we have just been given by Claudius. Hamlet is even consistent enough to know that for authenticity's sake he must turn his argument against himself: his 'inky cloak', tears, sighs and so on are superficial, mere conventional hints, imperfect signs of grief, and he does not want Gertrude to be mistaken: these things too only 'seem'; they are 'actions that a man might play'. He draws here on the language of the stage: human behavior, he implies, is a kind of drama, a mask of words and deeds, of ingenuity, metaphor and imagination by which we endlessly defer and conceal the truth. But it is important also to notice that Hamlet is not so stand-offish as to refuse to play the game: after all, he stages a play to catch the conscience of the king, and he plays at madness, though it may well be that he becomes mad in doing so, and he plays at swordplay at the end, and at elaborate verbal games throughout. Far from refusing society's game, Hamlet plays it much *more* ferociously, elaborately, ingeniously, than all the others, so that he ends up turning the game itself inside out. The critical cliché depicting him as a malcontent brooding on the edges of society is therefore too simple: he is much more threatening as the enemy within, a fact clearly enough realised by Claudius when he packs Hamlet off in a hurry to England with Rosencrantz and Guildenstern.

Hamlet's speech to his mother is thus turned against himself as a token of his uncompromising truthfulness. But also, Hamlet's truth has broken loose from the consensus, for it is intolerant of the merely conventional. It is as if the logic of Folly's perpetual parade of masks [in Erasmus's *Praise of Folly*] is pushed to the limit, for if language is a performance, a false front, a metaphoric illusion, it can never come to rest securely on any general statement, any idea which another might share. And so Hamlet's brilliant strategies do not so much enter into dialogue with others as fend them off, and in turn his deliberate alienation of others rebounds on Hamlet himself.

PV, 138–40

The following excerpts deal with the literature of modern Northern Ireland in order to show how the 'liberative transgressions' of art as a means of personal self-fashioning stand in contrast to the exclusionist, depersonalising binary oppositions and enmities pervasive in the culture at large. By way of these examples, I want to maintain that literature is fundamentally dialogical, in contrast to the monological discourses and 'negative transgressions' by which traditional boundaries are confirmed and separations deepened.

The Bloody Brae by John Hewitt is a dramatic poem in the form of a dialogue, and it provides a telling example of the interconnections among dialogue, transgression, and the personal.

Seamus Heaney's poem, 'Whatever You Say, Say Nothing' likewise shows how double-edged language is in managing the shifting boundaries between inclusion and exclusion, liberation and negation. Heaney also uses language here to reflect on the poem's own subterfuges, setting up a dialogue within a dialogue, the tentative resolution of which is the poem as a whole.

Finally, in order to confirm my main point, I draw on the teachings of the Buddha. Despite his austere views on non-attachment and the non-identity of the self, the Buddha throughout his long teaching career engaged in dialogue with a wide variety of interlocutors, adapting his discourse in a manner best suited to their personal needs and aptitudes. Again, dialogue is an effective means for bringing us to new knowledge and understanding by crossing over to the point of view of the other in order to effect the transvaluations that are central to the development of personal knowledge and mutual understanding.

15.

In John Hewitt's *The Bloody Brae*, a dramatic poem with six voices, an old man (he is an ex-soldier now living in penitential solitude) meets the ghost of a young woman he had killed along with her child as part of a Cromwellian pogrom against Catholics in the seventeenth century. The speaker, John Hill (John Hewitt?), while asserting 'This is my country', also faces his own guilt by encountering his victim, Bridget Magee, of whom he asks forgiveness. She offers this to him, but also reproves him for having dwelt so long in solitude instead of going out and actively promoting tolerance. She reminds Hill of how terrible his action was, but 'Pardon like rain must fall on every face / that's lifted up towards it', and through reconciliation the load can be shared and made 'a glittering web for God's delight'. Over and against this exchange, the voice of another soldier, Malcolm Scott, attempts to convince Hill that there is nothing to be guilty about: the troops had done their duty, and, besides, 'You forget who began the murder'. Here, the old, familiar binary resurfaces (those others started it), and Scott's untroubled, tough confidence is a reminder of a reality principle against which the language of mercy and forgiveness easily breaks – 'mumbling Mercy and Pity', as Scott says.

There are many good things in *The Bloody Brae*, but I want to concentrate on one only. At first Bridget seems reluctant to forgive, but she wants John to know that forgiveness has its own kind of truth and is not soft-centered: 'Truth is a lightning flash'. That is why he must understand how he has closed himself up in his own guilt: 'You have narrowed your mercy round you'. Instead, he should learn that 'every moment is the time for mercy' and he should go out and promote this message everywhere by direct, personal engagement with others. For his part, Hill realizes he can't demand forgiveness as 'a debt you owed me', but he has tried to school himself to be worthy of it. At last she tells him: 'as the woman you murdered, I forgive you'.

Although the text does not draw our attention explicitly to it, the opposition between Catholic and Protestant here entails a reversal of their typical positions on some fundamental theological issues. The Protestant becomes the hermit, has a vision, and asks forgiveness from another person rather than directly from God. By contrast, the Catholic gives a lesson in evangelical preaching and declares herself against the hermetic life, reminding Hill also of the fundamental Protestant principle that pardon 'cannot be earned / God is no huxter charging interest'. The poem offers no evidence that Hewitt realizes the import of this exchange, a crossing over between typically divisive religious positions that itself unconsciously effects something of the liberating reconciliation the poem recommends. Nonetheless, the verse is complicated and made more deeply resonant because of the deeply inter-personal exchange it registers.

BE, 56–7

16.

One of Seamus Heaney's best known poems about the sometimes dangerous consequences of equivocal speech is 'Whatever You Say, Say Nothing', from *North*. The title repeats a well known bit of Northern Irish folk wisdom, and the poem comprises twenty-two quatrains, the alternate rhymes providing a satiric edge, offset by the looser and more conversational intervening verses. The poem is bluntly contemptuous of journalists' pat questions and jargon ('escalate' / 'Backlash' and 'crack down', 'the provisional wing'), and of the social requirement to be 'Expertly civil tongued with civil neighbours'. Heaney is caustic also about religious hypocrisies on both sides of the community divide. Although '"Religion's never mentioned here", of course', Catholics none the less in their 'deepest heart of hearts' feel gratified that the Protestant heretics are at last being led 'to the stake'. Likewise, behind 'the great dykes' made by 'the Dutchman' (William of Orange), the Protestant community hunkers down, preserving the notion that 'to be saved you only must save face / And whatever you say, you say nothing'. Being 'saved' evangelically and saving face are conflated here, and the political imperative to maintain the *status quo* through a stony defensiveness rests on a barely suppressed sectarianism masquerading as self-righteousness. Religion is therefore the source of an equivalent hypocrisy on both sides, dangerously annexed to political violence in which each side mirrors the other in a mutual and mutually impersonal scapegoating antagonism.

As the poem explores this unfortunate situation further, Heaney looks again to the epic tradition, and specifically to the story of the Trojan horse. Northern Ireland, he suggests, is a land

> *Where tongues lie coiled, as under flames lie wicks,*
> *Where half of us, as in a wooden horse*
> *Were cabin'd and confined like wily Greeks,*
> *Besieged within the siege, whispering morse.*

Here, Catholic nationalists are the wily Greeks trapped inside Northern Ireland, which is like Troy defended by Protestant unionists, and yet the analogy is not quite accurate if only because Northern Ireland's Protestants know all too well that the nationalist community is by and large ready to bring them into a united Ireland; by contrast, the Trojans (except for the ill-fated Laocoon) think that the horse is a peace offering, and is just as it appears. Still, the stanza is less concerned with this precise correspondence than with the turn at the end, bringing Heaney back to language. The coded and whispered words of subversion are a result of the double siege (by analogy, the 'double minority' problem), and these coiled tongues are incendiary, provoking violence by refusing any personal, dialogical communication across the divide, just as does the tight reticence of 'whatever you say, you say nothing'.

Once more, then, for Heaney the epic returns us to the *agon* of language, and to a heroism represented by the poet's own labour, unveiling the hypocrisies concealed by conventional jargon. But although Heaney appeals in this poem to the epic to discover the 'fork-tongued' duplicities of Northern Ireland's sectarian factions, he does not (except by the widest indirection) engage the protest against sectarianism and religious hypocrisy registered from the heart of Christianity itself. If anything, poetic diction is offered here as a means of grace unmasking and bringing to consciousness the dangerous depersonalizing stereotypes and equivocations on which violence feeds.

BE, 49–51

17.

Although doctrine is important, it is abstract and prescriptive. By contrast, people's actual experience is typically complex, made up of passionate commitments, deeply felt loyalties, assorted ideals and aspirations, unconscious prejudices, occasional altruism, and the usual supply of good intentions. The means by which enlightenment might be discovered through the inconsistencies and contradictions of this kind of ordinary experience are exemplified especially by what we might call the literary dimension of the Buddha's Discourses – that is, the skilled and often ironic indirection through which the Buddha engages people (including the reader) dialogically.

For instance, the Buddha remains always mindful that people are nurtured by the group into which they are born and to which they remain attached by deeply felt personal ties. This kind of participatory experience is humanizing and should be seen as a preparatory ground for the Buddha's higher teachings rather than an impediment to them. Not surprisingly, these higher teachings remain closely tied to the deconstructionist (or, as Thomas M. Greene says, 'disjunctive') view of language that I began by noticing, aimed at freeing us from attachments and illusions. Yet, as we see, people's actual experience as participants in complex social and personal relationships needs to be addressed also by means of a more warmly engaging (let us say, again with Greene, 'conjunctive') and less austerely skeptical language.

And so, as persons who aspire to a freedom we do not yet have and cannot adequately describe, we need to conduct our conversations vigilantly in the space between these two broad views (conjunctive and disjunctive) of how language operates. My main claim is that throughout the Discourses of the Pali Canon, the Buddha understands and pursues this middle way with great skill, and the dialogical example he provides in doing so remains basic to the meaning and practice of compassion, the heart of his message.

SL, 6

18.

The interplay between these two broad tendencies (the first to disengagement from history; the second to engagement with many individual people through teaching the *Dhamma*) parallels the counterpoint I have described between disjunctive and conjunctive language, and how, despite their opposition, each requires something of the other. Thus, the Buddha remains disengaged from the world's turmoil because he is enlightened, and, especially in meditation, Buddhists continue to practice this kind of detachment. Yet the Buddha also engages with the world because he has teachings to impart to the unawakened, who are by definition recalcitrant, wrongheaded, and confused. As I have suggested, disjunctive language is especially effective for describing the Buddha's teachings about non-attachment; just so, his compassionate, dialogical engagement with the unenlightened requires a more personal, conjunctive discourse. Thus, the Buddha's assurance that each of us is an island does not preclude a recognition that we are also bound up with one another through interconnected chains of causation – language and enculturation chief among them. Some of the Buddha's profoundest teachings (especially in the *Suttas*, or Discourses) are imparted through a skillful management of these oppositions, as, on the one hand, he conveys something of the 'prodigious heightening' of his world-transforming vision and, on the other, acknowledges our common frailties and aspirations, frustrations and longings, anxieties and hopes.

SL, 18

6   IMAGINATION

Imagination is integral to desire and to our experience of the gap between desire and fulfillment, which is also the gap between body and language within which we are constituted as persons. Without imagination there are no ideals to aspire to and there is no way to consider the relation of means to ends or to reflect on the thoughts and intentions of others. Imagination therefore is fundamental to personal relationships and to the shaping of society, and there are no politics without imagination, if only because politicians make promises about a better, imagined future.

The most influential theorist of imagination in English is Samuel Taylor Coleridge, who makes a key distinction between primary and secondary imagination, and then also between imagination and fancy, as the following excerpts show. The philosopher Owen Barfield interprets Coleridge's view of imagination in a manner relevant for our personal self-fashioning in the modern age. Maurice Merleau-Ponty, Jean-Paul Sartre, and Northrop Frye, among others, are likewise concerned to develop a modern post-Romantic understanding of how central imagination is to human discourse and social organization.

1.

As Northrop Frye says, educating the imagination 'affects the whole person', entailing its 'social and moral development'. Consequently, education helps to reveal 'the real form of human society hidden behind the one we see', for what appears to us on the surface as real is often a tissue of illusions of the kind that 'propaganda and slanted news and prejudice and a great deal of advertising appeal to'. As Marx says, we are immersed in the ideology that we go on remaking, and a critical approach to culture can help us to understand something of how this is so; for, as Frye also points out, in a great work of literature, 'the whole cultural history of the nation that produced it comes into focus' as the context within which 'the whole person' emerges.

PC, 6

2.

At this point, where Merleau-Ponty's theory of imagination engages the paradoxical interplay between participation and separation characteristic of the human use of language, he echoes Sartre who also says that imagination is an irreducible act of consciousness (it is impossible, he claims, to describe the contents of a mental image). According to Sartre, imagination pre-eminently makes present an absence, and this fact is of signal importance because it is central to the exercise of freedom that we can hold the world at a distance, imagining a not-yet-existent state of affairs that calls on us to choose. The mental image itself is nebulous, but by summoning us to concrete action it is integral to our personal freedom and our limited capacity for self-fashioning.

In short, despite anti-Romantic attacks on privileged consciousness and creative individuality, it is difficult entirely to dislodge subjectivity from human thinking. In the myriad, irreducibly complex adjustments, *gestalten*, negotiations of feeling and skills of adaptation by which persons adjust to one another and explore the world, the sense of a self as agent having a degree of identity and continuity persists, and its shaping activity, even through the untellable complexities and constraints operative upon it, remains importunate. The fact is that in meeting another person we encounter a subjectivity akin to our own, and in negotiating the world we are active interpreters, makers of tools, choosers of directions. For so it is to be a person, and 'imagination' describes this many-sided and perpetual encounter and adaptation, interrogation and synthesis. In such a context, our claims for imagination might also remain quite modest, for imagination is a limited and contingent power, bearing the marks of our incompleteness and tentativeness: 'the best in this kind are but shadows'.

We might now propose that imagination comprises three main elements. The first is a configurating and synthesizing activity at work in perception, by which a thing becomes an object (that which I know and can talk about). The second is the capacity to produce a fictional world, in some ways an alternative to the one we live in, and which then also lets us interpret our familiar world in a new way. The third is the power to make present an absence and thus to hold out alternatives enabling choice and action. In a sense, the power of negation evident in the third element is operative in the other two as well, for the self we know in the object (first element) is never fully present, and our fictional worlds (second element) are not actual worlds. All three elements are therefore taken up within a dialectic of presence and absence, and are enfolded upon one another much as is our experience of past, present and future time. Thus, a critique of imagination will disclose how imagination engages with the temporal embededness which is basic to our condition as historical persons. Imagination's role in perception then is analogous to the presence of the past, in the sense that it deals with the givenness of a world and of history (Heidegger's 'factuality'). Imagination as fiction belongs in the present, where we recognize most intensely the production of new effects and fresh metaphors, at once constrained by history and yet novel, present yet figurative (Heidegger's 'fallenness', marked by ambiguity). Imagination as negation belongs with the presence of the future because it is concerned with openness and possibility (Heidegger's 'existentiality'). In all three, bodily immediacy and disembodied distance come together, and imagination, like language itself, emerges from an interplay of presence and absence, the tension of 'is and not-yet' within which the personal also is constituted.

PV, 104–6

3.

It is well known that Coleridge responded enthusiastically to Kant, though he also looked over Kant's shoulder to Tetens' *Philosophische Versuche*, on which Kant drew. For Coleridge, the capacity of human beings to 'superintend the works which they are themselves carrying on in their own minds' is the key to imagination, but the mind arrives at self-experience only by encountering an object, and becomes 'a subject by the act of constructing itself objectively to itself'. Thus we 'understand' ourselves in and through objects which in turn are partly products of thinking, and Coleridge calls this synthesis 'primary imagination'. In a much-cited passage, he defines primary imagination as 'the living power and prime agent of all human perception, and as a repetition in the finite mind of the eternal act of creation in the infinite I Am'. Imagination here is at once creative and finite, and in coming to know its workings, Coleridge argues, we participate in Reason, a kind of spiritual unconscious which could be described as nature's inner power of significance. But Reason itself has two aspects, for although it is super-individual and we participate in it as we do in being, it is also the principle enabling logic and analytical detachment. The paradox therefore recurs: we are to grasp Reason by analogy with the process whereby the classified parts cohere in an organic whole, just as the whole informs the parts, and yet grasping this principle is itself an act of imagination, which is irreducible.

Coleridge's 'primary imagination', then, is so instinct with 'thinking' but we are usually unconscious of how this reasoning process operates. But when we invent fictive images we deploy 'secondary imagination', which remains at one with primary imagination insofar as both draw on what we might call the creative unconscious. In turn, secondary imagination is distinguished from Fancy, which is a mere juxtaposition of similarities – a superficial, aggregative pursuit that does not synthesize the parts into a whole. And so weak poetry is fanciful rather than imaginative, because it does not create new meanings.

Clearly, Coleridge does not regard the self as a pre-established essence set over against an extended material world. Rather, subjects become conscious through objects which, in turn, subjects help to produce by an active configuration, and this, as I have been arguing, is part of what is entailed by the idea of the person. Nonetheless,

Coleridge also privileges self-consciousness and the notion that the mind can 'find itself' through imagination and thereby come to know its innermost unity with the powers and energies of sustaining nature. Coleridge's world and that of the post-structuralists could not, therefore, be mistaken for long, even though the path from Coleridge to Derrida through phenomenology is marked by continuity as well as contrast. As we have seen, among phenomenologists the status of the subject and the structure of perception receive intense scrutiny. For instance, Maurice Merleau-Ponty points out in a broadly Kantian way that perceiving is always perceiving something, and all perception is also imbued with a degree of general significance. But Merleau-Ponty goes on to suggest that because 'perception' entails active interpretation there is no need to introduce a further occult power into the transaction. The word 'imagination' consequently should describe our deliberately produced fictions.

Yet Coleridge is not so easily shaken off, and is already alert to this objection when he describes how pure thought and simple percepts are outside our normal experience. Perceptions are (as Merleau-Ponty says) thought-imbued, just as concepts, however rarefied, are shot through by traces of the concrete and perceptual. Coleridge points out that we repeatedly distinguish what we do not separate, and ordinary thought could not proceed otherwise. Just so, in analyzing an act of cognition we can distinguish between what proceeds from our thinking and configurating activity, and what impinges upon us. Indeed, Merleau-Ponty finds himself doing just this when he analyses perception as a single power uniting two forces (active and passive) which is precisely what Coleridge also does.

PV, 102–3

301

4.

Owen Barfield points out that in dealing with micro-particles, modern physics reveals more and more clearly that matter is fundamentally unrepresentable, and, consequently, modern science challenges the Cartesian co-ordinates upon which the development of physics depended. Barfield anticipates a reunion of science and religion brought about by new ways of understanding the material universe, and this reunion will be founded on a mutual appreciation among scientists and students of religion that the power of imagination in human thought and perception is transformative.

SA, 123

5.

Barfield points out also that polarity is not a logical concept, and must itself be grasped by imagination:

> *Where logical opposites are contradictory, polar opposites are generative of each other – and together generative of a new product. ... We can and must distinguish, but there is no possibility of dividing them. ... The point is, has the imagination grasped it? For nothing else can do so. At this point the reader must be called on, not to think about imagination, but to use it. Indeed we shall see that the apprehension of polarity is itself the basic act of imagination.*

And so the circle is neatly closed. Polarity is basic to the act of imagination by which polarity is to be grasped. Imagination therefore is the activity which transmutes the dichotomy itself between subject and object: only by knowing 'that' imaginatively can I know myself, and it is absurd to claim that mind emerged (as Darwin says) from a world of inanimate objects, because objects are but one element in a bi-polar structure involving subjects. Imagination, which unites them, bespeaks rather an anterior condition out of which our awareness of the autonomy of extramental things has developed to a degree equivalent to our self-consciousness. Only by an idolatrous mistaking of the material for the 'real' have we lost sight of this rootedness of things in the originally given meaning in which we, and the world before us, subsist.

However, because the polarity at the heart of perception is reproduced in the relation between images and structure in poetry, the experience of imagination in literature can become a guide to misdirected theories of perception. The poem, typically, shows us a passionate utterance quenched in an adapted form or frame, while the reader, a transcendent third, contains this polarity while also participating in it personally. This is explained in *Poetic Diction*, Barfield's first book, which, as he says himself, determined the future direction of his studies, leading him through Coleridge and Steiner to a fuller exploration of how we become self-aware as historical persons.

SA, 124–5

Fantasy is of special interest in the present discussion because fantasy thematises the process itself of imagination. It does so by causing us to hesitate between the acceptance of some inexplicable event and the laws that govern our familiar world. With this in mind, Tzveton Todorov describes how fantasy challenges our sense of having a unified personal identity while calling us to reconsider the structure and meaning of the familiar world on which that identity depends. G.K. Chesterton makes much the same point, albeit in a more bracing manner, and J.R.R. Tolkien echoes Coleridge's distinction between primary and secondary imagination in order to claim that fantasy is 'a human right', enabling us better to understand our personal desires and creative freedoms.

6.

The most concise introduction to Todorov's thinking is his *Introduction to Poetics*. Basically, he argues that literature is inseparable from human sign-making and cultural symbolism in general, and he sees 'poetics' as playing 'an eminently *transitional* role, even a transitory one' in the emergence of a general theory of discourse. In so doing, Todorov attempts to place himself historically, interpreting his special concern as 'the site we have reserved for the *other* since the Renaissance'. By this means, he tells us he is reaching towards such large questions as tolerance, xenophobia, colonialism, and 'assimilation of the other and identification with the other', which are basic to the idea of the person.

Todorov's reassurance about his historical concern is partly a defence against the standard accusation that structuralists ignore history. Yet his own writing is characteristically abstract, and the approach to fantasy in his well-known book, *The Fantastic: A Structural Approach to a Literary Genre*, is very much what the subtitle declares it to be. Todorov's key argument is that fantasy produces an effect of combined hesitation and wonder occasioned by the intrusion into our familiar world of an extraordinary event that cannot be explained adequately by the laws of that familiar world. The fantastic lasts only as long as the hesitation between belief in supernatural intervention on the one hand, and incredulity on the other. If the reader decides that the laws of the familiar world do after all offer a sufficient explanation, then the strange event can be described as uncanny. An example is Jan Potocki's *Saragossa Manuscript*, where "'the miracles" are explained rationally at the end of the narrative', as is the case also with many detective novels. If supernatural laws are invoked, then the event is marvelous, as in the *Arabian Nights*. But fantasy takes its life precisely from an uncertainty poised between these alternatives.

PV, 118–19

7.

With characteristic breeziness, Chesterton reminds us that we cannot say how an egg turns into a chicken any more than we can say how a bear could turn into a prince, and the fact that fairy tales make rivers run with wine reminds us 'for one wild moment' that they run with water. In short, such reflections force us to see what an 'eccentric privilege' life is, and, especially, how the human being is 'the Great Might-Not-Have-Been'. Realisation of this perilous condition causes anxiety, but also provokes action. Our world is full of pain but is also our home, at once an ogre's castle and our own cottage. Can we then 'hate it enough to change it, and yet love it enough to think it worth changing'?

PV, 122

8.

Faerie is for Tolkien a realm of enchantment where we discover the power of language in combining the elements of 'primary' creation to make a 'secondary' world of imagination. To enquire about the origins of faerie is therefore to ask about the origins of language, and, clearly, we must take seriously the enchanting, subcreative power of the human mind to make as it is made, for through it we explore some of the primal desires of our own nature. Fantasy, in short, is for Tolkien a human right, and only by unhappy misunderstanding were fairy stories dismissed, during the Renaissance, as unworthy of adult attention, and relegated to the nursery.

This unfortunate process was accelerated by the advent of industrialism, and the advances of technology in his own century occasioned in Tolkien a resigned pessimism, for he saw the mechanization of human society as directly opposed to the literary values he cherished. These, even though founded in imagination, Tolkien vigorously maintains are not escapist, because the power of subcreation lies to a large degree in the sense of an actual world that it communicates. Faerie is not just dreamland; dreams are subjective imaginings, whereas in faerie we meet the primal human desire for personal 'realization, independent of the conceiving mind, of imagined wonder'. As persons, we want the deepest desires of our nature to be fulfilled, and the power of faerie lies in showing us that they can be.

Tolkien here resorts to a neologism, 'Eucatastrophe', to describe the happy reversal or turn of events which breaks through the tragic frame of suffering in a successful fairy story to reveal, in a moment of poignant joy, that the reader's profoundest wish really is for the end not to be in misery and defeat. He gives an example:

> *Seven long years I served for thee,*
> *The glassy hill I clamb for thee,*
> *The bluidy shirt I wrang for thee,*
> *And wilt thou not wauken and turn to me?*

> *He heard and turned to her.*

SA, 105–6

The therapeutic dimensions of imagination and fantasy are addressed by the psychologists Bruno Bettelheim and C.G. Jung. Bettelheim deals with fairy tales and Jung with traditional myths and symbols to argue that a healthy personal identity requires a balance, such as imagination helps to provide, between our conscious understanding and the wellsprings of feeling and emotion reaching back through our evolutionary history. Yet the therapeutic efficacy of imagination and fantasy is not confined to the old stories, as modern assessments of Lewis Carroll, for instance, indicate.

As a counterweight to the fantastic worlds of fairy tales and myth, the Polish film director Krzysztof Kieslowski reminds us that close perceptions of the ordinary world can also put us in touch with the mystery of being. And so, if fantasy brings us to a renewed sense of the strange dimensions of ordinary experience, then also, by way of imagination, ordinary experience can be a portal to the encompassing mystery, likewise bringing home to us how, as persons, we go on being taunted and spurred on by desire, which simultaneously makes us all too aware of our own personal incompleteness.

9.

Jung's practice as a medical doctor allowed him access to mentally ill patients, and his extraordinary learning in mythology, philosophy, and the history of ideas enabled him to link the findings of his clinical practice to the world's great religions. In so doing, he was surprised to discover how the delusions, dreams, and fantasies of patients could reproduce mythological and traditional symbolic motifs of which the patients had no prior knowledge. Jung undertook to explain this interesting discovery by suggesting that there is an analogy between the evolution of the unconscious and the evolution of the body. That is, because of our evolution as a species, human bodies are basically similar despite the variety of actual human beings. So also, the unconscious is the result of an evolutionary development whereby patterns of behavior are set down, so that the mind's unconscious operations are similarly structured, despite the variety of individual manifestations. Jung named these basic patterns 'archetypes', by which he meant organizational tendencies that give rise to specific kinds of images and symbols, both in the dreams and delusions of patients and also in the productions of culture, such as art, religion, and mythology.

For Jung, archetypes declare themselves especially in symbols, which are a bridge to the unconscious but which do not encompass the underlying energies upon which consciousness floats like a bubble on the ocean. In the case of an ill patient, the spontaneous symbols in dreams or hallucinations can be messages indicating the kinds of rebalancing, or adaptation, necessary to restore the free flow of energy in which a healthy personal development consists. In a broader cultural context, the symbols and imagery of religion, mythology, art, and literature perform a similar function, helping to maintain a healthy equilibrium between consciousness and the unconscious – the busy waking world and the tacit dimensions of the dark powers that sustain it. 'All religions are therapies for the sorrows and disorders of the soul', Jung says. Likewise, psychoanalysis is 'a highly moral task of immense educational value' for understanding what it means to be a human person.

IM, 196–7

10.

The rise of fantasy as a kind of fiction supposedly for

children but taken seriously by adults is comparatively recent. A key figure in its history is Lewis Carroll, whose uniqueness lies partly in the fact that he wrote for children for the fun of it, without moralizing. But Carroll's genius has also been acknowledged in the twentieth century by a range of figures about whom Charles Dodgson might well have felt misgivings. For instance, he is praised in the first surrealist manifesto of 1924, admired and imitated by Joyce as well as by Wittgenstein, André Breton, Vladimir Nabokov and Antonin Artaud.

SA, 93

11.

Krzysztof Kieslowski's special magic emerges from a tension (a favourite word of his) between our immediate material circumstances and the more elusive dimensions of time, chance, and coincidence in which we also find ourselves inexplicably immersed. Yet Kieslowski never looks to theology or religion for answers to the metaphysical questions he poses; rather, he provides a sense of the mystery of existence itself, from which religion takes its own, different life. He knew there is too much that we don't know, and a reductive materialism or escapist supernaturalism merely betray the ambivalence and uncertainty of our status as persons.

Kieslowski once said that he doesn't trust movies, only audiences, and he wants his films to be the equivalent of sitting down and having a chat. Yet he also knew that his films would appeal to people whose sensibilities are attuned to the subtleties of feeling, intuition, and tacit communication that he especially investigates. 'Either you feel it or you don't', he says, commenting on *Three Colours*, and he admits that *The Double Life of Véronique* is 'a film for a very limited group of people. I don't mean an age group or a social group but a group of people who are sensitive to the sort of emotions shown in the film'. He goes on to insist that such people can come from all conditions in life and are not an élite, 'unless we call sensitive people élite'. An analogy might be to lyric poetry. People who read lyric poetry often and with pleasure are a minority among readers. They might come from all walks of life, and as a group they are distinctive only because they have a sensibility attuned to the subtleties and revelatory power of that special means of communication. Just so, Kieslowski is a lyric poet among filmmakers. 'Yes, absolutely' Kieslowski is a poet, says Jean-Louis Trintignant, reflecting on his experience in *Red*, where Trintignant and Irène Jacob played the leading roles. And so it might be helpful to consider briefly Kieslowski's own view of the creative process, and the kind of appeal his particular kind of filmic poetry has.

As we have seen, Kieslowski points to 'something like a barometer' within himself when he makes moral choices which, typically, he experiences as more complex than is allowed by a plain 'description of right and wrong'. In the same context he refers to an 'inner compass', a term he applies both to moral choices and to filmmaking. He explains that he doesn't film personal things 'in a certain way' so that critics 'will understand what it's supposed to mean'. Rather, the process 'comes naturally to me', and 'if you haven't got your own compass within yourself which clearly points you in a certain direction then you won't find it'. Elsewhere he says that 'I don't know how ideas come to me', and repeats that he doesn't 'analyze' or 'rationalize'. His ideas 'come of their own accord', arising not from a single principle or source, but 'from everything you've touched'.

That is, the creative process expresses an entire sensibility and has its own highly personal integrity ('authenticity', Kieslowski says) about which one ought not to be overly self-conscious, especially during the creative process itself.

In all this, Kieslowski describes what John Keats means by 'negative capability'. That is, the poet, like other kinds of artist, feels or senses the power of an image or metaphor without analyzing its implications. Analysis after the fact might provide understanding (more or less), but creative power emerges from a distinctive quality of imagination, an ability of the whole person to sense, feel, intuit, and shape the image as well as think about it. The image itself might well contain a great deal more than the artist understands at the time.

IM, 210–11

As I mentioned in Part 1, a key marker of personal agency is that we can construct counterfactuals. And yet our ability to do so is ambivalent because through imagination we can, chameleon-like, adapt rapidly – sometimes uncritically – to the requirements of changing times and circumstances. As we have seen in I,2 (b), Plato, Augustine, and Aquinas developed theories about imagination in keeping with a 'Sacramental' view according to which images mediate transcendent truths. In the age of 'Disenchantment and Discovery', John Locke explored a view of imagination divorced from the metaphysical presuppositions of the Sacramental Age. And yet, although metaphysical language in the age of Locke had lost prestige, it also sometimes took on new life as a kind of conceptual poetry, for instance in Thomas Browne. By contrast, for John Milton, the rejection of traditional metaphysics resulted in a disconcertingly materialized depiction of things traditionally regarded as spiritual, as we see, for example, in his description of the digestive tracts of angels and in his belief in mortalism. In Milton, the gravitational pull along a horizontal axis that privileges history and material actuality draws us already towards a modern, secular materialism in which imagination looks primarily to its own ordering principles for validation, and in which personal identity is imagined in ways not available to the Middle Ages. Yet, as the example of Thomas Browne reminds us, the transition from Medieval to Modern was not straightforward. The old did not simply replace the new but remained interwoven with it, contributing to how we understand ourselves, as the following excerpts show.

12.

In Plato's *Republic*, the poets are banished because they are second-hand imitators of the transcendent world of Forms. That is, poets give us a copy of things which are themselves copies of eternal Ideas. Nevertheless, poetry returns at a crucial juncture of Plato's argument to provide a myth serving to unite the will of the Republicans, enlivening them, however high or low their caste, to the ideals by which the state should be governed.

But in the *Ion*, Plato speaks of poets in another sense altogether. As inspired seer (not just imitator) the poet now brings insight from a higher-than-ordinary source, and this, in a way, is the effect achieved also by the (inspired) author of the *Republic*, so that we are left to meditate the spectacle of a poet, Plato himself, whose very sense of the power of poetry leads him to denounce it. Yet, Plato is especially concerned with how images reflect their originating principles, and for the Greeks in Plato's tradition, the mind's images, like those in literature, are valuable because, by the nature of things, the One is reflected in inherently meaningful ways through the multivalent world of becoming, even though the One, like ideal Goodness, cannot be adequately described or encompassed by the images that reflect it imperfectly.

LM, 28

13.

On the lowest, 'corporeal' level, Augustine posits an interaction between the body and the object by means of which the mind creates an image representing the object, and commits it to memory. But because human thought responds immediately to the perception of objects in the formation of 'spiritual' images, 'corporeal vision' is never experienced by itself, without some intellectual component. Presumably the fact that Augustine never seemed to doubt the independent existence of things encouraged him to posit 'corporeal vision' on logical grounds, though it seems we cannot otherwise verify it. But the main point is that 'spiritual vision' involves a mixture of mutability (derived from the corporeal) and immutability (derived from the intellectual), and the hallmark of 'spiritual vision' is the image. Thus, the meaning of images, like that of a human life in time and history or the unfolding words of a sentence, becomes clear by reference to the imageless source of intelligibility, the final object of faith. It follows that images are subject to the same imperfection as are human beings in time, and must be accepted in the same trust that meaning will be revealed in light of the vision they signify. On the one hand the object of faith is therefore transcendent and imageless (intellectual vision), but on the other the eternal species of temporal things is really, if imperfectly, represented by the images in our minds ('spiritual vision'). From this point Augustine is free to stress how rich are the analogies between our images and transcendent Ideas. The free range of the analogy-making faculty is therefore encouraged because we can discover by this distinctively human means (animals and angels do not have 'spiritual vision') something of our distinctive place in the world.

II, 8–9

14.

Like the author of the *Timaeus*, Augustine is forced to a kind of 'spurious reasoning' as imagination attempts to approach the original corporeal stuff of the universe which exists on the very verge of the intelligible. 'So that when thought seeketh what the sense may conceive under this … it may endeavor either to know it, by being ignorant of it; or to be ignorant, by knowing it'. Augustine engages in a good deal of this kind of verbal juggling to explain how matter has less identity than words can say. In his attempts to grasp it, he tells us, he eventually stopped questioning his imaginative 'spirit' altogether, 'it being filled with the images of formed bodies'. The formless matter created from nothing by God's act is, he concludes, itself 'almost nothing' – a fluid, mutable, invisible and unorganized realm that can scarcely even be said to exist. In it the image of God can be faintly traced by a strenuous reduction whereby imagination works against itself, imaginatively.

The interest Augustine demonstrates here in the elusive relationship between images and matter shows, as I have said, his desire to preserve both his Biblical conviction and his Platonist theories, and one result is that matter, being good, is the foundation for the formation of images. It is then easy to see how the knowledge of material things can be used to elucidate signs, just as signs, properly interpreted, lead towards the vision of eternal realities, so that the unique privilege of human beings is to refer, in praise, the meaning of the creation to God.

II, 12

15.

For Aquinas, just as for Augustine, writes Gilson, 'if a physics of bodies exists, it is because there is first a mystical theology of the divine life'. Admittedly, Aquinas does allow a good deal less to human knowledge than Augustine, who claims that in this life we can sometimes have the imageless experience of intellectual vision. For Aquinas, the mind must rather infer the forms indirectly from the effects of sensible bodies and be content with only a 'tiny ... connatural' light which is 'enough for our knowing', but which leaves us with the arduous responsibility of building certain knowledge by slow degrees. By insisting on our imperfection, Aquinas underlines the Augustinian precept that knowledge must be founded on faith which will pass away only when happiness is attained in the vision of God.

As a result of these similarities, and despite the different emphases, Aquinas's theory of art and beauty is not conceptually far removed, either, from the basic teaching of Augustine's *De Doctrina* on signs and images as representations of mysteries. Art, Aquinas explains, is a human act that reveals a harmony and radiance shining out from the ordered matter which the artist has arranged according to his conception and by way of images, and through which we apprehend something of Beauty itself.

II, 15

16.

Locke warns especially against the deceptive imagination which he associates with the mind's proclivity for presenting fantastical, inadequate, and false pictures of things as true. For Locke, the most insidious trick of imagination is to have us take names for actual things. He consistently warns against this, claiming that in poetry we are swayed by associations of images, so that the conformity between our ideas and the real nature of things is likely to be distorted:

> But yet if we would speak of things as they are, we must allow that all the art of rhetoric, besides order and clearness; all the artificial and figurative applications of words eloquence hath invented, are for nothing else but to insinuate wrong ideas, move the passions, and thereby mislead the judgement; and so indeed are perfect cheats.

How seriously Locke took this argument is indicated by his definition of madness as a too lively imagination.

So far, I have discussed imagination in Locke not in terms of a difference in kind between images and ideas, but a difference in degree, with imagination linked to rhetoric, wit, fancy and metaphor and having a power to distract us from simplicity and clarity. And yet all our knowledge, according to Locke, comes through images because knowledge is rooted in the senses. Our simple ideas are not therefore reflections of transcendent Forms, but the basic irreducible images of colour, shape, and so on, which we put together in complex ideas. So although he does not say much in the *Essay* directly about imagination, it is everywhere indirectly the subject of discussion because for Locke it is the medium of thought itself. In thus combining images and ideas to root them in physical reality, Locke denies the relevance to human knowledge of a transcendent dimension and assumes instead, because it seems the best hypothesis, that God has created us able to make the ideas which each of us experiences: 'We are like God in our understandings; he sees what he sees, by ideas in his mind; therefore we see what we see, by ideas that are in our own minds'. The human being, as the shaper of ideas through images, is therefore now in an unprecedented way an autonomous agent.

II, 198–9

17.

Whereas poetry describes the links between human nature and the world through an affective appeal to concrete particulars, metaphysics, traditionally understood, does so by abstraction: its object is the unity of being, and its procedures are logical. As a consequence of the discovery of method, traditional metaphysics was widely regarded with suspicion, and often seemed just another kind of imagination. Consequently, a scientist with old-fashioned leanings, such as Thomas Browne, had to choose either to defend traditional metaphysics philosophically or, by deploying metaphysical language imaginatively, to run the risk of confirming its fictional status. As Digby and Coleridge detect, the second option best describes Browne's practice. Of angels he writes, 'there is not any creature that hath so neare a glimpse of their nature as light in the Sunne and Elements … in briefe, conceive light invisible, and that is a Spirit'. Metaphysical intuition here takes the form of imaginative insight; the aim is not an abstract and systematic analysis of light, or God, or of the limits of human intelligence (though all these pertain to Browne's subject), but an invitation to readers to feel how interesting it is to imagine the angels in such a manner.

DM, 104

18.

Browne's predicament is therefore that he thinks of himself as one of the new philosophers, and in some respects he behaves like one, for he is an empiricist who is judiciously skeptical about metaphysics and the relationship of language to things. But he remains an old-fashioned metaphysician nonetheless, convinced that things in this world are hieroglyphs of a higher, spiritual reality. Besides, his metaphysical practice is so informal, and is conducted in a style so personal (at once epistolary and meditative), that he makes of the topic something subjectively pleasing and imaginatively coherent, rather than something conceptually rigorous and logical. While we may see Browne in one sense as rescuing metaphysics from pedantry (by reaffirming it as creative), in another sense he threatens to reduce metaphysics to fiction by the very fact of his treating it imaginatively and without critical rigour.

DM, 109

19.

Milton's depiction of God the Father has been widely criticized for its literalness, and Dante's suggestive indirection admired by contrast. I have suggested that a similar response to a world increasingly regarded as constituted of quantifiable material reality causes Crashaw and Milton alike to strain in representing the spiritual in physical terms. Yet their responses to this challenge are diametrically opposite. Crashaw rushes to a Catholic sacramentalism and the Platonist traditions of the Capucins to transubstantiate the physical 'vertically' into the higher mystery which spiritualises it. Milton rejects this Neo-Platonist ontology with its accompanying sacramentalism, and his 'horizontal' spirituality is oddly materialised, not because the soul is unlike matter, but because it is similar.

The exegetical theory behind Milton's attitude to poetic imagery, which consistently reflects these other concerns with matter and time, history and progress, is well described by William Madsen. He contends that Milton's 'shadowy types' should not be read as Neo-Platonist intimations of higher ineffable mysteries, but according to Protestant methods of Biblical exegesis, as foreshadowings, just as the types of Old Testament history indicate things to come. Milton uses imagery in a Platonist sense only to describe Adam's condition before the fall and the 'grateful vicissitude' of heaven, where time, unbroken by sin, moves in cycles. But in fallen time this original perfection is damaged, and is restored by Christ. Before the Incarnation, human history provided only *shadows* of truth, a series of images and types of what will happen in the fullness of time. Then, with Christ, such images and types are abolished and he alone is 'the image, as it were, by which we see God' and the 'word by which we hear him'. The usefulness of images is not, in consequence, denied by Milton, for they still can be used like the Old Testament types to enliven and illuminate truths already known in Jesus. Read in this way, Milton's imagery, like his theories of time, matter, politics, and history, turns out not to be 'mysterious' in the Neo-Platonist sense, for in his poems the thing pictured, the event alluded to, the tableau exquisitely presented, do not mediate any transcendent Idea, and the emphasis is historical and psychological, horizontal rather than vertical.

II, 136

The following five excerpts deal with literature from the early modern period to the present. Each of the selected authors deals with imagination in relation to the shaping of personal identity within a specific cultural context. Edmund Spenser's depiction of the connection between courtesy and holiness shows how imagination shapes us as individuals. For Desiderius Erasmus, imagination, although salutary, lets us see also how precarious our sense of personal identity is. Samuel Johnson seeks to balance imagination and reason in order to preserve some sense of personal integrity and stability in a world full of dangerous deceptions. Wordsworth (drawing on Coleridge), calls upon poetry to shape a healthy human identity in an industrial age when people are increasingly alienated from nature. For Seamus Heaney, imagination returns us to the organization of the poem itself as a token of the personal integration to which we aspire.

20.

In Book VI of Edmund Spenser's *Faerie Queene*, Sir Calidore is the knight of courtesy, which Spenser describes as virtue's fairest flower: extravagant praise, one feels, for a mode of behavior commonly thought of today as roughly equivalent to etiquette. But in the age of Spenser, courtesy had a special meaning. He tells us that there are no explicit rules governing it; rather, it requires discernment, as poetry itself does, and it stands in relation to the rules of decorum as does poetry to the rules of prosody. Courtesy then is the poetry of conduct, at once distinct from literature, and yet analogous to it. Once Spenser had made this point, exhorting his readers to fashion their lives like a poem, he continued the *Faerie Queene* no further.

There is no clear reason why Spenser stopped when he did, but Book VI seems both to complete and complement Book I, the topic of which is holiness, virtue's fairest flower in another sense. And so poet and saint find themselves at last in complementary opposition. In Book I, we are asked to acknowledge that holiness is the aim of all the virtues, and also that poetry cannot describe holiness adequately. In Book VI, we learn that the heart of virtue (the empirical test of holiness, as it were) lies in conducting ourselves in a manner analogous to a poem, in the process of our own self-fashioning. Spenser seems thus to believe that imagination can give us some real sense of the transcendent mystery, but poetry pronounces also its own limitations and Sir Calidore's most serious, because undefeatable, enemy is the Blatant Beast, a monstrous rumour-mongering distorter of *words*. Calidore, after all, in fashioning his identity with a poet's craft, is not free from the poet's entanglement with language, if only because the distortion of words can cause us to act in harmful ways.

LM, 33–4

21.

In Erasmus's *Praise of Folly*, at one point Folly asks, 'what else is the whole life of man but a sort of play', and she goes on to suggest that in the public world all we ever meet are the masks people assume in order to perform their various (and variable) parts in life. According to this view, the real core, or soul, or identity of an individual person eludes us, and the fact that true ecstatics seem crazed in the eyes of the world shows that what you see of a person does not really tell you about that person's inner state and condition.

Yet there is a nightmarish side to this argument, though Erasmus does not explore it in detail. If all we encounter in another person is a series of performances, and if life is entirely a theatrical play, perhaps there is no real self but only an endless shifting of appearances, a kind of vertigo of loosely-connected illusions, and spiritual ecstasy might just be another of these. At one point, Folly tells us that many people do not believe in the soul because they cannot see it; we might recall that, with some slight variation, Hume would later argue that this is indeed a good reason for unbelief. Thus, Erasmus's doctrine of an ecstatic soul that nobody can see threatens to leave us merely with the peculiar behavior of human bodies that everyone can see. Already we might feel an uncomfortable closeness to the world of Samuel Beckett, Foucault's panopticon, and Freud's scopophilia.

PC, 96

22.

From the start, Samuel Johnson's *Rasselas* sets out to indulge our fancy. There is an exotic Eastern setting with a paradisal valley, an adventurous escape, a kidnapping, strange castles with secret passages, a trip into the interior of the pyramids, and more. The reader is therefore attracted by the same promise of adventure and discovery as Rasselas, and Johnson ensures that both are brought to the same relentlessly sobering disappointments. Moreover, and with splendid irony, it turns out that the apparently reasonable notion underlying Rasselas' pilgrimage – that he should make a survey of how people live and then choose what to do with his own life – turns out to be among the grandest illusions of all. Initially, Rasselas assumes that he is free to stand outside and observe things neutrally. Yet, the advocates of this kind of detachment whom Rasselas meets are unhappy because their imagined autonomy breaks down under pressure of the reality it seems to preclude. Once again, the 'hunger of imagination … preys incessantly upon life', and in this context Johnson's allusions to rivers are especially suggestive.

When Rasselas first experiences discontent in the Happy Valley, he seeks seclusion and spends 'day after day on the banks of rivulets', telling himself 'I am not at rest'. The agitated water here resembles his uneasy state of mind, and Johnson quickly establishes a link between the river and the book's psychological themes. Later, Rasselas confesses to Imlac his desire to 'mingle' with the 'mighty confluence of nations' outside the valley. But as we see, 'mingle' is not quite what he intends, as he ventures forth to survey his options. This tension between participation and detachment recurs when Imlac lectures Rasselas on not endeavouring 'to do more than is allowed to humanity', and then confirms his advice by alluding to the river: 'no man can at the same time fill his cup from the source and from the mouth of the Nile'. The river is life, and we must take our appropriate pleasures at the appropriate points: the freshness of the source and the fullness of the river mouth are different, and we should not try to have them both at once. Filling our cup suggests that we are not only travellers, lookers-on during the course of a voyage, but also participants in the river's substance. Also, the waters suggest life's fluid and restless course, mirroring in turn imagination's fickleness and turbulence. In the concluding chapter, the Nile has overflowed, and the company cannot take excursions. Instead, they discuss 'the different forms of life which they had observed'. Each describes the most desirable existence, including Imlac's wish 'to be driven along the stream of life' without taking any particular course, but they all know at last that the ideal cannot be attained, and so they return to Abyssinia.

The river in all this is something to travel on and mingle with, simultaneously. It is within us, as the stream of our pleasures and discontents, the fluctuations of imagination and desire, and although its waters can overflow, they normally take their course between the containing banks. Indeed, only because there is a containing structure can there be a river at all, making its way from source to ocean. And in a sense Johnson depicts here imagination's relation to reason, the general, containing structure within which run the currents of a disturbing, necessary energy, at once potentially fertilising and destructive. The river then is also a symbol for the balance between the contrary elements necessary for a stable personal identity as we pursue a course on the river of life.

PV, 214–15

23.

A certain set of terms now confronts us: *Matter*, that of which we are conscious, as Coleridge says, and which is not conscious itself; *Spirit*, which operates in the openness to experience which we know through the limits imposed by matter and in our partial freedom from such limits; *Imagination*, the characteristic psychic life of human beings, a power of apprehension and of synthesis in which, as Wordsworth says, 'bodily eyes / Were utterly forgotten, and what I saw / Appeared like something in myself'.

As Coleridge recognized, Wordsworth took 'primary imagination' as his theme: that is, the primordial, creative contact of the human mind and nature. But in the very act of thematising 'primary imagination', Wordsworth's poetry makes clear the gulf that can exist between capturing such experience in words and following out its consequences theologically. With the decline of his creative powers after the great decade of 1798–1808, Wordsworth's life-story remained complex, but it was not a story of private turmoil finding direction through contemplative vision and 'heroic virtue'. Wordsworth, we might conclude, was a poet but not a saint, and Bertrand Russell's quip on the subject catches the main distinction:

> *In his youth he (Wordwoth) sympathized with the French Revolution, went to France, wrote good poetry, and had a natural daughter. At this period, he was a 'bad' man. Then he became 'good', abandoned his daughter, adopted correct principles, and wrote bad poetry.*

The point here is that for the Romantics, personal self-fashioning develops from the profound interconnections between ourselves and nature, as imagination is uniquely ordered to show. The vertical transcendence of the Sacramental age is now re-imagined as emerging from the depths within, as M.H. Abrams' inspired title, *Natural Supernaturalism* suggests.

LM, 32–3

24.

What I am calling Heaney's 'figural' explorations are produced by his much-praised descriptive talent, holding carefully observed phenomena on the edge of some broader significance that does not always harden out conceptually, but which is felt as real and immediate rather than abstract, and which often returns us to the craft and achievement of the poem itself. The difference between this provocative poise and Heaney's admired Dante – master of the figural – is that an architectonic set of explanations of nature's inherently meaningful order, together with a particular kind of eschatological expectation, still frame Dante's world, but not Heaney's, even though Heaney retains a good deal of the Catholic sensibility of his youth that (partly) draws him to Dante's vision, with its incarnational radiance and sacramentalism. For Heaney, however, an objective trust in the hierarchies of the chain of being is replaced by a Wordsworthian sense of an implicit, deep resonance between the creative mind and the powers of nature, and also by a trust in the ordering effect of the poem itself, reflecting a typical Modernist self-consciousness (especially evident in Heaney's interest in Mandelstam) whereby the poem charts and frames our personal bearings in search of wholeness in a fragmented world. Yet Heaney does retain something of Dante's sacramental reverence ('something priestly in himself', as Foster says), even as he turns to Wordsworth to adapt the figural mode to a less explicitly Catholic view of the world than that imparted by his early upbringing. He then effects a resolution – by way of Modernism – offering up the poem itself as a quasi-sacramental act. We might describe the combined effect of these elements as 'post-Romantic figural' – a shorthand way to indicate the typical Heaney qualities I have noticed in the *Clearances* sequence.

BE, 60–61

No European painter has left such an extensive written account of his own practice as has Vincent van Gogh. In his letters, he attends frequently to how imagination transfigures the natural world while remaining rooted in it. However, he resisted working directly from imagination because he thought that he would then become too removed from actual material things, and his tempestuous, career-changing quarrel with Paul Gauguin arose out of this conviction, with which Gauguin strongly disagreed. Yet, for Van Gogh the quarrel was not just about aesthetics; he knew that he was mentally unstable and he feared becoming disconnected from the reassuring immediacy of ordinary things. Also, he believed that art is therapeutic, and he felt that he needed to paint to preserve his mental health. Consequently, for Van Gogh imagination was both therapeutic and potentially dangerous, and balancing these opposites was as perilous for him as it was necessary for his personal well-being and his work as an artist.

25.

In Arles, as a means of attaining the kind of expressive impact he valued in a painting, Van Gogh emphasized the effectiveness of exaggeration and even of ugliness in his work. For instance, he describes his portrait of a Zouave – a member of one of the French infantry units recruited originally from an Algerian Berber tribe and subsequently associated with exoticism and fierceness – as 'a coarse combination of disparate tones' and goes on to say how he would 'always like to work on portraits that are vulgar, even garish like that one'. He praises his painting, *Night Café*, by claiming that it is 'one of the ugliest I've done', expressing, as it does, 'the terrible human passions'. He describes *The Sower* and *The Night Café* as 'exaggerated' and as seeming 'atrociously ugly and bad', except that they achieve 'a more important meaning' because of these very qualities. He recognizes the 'external beauty of things', but 'I make it ugly in my painting, and coarse', and he will not 'contradict the critics who will say that my paintings aren't – finished'. Here, he again draws attention to imperfection as an aesthetic value, implicitly correcting the perfectionism that he had, to his cost, found untrue to life – not least in his own idealizations of religion and love.

In light of these opinions, Van Gogh's discussions with Gauguin about imagination became especially pressing. The key problem is clear in a letter written to Theo from

St. Rémy in 1889, in which Vincent explains how he has written to Gauguin and Bernard to complain about their 'dreaming', by which he means their use of imagination divorced from direct observation of nature. By contrast, Van Gogh says he paints olive trees and cypresses, and 'what I've done is a rather harsh and coarse realism beside their abstractions'. The 'harsh and coarse' here reminds us of Van Gogh's comments about the Zouave and *The Night Café,* and about how a deliberate lack of perfection can bring a painting to life. This way of thinking stands opposed to Bernard and Gauguin's 'abstractions' – which is to say, their misunderstanding of the proper use of imagination.

Still, Gauguin did make some headway in changing Van Gogh's mind. As Vincent explains to Wil, 'he encourages me a lot often to work purely from the imagination'. Elsewhere, he tells Theo, 'I don't find it disagreeable to try to work from the imagination', and 'Gauguin gives me courage to imagine, and the things of the imagination do indeed take on a more mysterious character'. Gauguin, he writes, 'has proved to me a little that it was time for me to vary things a bit – I'm beginning to compose from memory'.

However, in the end Van Gogh was unconvinced, and when the breakup occurred and Gauguin left Arles hastily, Van Gogh regretted having compromised. In January 1889, he writes to Theo denouncing Gauguin's 'castles in the air' and goes on to interpret Gauguin's ideas about imagination as a moral matter: 'but I, who saw him at very, very close quarters, I believed him led by his imagination, by pride perhaps but – quite irresponsible'. In short, for Van Gogh, imagination broken loose from its anchorage in everyday reality runs the risk of becoming escapist and of fostering pride. Irresponsibility then follows from an insufficiently conscionable engagement with the world and with other people.

Whether this is fair to Gauguin matters less, here, than what it tells us about Van Gogh's struggle to formulate an understanding of his own practice as a painter that would sustain him through the crisis with Gauguin and through his ensuing illness. Not surprisingly, during his illness, he wanted his work to ground him in the reassuring common world of ordinary objects and people. His hallucinations were 'unbearable' and work was the antidote, 'unless my work is yet another hallucination'. The fear of madness haunts him – 'I'm a madman or an epileptic, probably for good' – even though he tries 'to consider madness as an illness like any other'. He is troubled by the fact that during his attacks, 'it seemed to me that everything I was imagining was reality', but he concludes, brusquely, 'I don't want to think or talk about it'. Rather, he asks Theo to let Dr. Peyron know that 'working on my paintings is quite necessary to me for my recovery', and he also tells Theo, 'I'm struggling with all my energy to master my work, telling myself that if I win this it will be the best lightning conductor for the illness'. The interconnections here between Romantic imagination, art, and the difficult courses of Van Gogh's personal self-fashioning remain central to his extraordinary appeal today.

LV, 64–5

26.

Throughout his painting career, Van Gogh insisted on working directly from the model – whether a person or an object. This preference reflects his concern to anchor imagination in some recognizable aspect of the common world, as he thought all good painting should do. But he was careful to maintain a balance between the contribution made by his models and by his imagination. Too much attention to 'the figures' can dampen imagination, which must be allowed free expression, and Van Gogh points to Rembrandt as an example of how imagination's transcendence of nature is 'a revelation', even though Rembrandt's departure from strict verisimilitude may seem exaggerated. Just so, simplification, when it is inspired by imagination, can catch 'the expression in a figure' beyond what a stricter verisimilitude could provide and 'instinct – inspiration – impulse' often are better guides than some 'calculating' people might think.

Yet Van Gogh insists also that technique, practice, and the patient production of studies in which 'no creative process may take place' help to keep imagination grounded in the world of common experience. At one point he even worries that Theo will think his letters are merely 'a trick of my imagination' and his words 'without foundation'. What applies to painting applies here also to writing, and Van Gogh shows that as a writer he was self-conscious in assessing what we might justifiably describe as the literary impact of his words.

Van Gogh returns frequently to the idea that the creative imagination takes one out of oneself and into an enhanced, dreamlike state and that to lose oneself in a task is the 'surest way' to be creative. The great painters 'forget themselves in – being true', and for Van Gogh, such an experience is exalting. He describes the loss of self in the creative moment as dreamlike, the result being that painting is less difficult than the tedious work of making studies. Nonetheless, studies enable a painter to learn 'by heart', which in turn enables the creative imagination to soar while remaining grounded in nature. The creative intuition that Van Gogh describes as taking us beyond the ego and into a sense of deep interconnectedness with nature and with other people is, in turn, a hallmark of the personal such as art discloses to us as deserving of our imitation.

RV, 117–18

7 METHOD IN ART AND SCIENCE

Rapid advances in modern information technology combined with secular freedoms of unbelief have enabled access to a vast range of cultural resources, so that today the choices involved in shaping one's life meaningfully are often all but overwhelming. Information overload is now acknowledged as a cause of illness, and one reason for this disturbing phenomenon is that information alone does not prescribe the values that might provide people with stability and a sense of purpose. Instead, the relentless tsunamis of information, misinformation, and disinformation that are now part of everyday life leave people often confusingly and perilously suspended and without bearings. In response to this state of affairs, what is loosely called post-modernism affirms the eclecticism itself, and one result is that a fashionable, radical skepticism undermines whatever apparently firm ground seems to be beneath anyone's feet. Ironically, however, this includes its own feet, so that the basic problem remains, namely that an unceasing play of difference cannot engender the values whereby the common good could be understood also as the personal good of each.

In this broad context, it is helpful to step back to consider the characteristic modes of thought underpinning the scientific revolution during the period of 'Disenchantment and Discovery' from which modern technology and the juggernaut of instrumental knowledge, together with its main ally, free enterprise capitalism, have developed, giving rise in turn to the deracination and wild skepticism so prevalent in the present times.

One fairly standard view of scientific progress and instrumental knowledge in general is that they occur by accretion and are increasingly objective. This view is not entirely wrong, but it needs to be complemented by the fact that science is always implicated with what Michael Polanyi correctly describes as 'personal knowledge'. That is, the growth and development of scientific knowledge is a facet of the culture that brought it about, and science remains interwoven, however tacitly, with the values promoted by that culture with which science needs to be self-consciously integrated, even as it effects change.

1.

One fairly straightforward view suggests that scientific progress occurs by accretion and is therefore increasingly objective. Another opinion, however, suggests, for example, that Newton's universe is *transformed* by Einstein's and reconceived from within, rather than just added to. The physical events that Newton described remain before us, but they are observed in a new way, and 'to make sense of Einstein's universe', writes Thomas Kuhn, 'the whole [Newtonian] conceptual web whose strands are space, time, matter, force, and so on, had to be shifted and laid down again on nature whole. Only men who had together undergone or failed to undergo the transformation would be able to discover precisely what they agreed or disagreed about'. Karl Popper likewise points out that the new theory explains the same things as the old theory, but it '*corrects* the old theory: it contains the old theory, *but only as an approximation*'; 'similarly', Popper goes on, 'Einstein's theory contradicts Newton's, which it likewise explains, and contains as an approximation'. Yet, as Popper elsewhere says, Einstein in turn is not proof against the process that led him to correct Newton, and Einstein assumed that his own theory was provisional and he hoped to find it wrong: '*Einstein consciously seeks for error elimination.* He tries to kill his theories'. He tries, that is, to make the ideas of the past obsolete, and, in so far as such an impulse is necessary for scientific progress, science indeed remains anti-historical. It declares the old theories wrong, because the new theory is more comprehensive, stands up to tests better, is less easily falsified.

The value of this second view of scientific progress is that it respects objectivity without being overconfident, for it acknowledges that science does not develop by starting from scratch, basing knowledge on certainty and proceeding, step by step, to clear conclusions. Einstein appreciated this by the very fact that he assumed his theories would be found wrong, just as, presumably, countless working scientists admit that their own ideas are not likely to be the last word. But such an admission can, in turn, entail varying degrees of imaginative range. Spoken from a conviction, for instance, that today's science is the best and most sophisticated, it can mean simply that progress *has* been cumulative, so that (no doubt) more will be added to what we have so far achieved. Such thinking, I am keen to stress, is a far cry from the kind which sees progress as an imaginative reconstitution perilously and ambiguously dependent on cultural and historical circumstances, mingling the familiar with the new, old vocabularies with fresh insight: a sense, in short, of the development of science which makes it sound more anxious than assured, more organic than structured, more reminiscent of the development of literature and of personal self-fashioning, and so more fully a participant in a society which also expresses itself in art and history as well as in the languages of quantification.

DM, 5–6

2.

On the one hand, therefore, we must avoid assuming that Ramus and Bacon and Descartes and Hobbes used the term 'method' (which they used often) in an univocal sense, to indicate some shared objective notion which could be developed and added to as knowledge progressed. On the other hand, we must avoid losing sight of the revolutionary fact that a new scientific attitude and set of procedures did emerge with striking distinctiveness during the Renaissance, and have subsequently transformed Western thought and culture. Many useful studies illuminate both sides of this issue. Neal Gilbert's *Renaissance Concepts of Method*, for instance, reviews uses of the term 'method' from Plato through the Middle Ages and into various areas of Renaissance speculation. In its original sense, says Gilbert, 'method' means 'following after', and indicates both the acquisition of a sound knowledge of an art, and the qualification to teach it. We are reminded that 'However divergent the various trends of this discussion may appear, the ancient Greek basis of it can always be traced'. In his introduction, not surprisingly, Gilbert points out that much 'talk of method in the Renaissance may not have concerned *scientific* method in our modern sense at all', and he provides a great deal of information on the application of the word to theology (Erasmus), to history (Jean Bodin), to medicine (Galen's commentators), to logic (Peter of Spain), to the arts (Sturm), and to the general educational curriculum (the *Ratio Studiorum* of the Jesuits). He discusses a single method for the teaching of all subjects (Ramus), and proposals for a plurality of methods, each appropriate for a different area (Giulio Pacius). At the same time, he acknowledges the emergence from all this of a modern scientific attitude, and, in consequence, of a distinctively modern temper in seventeenth-century methodologies, such as Descartes'.

We are thus provided with a great many uses of the term, from which a 'modern' sense of what 'method' means gradually emerged. Nevertheless, it did emerge in a strong form, and Herbert Butterfield puts the main issue plainly: the scientific revolution, he says, is so momentous that it

> *Outshines everything since the rise of Christianity and reduces the Renaissance and Reformation to the rank of mere episodes, mere internal displacements, within the system of mediaeval Christendom. Since it changed the character of men's habitual mental operations even in the conduct of the non-material sciences, while transforming the whole diagram of the physical universe and the very texture of human life itself, it looms so large as the real origin both of the modern world and of the modern mentality that our customary periodization of European history has become an anachronism and an encumbrance.*

There *was* a palpable challenge to old authorities in the name of new modes of inquiry which involved different presuppositions, which the phrase 'discovery of method' can describe. For instance, despite Galileo's indebtedness to medieval impetus theory, his special genius is expressed in the declarations of *Siderius Nuncius* and in the mathematical results of his experiments on motion. Likewise, despite a covert attachment to Aristotle, Bacon remains significant for the history of science through his strenuous insistence that progress lay with the kinds of experiment which would vex nature and would be conducted in an atmosphere of co-operative mutual criticism. Those who appreciate Kepler's laws of planetary motion do not need to dwell on his magical reverence for the sun; nor did the followers of Newton need to consider seriously his alchemy and theological opinions. The New Philosophy, which for Donne called all in doubt, may indeed have arisen along no clear or single line of development, but rather as a kind of organic upheaval occasioned by a number of causes working together, but it was a palpable and disturbing process, felt as such, both implicitly and explicitly. In Galileo's case, we might say, the departure from tradition was predominantly explicit; by contrast, in Descartes's careful submission to orthodoxy in the *Principia* (as in his equally careful avoidance of outright Atomism), we can detect a tacit awareness of the unsettling implications of the kind of enquiry he, no less than Galileo, knew himself to be promoting.

How, then, should we describe the new thing? Walter Ong's common-sense suggestion that scientific method entails a certain 'routine of efficiency' in collecting, organizing and promulgating knowledge about nature is a convenient place to start. But Giorgio de Santillana is also correct to avoid defining such a 'routine' conceptually; rather in terms of a disposition or attitude, a distinctive habit of mind or desire based on a certainty for which one assumes responsibility: 'It is the resolute assumption of responsibility', he writes, 'which forms the criterion'. Thus, Galileo faced the anti-Copernican decree of 1616, and in so doing 'he stated in no uncertain terms that in such grave matters his authority was fully equal to that of the Church Fathers themselves', and this new attitude entails something like a 'feeling of *immanence* as against the former sacramental transcendence'. The visual arts especially exemplify the point: whereas the invisible field of force in the background of medieval paintings is God's mysterious presence, in the Renaissance this background is space, not manifesting transcendent mystery, says Santillana, but asserting intelligible reality.

Santillana also highlights the importance for the rise of science of painting and architecture, and his argument draws heavily from these fields. But the attitude he describes has to do, in a larger sense, with the objective world itself – the book of the world, as it were – conceived not primarily as the bearer of ontological mystery, but as a configuration of things in space: the book of the world, as Galileo says in a famous phrase, which is written in mathematical symbols. The 'routine of efficiency' which marks the discovery of method, we might therefore venture, deals especially with matter moving in space; its procedures are mathematical and empirical, and its disposition is to treat nature as intelligible, not mysterious. It follows that Copernicus is revolutionary because he deployed mathematics to describe the spatial movements of the heavenly bodies, and Galileo's 'perspective glass' vindicated not only the Copernican theory, but also the spirit of Copernican inquiry, just as his experiments with the pendulum and with rates of acceleration of spheres on an inclined plane took as their first concern the movement of mass in space, empirically observed and accounted for in terms of quantity. Likewise, Brahe's careful observations of the heavenly bodies (albeit for astrological reasons), when interpreted mathematically by Kepler, resulted in the laws of planetary motion: the movements, that is, of mass through space. Although Bacon did not accept the Copernican theory, by his resolute empiricism he confirmed his allegiance to the new method; his House of Solomon was a model for the Royal Society, and the experimenters who belonged to the Society – such as Boyle and Hooke – saw him as their admired predecessor. Although Descartes, in turn, was not an empiricist on Bacon's model, his mathematical method – arising from his invention of analytical geometry, which represented relations in space by arithmetic or algebra – assumed that scientific knowledge was fundamentally mathematical. His theory of vortices – whereby the ether, or prime matter made up of corpuscles, was held to move in a series of whirling centres – was an attempt to render the universe amenable to mathematical analysis by representing its basic components as material bodies in motion. And in England, when Sir Kenelm Digby introduced his friend Thomas Hobbes to Cartesian thought, Hobbes combined parts of Descartes with elements from Galileo and Bacon, intending to explain reality solely in terms of bodies moving in space. One result was that for Hobbes thinking itself became a kind of motion, and agitation of the primary corpuscles, a mechanical function to be conceived in material, quantifiable terms. And for Newton (as the title of his *opus magnum*, *Philosophiae Naturalis Principia Mathematica* – Mathematical Principles of Natural Philosophy – suggests), mathematics also was fundamental, though Newton insisted on the empirical verification of mathematical deductions. Like the others, he held a corpuscular theory of matter and suggested, even, that new, powerful microscopes might enable us to see the atomic particles themselves. Despite his quasi-theological notions about ethereal spirits and space conceived as God's *sensorium*, Newton's major contribution to science rendered cogent, as never before, an interpretation of nature as a vast system of mechanical motions definable mathematically in terms of mass, space and time.

The discovery of scientific method I therefore take to mean a certain efficient organisation of knowledge, based on the assumption of responsibility for a mathematico-empirical investigation of nature, espousing a corpuscular theory of matter and, for practical purposes, depicting the universe in terms of geometrical configurations of mass in space. The new method departed not only from the standard medieval model of the universe based on Ptolemy, but also from the metaphysical spirit which had informed and regulated it. The assumption of personal responsibility of which Santillana talks therefore entails a willingness to do without traditional metaphysics as far as possible, for practical scientific purposes.

DM, 7–11

3.

It was no offence to the new method to posit God as the first cause, even though this pious acknowledgement could also conveniently protect science from theological interference by pointing out that the Supreme Cause was beyond investigation by human reason alone. Because of his 'extremely weak' created nature compared to God's infiniteness, Descartes concludes, 'this is enough by itself to show that what are called final causes are no use at all in Natural Philosophy'. 'For certain it is', says Bacon, 'that God worketh nothing in nature but by second causes', and too ready an appeal to final causality has 'strangely defiled philosophy'. Insistence on God's transcendence and on the inscrutability of his will therefore enabled science to get on with investigating nature unencumbered with theology or the kind of metaphysics which would raise the mind in a non-utilitarian fashion to the mystery of being.

DM, 14

4.

When placed in this context, Francis Bacon's well-known engagement with similar problems will seem less exceptional and more a particular (if unusually forceful) treatment of ideas which were in the air. On the one hand, Bacon is a mechanist who, for instance, berates physicians for neglecting anatomy. Doctors 'quarrel many times with the humours, which are not in fault, the fault being in the very mechanical frame of the part', and medical practice can be best improved by a 'silent and long experience' based on, among other things, comparative anatomy. Bacon attacks Galen especially for being non-empirical and non-progressive ('Is that Galen I see there, the narrow-minded Galen, who deserted the path of experience and took to spinning idle theories of causation?'). But the Paracelsians are worse even than the Galenists because their ideas about sympathies and correspondences are so much further removed from the patient inquisition of material facts.

On the other hand, Bacon is also full of pious reassurances: the effects of the body on temperament must not derogate from the sovereignty of the soul. The very explicitness of this caveat, as with so many contemporary writers on the subject, shows Bacon's sensitivity to the fact that a predominantly 'methodical' approach to the human body – based, that is, on experimentation and divorced from the traditional, metaphysically oriented Galenism – could all too readily entail a thoroughgoing materialism.

To summarise: the mechanization of spirit, the development of comparative anatomy, determinist theories of the passions, the empirical enterprises of apothecaries, barber surgeons, cunning men and wise women combined during Bacon's century to undermine the metaphysical bases of traditional Galenism. The root challenge offered to Galen by the discovery of method was, therefore, basically straightforward, and lay in certain assumptions about what was most real about physical bodies. Galen had opposed the atomists, and his medieval commentators followed him on this point. He thought that qualities are real, and that they inhere in a material substrate, the *ousia,* called *soma* or *hyle* ('wood', body). For Galen, the primary qualities (hot and cold, dry and moist) have an independent, objective existence; density, rarity, smoothness and hardness are therefore secondary. This interpretation is precisely opposite to that held by Galileo, Bacon and Hobbes, who, like the ancient Atomists, declared those aspects of matter to be primary which are pre-eminently measurable. Yet at the same time they acknowledged that a thoroughgoing materialism does not account for the complexity of human beings and the traditional values by which they direct their lives.

DM, 60–61

5.

For the new scientists, the most real things are those which are measurable, but there was also a good deal of fudging on this point, because many scientists were also orthodox believers who understood the complexities of experience beyond what can be measured. One way around the problem, shared for instance by Bacon and Descartes, was simply to stress the ineffability of the divine mystery. A scientist could then cite humility as a reason for turning the enquiry away from a transcendent God and towards a less presumptuous investigation of second causes – the material world and its operations. Conveniently, the realms of spirit and matter are then conceived as belonging in different camps, calling for different kinds of explanation and enquiry.

The idea that real things are measurable gave rise also to the influential distinction between primary and secondary qualities. Because weight, volume, and dimension can be measured, they are primary; by contrast, secondary qualities such as colour, odour and sound depend so much on the perceiver that they cannot be said to belong entirely to the object (even though they are founded in it), and cannot be directly measured. For the new science, mathematics therefore becomes the pre-eminent tool for describing what is primary in nature, and replaces metaphysics, which is increasingly held suspect as an empty verbiage concerned with non-existent entities and productive of nonsense and superstition. Throughout the scientific revolution, the conflict between mathematics and metaphysics remained complex, and people's allegiances were often not clear-cut.

PC, 76–7

During the seventeenth century, the emphasis placed by the new science on secondary causes and primary qualities was itself rooted in developments within late medieval thought, and it is helpful to acknowledge how modern science emerged from its cultural antecedents even as it initiated powerful new ways of investigating nature. The clearest statement of the autonomy of modern science was provided at the beginning of the twentieth century by the Vienna Circle, but more recently philosophers of science have argued for a more complex view of how science is interwoven with other kinds of cultural formation.

6.

William of Occam (c. 1300–1350) speaks for the new tendency, and a key element in his thinking deploys a distinction between God's absolute and ordained powers. God's *absolute power* cannot be estimated from things as they are because God could have chosen other kinds of creation and other means of salvation. God's *ordained power*, by contrast, is what God has in fact willed and brought about.

This distinction is crucial to William of Occam because, by using it to demonstrate the non-necessary nature of things, he is able to stress that God has brought into existence a certain order of creation in which contingency is a divinely appointed means of our salvation. The epistemological consequences of this emphasis are evident in Occam's interest in perception, and what he calls 'intuitive cognition'. That is, we know individuals primarily; concepts are in the mind only ('*in anima et verbo*'), and are not essences shared by the things with other members of the species.

It is easy to underestimate Occam's complexity on this point and to conclude that universals must be, for him, subjective. To the contrary, he argues that there is a foundation for universals in nature, and so he does not, in the end, break entirely with scholastic realism. But his drift is clear: the mind's task lies in deciphering and processing linguistic events, which have an attenuated link with things and are constantly in need of clarification. For Occam, as for many of his contemporaries, mental images were in process of becoming divorced from concepts.

The development of Occam's way of thinking during the next century and into the period of Renaissance and Reformation is complex. But its effect in one respect is certain: discontinuity between the mind's images and the Ideas to which created species were held to conform, became a premise of the new philosophy of nature which grew out of nominalism and into the scientific revolution. Descartes stands at the parting of the ways. He held that the realm of extension is real because primary qualities are measurable. The mind then stands opposed to extension, investing it sometimes with a fanciful or analogical significance not inherent in the thing itself. Imagination must yield, therefore, to the rational processes of measuring and weighing if the laws governing matter are to be understood.

Descartes, of course, preserved the idea of God, and also much of the scholastic language of his early education, though subsequent thinkers did their best to divest him of both. But God, the first cause, was now so emphatically transcendent that legitimate human knowledge was limited to secondary causes operating within the natural world. Two plus two, Descartes repeated, echoing the nominalists, could be, for God, something other than four. Such fideism on the one hand piously affirmed the divine omnipotence, but, in so doing, also guaranteed the order of the created nature that we inhabit. On the other hand, however, it divorced God, the originator of that order, from the world, except in so far as we might come to appreciate an architectural structure which suggests a designer, now absent or remote.

Descartes also retained the scholastic doctrine of

substances. A material substance, he held, underlies extension, and a spiritual substance underlies our thinking selves. Subsequent developments of Cartesian thought, especially in England, devoted considerable energy to getting rid of these medieval elements. First Locke, then Berkeley and Hume, stripped Descartes of his innate ideas and substances, first material, and then both material and spiritual. Hume at last admitted the world a queer place, but allowed us to assert no more, epistemologically, than an association of sense impressions. Hume's most famous reader, Immanuel Kant, went on to conclude that we cannot know the world as it is in itself at all: the 'noumenal' eludes us. We must rest content with the 'phenomenal', that which we construct by perception, through the categories of space and time.

LM, 54–5

7.

The term 'positivism' is often loosely used to indicate a trend in science and philosophy holding that if truth claims are not empirically verifiable they should be rejected. Strict positivists consequently regard metaphysics as nonsense, and propose that scientific truth – which is the only kind – is value free. They hold that general, covering laws are the same for all sciences, and that these laws are confirmed by controlled tests. Historically, positivist attitudes might be traced to the ancient sceptics and medieval nominalists, but the trend assumes a distinctive modern form during the scientific revolution, especially through the methodological prescriptions of Francis Bacon (1561–1621). Auguste Comte (1798–1857) was especially influential in the development of modern positivism by describing the course of history as a gradual emergence of science from an immature age of metaphysics, preceded by an age of religion. The positivist phase thus marks the development of mature thinking freed from empty speculation and superstition.

In the twentieth century, positivism is mainly associated with the Vienna Circle, which focused especially on logic and linguistics, thus giving rise to the descriptive label, 'logical positivisim'. The Circle included Moritz Schlick, Rudolf Carnap, Otto Neurath, and Hans Reichenbach, with Ludwig Wittgenstein on the fringe (as ever), influential but not quite sufficiently partisan. Basically, these thinkers proposed that meaningful propositions deal either with matters of fact that are empirically verifiable, or with logical relations between concepts. Propositions about logical relations (analytical propositions) provide no knowledge about facts, but are seen to be true by analyzing the terms of which they consist, as is the case pre-eminently with logic and mathematics. Other kinds of propositions – such as those of religion and ethics – are, strictly speaking, nonsensical, even though they might have hortatory force. Logical positivism thus aims to show that if philosophical problems are not scientific they are meaningless, so that philosophy becomes a branch of science, constrained to clarify scientific propositions.

Today, the Vienna Circle's brand of positivism has been modified in a number of ways, but the claim that science attains to objective truth confirmed by empirical tests and subsumable under general laws providing approximate descriptions of actual entities has remained dominant in explanations of how science works. This broad position is set out clearly by Carl C. Hempel in *Aspects of Scientific Explanation*. Hempel claims that 'if a proposed explanation is to be sound, its constituents have to satisfy certain conditions of adequacy, which may be divided into logical and empirical conditions'. He then asserts that 'the explanans must contain general laws', and 'must have empirical content; i.e., it must be capable, at least in principle, of test by experiment or observation'. Hempel stresses that knowledge attained on this model is value-free, for although a scientist might choose to work on a problem for moral reasons, the resultant hypotheses are acceptable as scientific on the basis of how empirical evidence confirms them, and not because of any moral evaluation. Clearly, from Hempel's point of view, literature and criticism are not scientific because opinions about a poem involve value judgements not subject to empirical tests or subsumable by known covering laws.

One way to counter Hempel's position is by pointing out that scientific frameworks are always governed by the historical character of what is held to be objective, as well as by the observer's personal and social situation. As we have seen, this kind of argument was broached by Dilthey in the nineteenth century and assumes a variety of forms in Heidegger's critique of post-Cartesian 'technicity'. A more recent, influential development is offered by Jürgen Habermas, who argues that human sciences have different goals from positive sciences because the human sciences draw upon empathy and self-reflection to enable understanding. Consequently, the rules of positivist explanation and verification are not the only rules by which truth claims can be established.

By way of assessing some implications of this critique, I would like briefly to consider the influential contribution of Karl Popper, who was connected to the Vienna Circle, but as 'the Official Opposition' as Otto Neurath put it. Popper was born in Vienna in 1902, and grew up in the climate of logical positivisim; however, while contriving to maintain an objectivist view of science, he developed positions strongly critical of the Vienna Circle. As we have seen, according to logical positivism, empirical verifiability is the key distinguishing factor between science and nonsense. Popper attacked this view on the grounds that general covering laws are not verifiable but are taken up because of their convincing power, imaginative appeal, and so on. Indeed, far from being meaningless, metaphysical statements might be true, and although we cannot test them empirically we might still assess them critically. Against the sharp demarcation between science and metaphysical nonsense Popper set his principle of falsifiability: the distinguishing mark of scientific theories is that they are falsifiable, and unlike metaphysical statements the general laws of science can be tested by systematic efforts to refute them. Refutation then leads either to abandonment or modification of the law in question, and knowledge proceeds in a tentative and piecemeal fashion, open-ended and unplanned, approximating to a truth we can never fully know.

To develop his position, Popper assumes with the hermeneutic critics that all human observations are theory-infused. He points out that this is true even at the level of organic processes, which have a built-in capacity for adaptation and reaction to the environment. As our abilities to adapt and solve problems develop, we construct theories, some of which are testable in so far as we can attempt systematically to falsify them.

Although Popper's position can help us, as literary critics and theorists, to explain how texts have a serious bearing on a common world, the fact remains that a literary-critical evaluation is not a falsifiable proposition in Popper's sense. The person who holds *King Lear* in contempt because it oscillates between boredom and morbid sensationalism cannot be proved wrong in the same sense as a person who disagrees that all the ping-pong balls in this box are transfixed with nails. That is a simple distinction, but it will help to clarify how, despite his useful critique of positivism, Popper's principle of falsifiability still does not apply to literature.

Not surprisingly, Popper in turn has been attacked for not pushing the hermeneutic elements in his own arguments far enough and, consequently, for failing to describe how scientists actually proceed. In *The Structure of Scientific Revolutions*, Thomas Kuhn draws widely on the history of science to show that scientific communities most often try to confirm existing theories rather than falsify them, and that established practice guides the process of 'normal science'. Kuhn's theory about paradigm shifts (showing how the received view of a whole field can be transformed and replaced by another, incommensurate one) has had widespread influence outside his immediate subject, but Kuhn describes himself surprised to find his position frequently taken to imply the extreme hermeneutic claim that theory-choice is relativistic, and that 'might makes right'. He has been careful subsequently to point out that there are good reasons for choosing one theory over another, and in the end he departs less drastically from the positivist model than he is sometimes thought to do.

More adventurously, Paul Feyerabend attacks Popper and his disciples the 'critical realists' for self-righteous smugness. Feyerabend claims that if falsification theory were strictly applied nothing would get done, for science could not even begin. He proposes that science is a lot 'more "sloppy" and "irrational" than its methodological image', and calls for a kind of pluralistic anarchism. Feyerabend thus develops the side of Popper stressing how all observations are shot through with theory, and at the same time he questions the falsifiability principle, Popper's key guarantor of objective testing. Feyerabend proposes, rather, that discoveries come in unplanned ways, often as a result of following up seemingly irrelevant notions, and through the sheer, pleasurable process of play. He denies that there is any such thing as scientific method (let alone 'normal science'), and welcomes a pluralism wherein ideologies contend and standards are chosen by preferences for certain options. Feyerabend's basic principle is, as he says, that 'anything goes', and he thus repeats Habermas' position that there is not one privileged way of knowing. With others, such as Richard Rorty and Bas van Fraassen, Feyerabend is part of a broadly-based modern critique of positivism, stressing that science is a historically developed, specific kind of knowledge.

It is easy to detect a Scylla and Charybdis in the argument so far: too strong an adherence to positivist principles falsifies the historical embededness and complexities of scientific practice; yet the hermeneutic position courts a relativism whereby it is easy to feel that nothing is certain, and that critical and methodological procedures are irrelevant. This opposition is the main subject of Richard Miller's *Fact and Method*, which sets out to span the gap between the positivist and hermeneutic poles without surrendering certainty and well-foundedness. Miller's position is, as he says, 'a series of piecemeal defenses' rather than an over-arching argument, but he does propose a set of basic criteria. Explanation, he claims, is 'an adequate description of underlying causes bringing about a phenomenon. Adequacy here is determined by rules that are specific to particular fields at particular times'. A cause centers on 'a diverse and stable core of cases', and confirmation of a theory must be comparative as well as causal. Thus theories, causes and explanations evolve, and scientists at a given time rely on 'topic-specific truisms as their essential framework'.

For Miller, adequate theories and explanations are more contingent and historically conditioned than for positivism, but are rationally determinable nonetheless. Shrewdness, skill and connoisseurship combined with respect for evidence, sound reasoning and critical scrupulousness provide dependable explanations within specific fields of enquiry. Thus physics and chemistry by self-definition choose questions to which rigorous answers can be given. Questions that cannot be answered so rigorously are consigned to other fields—for instance, to geology or biology. History is by and large distinct from physics and chemistry because it does not have the privilege of confining its subject matter in the same way, and in the most influential aspects of Freud and Marx, theory takes the form of 'a repertoire of causal mechanisms' rather than a set of propositions or general laws serving as premises for deductions. Miller thus posits a scale of questions framed in the context of field-specific maxims, and more or less susceptible of rigorous or experimentally testable answers.

PV, 53–7

The overlap between science and other kinds of enquiry is especially intriguing in the case of psychoanalysis, which Freud held to be scientific but which in fact merges with the more personal modes of enquiry familiar to hermeneutics and literary criticism, such as symbolism, narrative, unconscious motivation, and so on. Anthony Storr is a hermeneutically inclined analyst, and Frederick

Crews is a literary critic who holds Freud to account for being un-scientific. In contrast to Crews's empiricism, Storr emphasizes that the suggestiveness and hermeneutic potential of Freud's theories make them useful for therapeutic purposes. The apparent reversal of roles here between the scientist and the humanist helps to clarify how the sovereignty of different kinds of specialization is uncertainly defined in relationship to their interconnectedness.

8.

I would like now to return briefly to the hermeneutically inclined analyst, Anthony Storr, and the empiricist literary critic, Frederick Crews. At one point, Storr describes the Oedipus complex as a kind of extended metaphor. He points out that we can notice generally in our society how small boys are vulnerable to taunts about their size and weakness, and are likely to experience rivalry with their fathers. By contrast, girls often consider themselves inferior and despised in a world where men hold power, and thus feel that their ability to produce babies is an equalizer. This 'metaphoric extension', Storr says, gets us closer to 'what Freud was getting at' in proposing that boys want to kill their fathers and marry their mothers, whereas girls feel their inferiority (which they blame on their mothers' lack of a penis) and then desire to be impregnated by their fathers.

For Crews, however, this kind of 'metaphoric extension' is an evasion. No one, he says, challenges 'the watered-down, conversational apprehension' of Freudian terms; the point is that these terms have a 'technical meaning' within psychoanalysis, and must be judged and tested accordingly. Repression is, once more, a key example. For Freud, it is an 'unconsciously compelled and traumatic forgetting' that occurs in early childhood and can cause disturbances in adult life. However, an alternative and fairly widespread use of the term takes it to mean that a consistent denial or refusal to face certain emotional or physical needs can cause a great deal of suffering and anguish. Deeply ingrained habits of defense against our emotional lives can cause us to fall ill, or to express the problem somehow indirectly and symbolically by unusual behavior. This second kind of explanation is closer to everyday experience, but Crews would regard it as a soft interpretation of a term that has a much more precise sense in Freud. So it is also with the Oedipus complex, which, in Crews' view, describes, precisely, a traumatic and repressed early experience. And so, turning the theory into an extended metaphor diminishes its specifically Freudian element, and by such means psychoanalysis as a whole can easily be reduced to a quasi-literary or quasi-religious exploration of the self that masquerades as scientific. The confrontation here between empirical objectivity and metaphorical suggestiveness is not finally resolvable and is reproduced in the personal positioning of each of us within the interplay itself of subjective experience and the world as encountered over and against us.

PV, 83–4

An extreme objectivist position such as we find in De la Mettrie's *L'Homme Machine* regards the human being as nothing more than a complex mechanism. De la Mettrie focused exclusively on the Cartesian idea that the body is an extended substance, and by and by his conclusions gave rise to concerns such as those expressed by Michel Foucault about the instrumentalising of human relationships in modern technological societies. In this broad context, a re-affirmation of the meaning and value of personal agency stands as a corrective that nonetheless can affirm the value of science as a liberator of human potential. During the twentieth century, much work has been done, attempting to mediate between the domains of imagination and empirical investigation, art and science, religious belief and secularism, as we see for instance in Michael Polanyi's important study, *Personal Knowledge*.

9.

In particular, under the influence of Cartesian philosophy, the category of the person, with its links to the metaphysical idea of a soul, soon yielded to a new interest in the self. This is especially clear in Locke, who was much influenced by Descartes and who saw human identity as residing in consciousness, a concomitant of the Cartesian 'spiritual substance'. Just as the person is marked by a soul, so the self is marked by consciousness, and this shift of emphasis in Locke's psychological theory reflects also in the larger domain of politics, as Frye suggests. Thus, Locke, together with other proponents of the social contract theory, held that individuals (each one a self, with a private consciousness) assemble and agree about the government they wish to have. On this model, each person is imagined first as a monad, initially independent and then entering into society.

The idea that we are individuals first, and then citizens, receives a strong impetus from the division between spiritual and material substances, emphasising as it does, the essentially private nature of the self. The Reformation, together with some strands of Renaissance Humanism, argued for much the same view of our individual singularity by way of championing freedom of conscience. In short, Protestantism, science, and the new political theorists insisted alike on the inner spiritual freedom of individuals as a pre-eminent value in a world, which, as we see, increasingly was interpreted as most real in those aspects which could be measured, controlled and put to use.

In this new climate, the old idea that the soul is the form of the body was seen to depend on an outdated metaphysics, and was scorned by scientists and reformers alike. The clearer dualism of mind and body, or consciousness and matter, seemed preferable, however problematic it was in its own way. Because bodies occupy a public space which is also the domain of the state, governments could now all the more easily see their task as the normalizing and regulating of behavior, treating people as the material units within the body politic, to be produced as the state determines.

Michel Foucault has claimed that the Age of Enlightenment, which indeed did much to free Western societies from the infamy of superstition and ecclesiastical tyranny, nonetheless also exercised its own form of oppression through institutions systematically compelling human bodies to conform. The rise and development of modern penal institutions, insane asylums, examination systems, regular armies, hospitals and so on, show how effectively state power reproduces itself by treating the body as a mechanism or material entity to be shaped and fashioned in the state's own image. De la Mettrie's book *L'Homme Machine* (1747) took a step beyond Descartes that was dangerous but all-too inviting: if each individual is a private self, why not leave that private self – if it exists at all – in the hands of each individual, while getting on with regulating that individual's public behavior? Foucault's well-known image of the panoption, borrowed from Bentham, is a metaphor for this radically depersonalizing process. The inmates of a panopticon (whether a hospital, school, or prison) are at all times visible to those who control them. But the reverse is not the case, and the inmates do not know whether or not they are being watched.

PC, 78–9

10.

Owen Barfield is a literary critic in the Romantic tradition, who looks to the history of science for clarification of the relationship between poetry and religious belief. Michael Polanyi is a scientist who looks to the language of religious faith to help illuminate the function of science in an open society, which he sees beginning in the seventeenth century and which he wishes to defend in the twentieth. The theories of both men meet and overlap on the questions of imagination and the place of art in society. Polanyi contends that appreciating the structure of a work of art can help us to acknowledge the importance of similar principles in procedures of scientific investigation. Barfield sees the poem as a structure wherein forgotten original meanings are made conscious by the yoking of incompatibles as metaphor, and argues that the nature of metaphor in modern literature is deeply influenced by the scientific revolution. From divergent starting points in the fields in which they are distinguished, both men find themselves concerned alike with science in relation to the creative imagination and to the shaping of personal values.

SA, 121

As persons, we remain a 'subtile knot', as John Donne says, tied into relationships that exceed our ability to make fully conscious, and which for that reason require vigilance and discernment. Today, the integration of science and technology to promote the good of individual persons within the culture at large also demands a similar discerning and creative attention. With these points in mind, I give the last word in this section to Erasmus' English follower, Thomas More, who wrote at an early phase in the development of modern English literature, at a time when Renaissance Humanism was also laying the groundwork for the development of the new science. Although there can be no return to the ideals of Renaissance Humanism, some understanding of the historical genesis of certain key problems and challenges of our modern civilizational phase point us in the direction of a new *studia humanitatis* adapted to the times so that we might move beyond the stop-gap solutions of Romanticism and the skeptical self-cancellations of post-modernism in assessing a viable personalism suited to the period in which we live.

11.

A commentator on Thomas More's execution wondered how the condemned man could joke at such a time. Part of the answer is that he had the confidence to do so – a confidence born of his awareness that the play of language depends on the binding of words to meanings, and also on a sense of their freedom, their evasive distance from things. Too rigid a binding, or, equally, too much volatility, has a way of becoming tyrannous. More's language as a literary practitioner, as we see in *Richard III*, is (like his jokes), most fully human, finding a place between. So, we may say (as with Humanism at large) that More's thought at once promotes those aspects of method which have to do with a self-critical attitude to language and its referents. This attitude entails a suspicion of secrecy and intellectual elitism. It favours common sense and plain speech, supported by accurate scholarship which is co-operatively developed and has a strong secular orientation. This kind of Humanism was not interested in experimentation or mathematics. But More's place at the beginning of modern

English letters is important not least because he provided a version of the continental Humanism which not only created the climate in which the discovery of method was nurtured, but also gave shape to certain of its main preoccupations. That these entailed a division between material, secular power and disembodied spiritual authority (the two faces of tyranny) is a principal reason for including More here, for already he deals self-consciously with a version of the very determinism with which the scientific method in its developed form continues to challenge us. In turn, More's creativity is expressed in the literature that he produced, engaging and transcending the cultural tensions and contradictions that simultaneously constrain and enable it.

DM, 46–7

8 THE ENCOMPASSING AND THE PERENNIAL PHILOSOPHY

A person has no internal sovereign territory, Bakhtin says, but stands on the boundary, *en route*, attempting to shape itself meaningfully. In turn, this adventure of self-fashioning is dependent on language, through which we reflect on what we know, knowing that we know. Memories are then shaped as narratives, and to give ourselves bearings we extend our story forward, imagining what would make us more fulfilled, more complete. Yet, in fact, desire remains always unfulfilled and we do not know exactly what a final happy ending would be, or the conditions under which it could take place, just as we do not know the 'concealed originality at the source' of our being, as Heidegger says. In short, we do not know where we have come from or where we are going, and in the interim we tell ourselves stories to make better sense out of our strange predicament. Even the assurance that, as Derek Parfit says, there is no 'deep further fact' is itself a story, however different from the other stories developed by the world's mythologies, religions, and wisdom traditions. Certainly, as Parfit suggests, we should stick to the facts. But one of these facts is (as Jaspers says) that we are always more than we know about ourselves, and so it is scarcely surprising that what he calls the 'encompassing' mystery of ends and origins and of the meaning of life should persist and invite explanation, and that reports about such matters from the frontiers of experience should merit attention. As far as these reports are concerned, the core principles that they express and that recur across the world's main wisdom traditions are sometimes referred to as the Perennial Philosophy.

As C.G. Jung points out, humans share a common biology and so it should not be surprising that our shared brain structure should produce similar symbols of our basic human condition. Just as a common biology supports a wide variety of individual physical differences, so the basic patterns of imagination – what Jung calls archetypes – inform a wide variety of individual myths and narratives through which we attempt to explain ourselves to ourselves. Also, the core insights of the Perennial Philosophy converge on a set of moral principles which, by and large, ethical atheists and unbelievers are likely to find acceptable, even though the Perennial Philosophy looks beyond the ethical to a transcendent dimension which it sees as the ultimate ground of morality.

Mainly, the Perennial Philosophy affirms that there is a ground of being which is the unmanifest principle of all manifestation and which is simultaneously transcendent and immanent. Humans can have some direct experience of this unmanifest source, and the way or path towards such experience entails a shift from self-centredness to reality-centredness, as a result of which self-centredness is recognized as the source of suffering. Yet, in the world as we know it suffering endures and an acknowledgement that this is the case calls upon compassion, which is inseparable from enlightened understanding.

The Perennial Philosophy can best be grasped through one's own cultural traditions, one's 'mother tongue', so to say, as long as we are mindful that, especially in today's world, the truth-claims of no single religion can credibly exclude all the others. This being the case, studying another major religion or wisdom tradition is helpful both for revealing the shortcomings and blind spots of one's own enculturation, and also for highlighting the shared or perennial dimensions of both traditions together. In addressing these points, the following excerpts deal with the Perennial Philosophy and its validation mainly within the cultural and historical circumstances of Western civilization, but also in relation to some aspects of Buddhism.

1.

The heart of what is loosely called mysticism in Western Christianity lies in experiences that our capacity for solitude reveals. Mystics claim to know the secret things of God disclosed in a particular way to their innermost selves, and then undertake to express their knowledge for the benefit of humanity at large. While stressing that the mystery is within, however, mystics deny that their experience is entirely subjective. As the familiar paradox maintains, God is transcendent and immanent, the soul-spark in each of us as well as the single goal outside us towards which we strive. When mystics write about such matters, they, not surprisingly, stress the inadequacy of words, though using words to do so, and therefore depending on language to proclaim the limitations of language. And yet, although caught with something utterly unique to say, they also reassure us that we are more alike with respect to the ineffable than we might think. They remind us how, habitually and for practical purposes, we ignore the immensely queer fact that we know at all. Attention to facts at the expense of attention to the mental processes from which facts emerge, they tell us, blinds us to ourselves and to the essential solitude 'wherein', as St. John of the Cross says, 'the soul attains to union with the Word, and consequently to all refreshment and rest'. The ground sustaining our everyday acts of perception should itself therefore receive our constant attention, however difficult this is to do.

LM, 1–2

2.

Despite their stress on subjectivity, mystics are inclined to be empirical. They are not overly concerned with definitions and they attend hardly at all to the formal word, 'mysticism'. If a vision is not testable, says the Irish spiritual writer, AE, ignore it:

> *The religion which does not cry out: 'I am today verifiable as that water wets or that fire burns. Test me that ye can become as gods'. Mistrust it. Its messengers are prophets of the darkness.*

If character is not transformed, if good works do not follow, we are to doubt that we have had an authentic religious experience. 'If you see a sick woman to whom you can give some help', writes St. Teresa, 'never be affected by the fear that your devotion will suffer, but take pity on her. ... That is true union with His will'.

Verification by works, however, is not the same thing as a scientist's empirical verification. The mystic, after all, talks about a transcendent reality that we cannot test as we can, say, the specific gravity of water. Yet concepts such as 'beauty' and 'goodness' are not meaningless because we cannot observe or handle or measure them directly. They are, rather, ideas which enable us to see ordinary things differently, with greater coherency and richness. 'God', as John Wisdom points out, is a preposterous notion that calls for our serious investigation because it enriches experience and because such enrichment results in a transformation of character.

LM, 2–3

3.

I thought you might like the Eric Gill woodcut, and your story about the girl on the bike, tossing her hair, was the trigger, the right moment – *kairos*. I once wrote about the literature of mysticism, and used the phrase 'intense ordinariness' to describe a recurrent phenomenon among those writers. Intense ordinariness has a moral and a creative dimension and so it is different from aestheticism: 'less a flash than a steady attitude of attentive wonder in which even the most banal occurrences are experienced as eternally precious'.

In *The Image of the City*, Charles Williams writes about how 'the wonder, the thrill, of a shoulder or a hand awaits its proper exploration. At present we have simply nothing to say to anyone in a state of exaltation, watching for "meaning", except something that sounds very much like: "Well, don't look too intently". The hungry sheep look up for the profound metaphysics of the awful and redeeming body, and are given morals'. He is right, 'morals' alone won't do, and the 'wonder, the thrill' of the shoulder – or tossed hair – call for a different language, a different discernment. Vincent knew this very well.

BH, 39–40

4.

In this context, I want to propose that the mystical centre of the Christian faith resides in a conviction that God is present in a discovery that our personal good is served by the good we do to others. This is what is meant by the

'Great Commandment' (Mk. 12:29 ff.; Mtt. 23:37 ff.) to love our neighbor as ourselves for the love of God. Some such insight is perennial in the world's major religions, and is sometimes referred to as the golden rule. Yet as persons we are historical creatures, and the spirituality of the golden rule involves us often in contradictions, so that adherence to it is not straightforward. Throughout this book I want to suggest that the gospel story of the Transfiguration is an especially effective representation of the difficulty of reconciling the ideal of the Great Commandment with our experiences of historical contradiction.

SD, 7

5.

According to St. Teresa, we need to help others in whatever way we can; we need to be instructed; we need to clarify our experience to ourselves. Her teaching involves the constant interaction of these three elements, suggesting that, in various combinations, they open up different possibilities, different directions for different readers. Teresa well knew that the 'ways' in which God leads souls are varied, so that it is impossible to be completely clear on the subject. There is 'no infallible rule', and 'no reason why we should expect everyone else to travel by our own road'. The castle which, as her title indicates, is Teresa's key metaphor, has many mansions. One Lord dwells at the centre, but the rooms arranged in concentric circles around his chamber are innumerable: 'there are so many of them that nobody can possibly understand them all'. There is order here, though we do not fully comprehend it, and we are left with a sense of how Teresa is discovering the 'way' as she proceeds along it. Fifteen years ago, she reminds us (referring to her *Life*), she had described the prayer of quiet differently. Things are now more clear, even though 'Both then and now, of course, I may be mistaken in all this'.

LM, 141–2

6.

Contradictions among religious faiths are likely to be overcome less by an anxious abandonment of one's position than by practice of openness to others and the gradual appropriation of other points of view, a process in which one's own dogmas and symbols can take on an enhanced life, discovering, as it were, their own deepest possibilities. In such an exchange, the kinds of differences that cause division (rather than variety) should dwindle by neglect. To assist in this process we have to be willing at least to stand on the boundaries of our own tradition, reaching to all that our tradition seems to reject: a position, that is, analogous to the poet's, using the common language to test common meanings in a singular manner.

LM, 153

7.

John Hick points to a recent change of attitude among many theologians to the plurality of religions. Exclusionist models of salvation have now faded from the mainline Christian Churches, though not from fundamentalist groups. In particular, Wilfred Cantwell Smith pioneered a pluralist theology whereby religious traditions are regarded as living and varied, and where dogmatic consistency is less important than the transformation of one's life – as Hick says, a 'transformation of human life from self-centredness to Reality-centredness'.

Clearly, there is a perennial tension between the cumulative weight of traditional teaching and enculturation and the individual experiences of personal transformation that Hick describes. A 'changed and elevated' life rather than conformity of belief is the main evidence that such transformation has occurred, and Hick argues that the world's main religious traditions provide examples of this salvific change from self-centredness to Reality-centredness. But because cultures differ, the conceptual apparatus used to explain the supreme Reality and the individual's experience of it also differs among religious traditions. In particular, there are differences in the concepts used to describe how the supreme Reality transcends our names for it, and also how it is made known through particular people and historical events. Thus, there is a contrast between what Hick calls the divine *impersonae* (the Absolute, One, Tao) and the divine *personae* (Adonai, Shiva, Christ). Nonetheless, Hick argues that these alternatives remain valid ways of describing our experiences of the Divine, and are not necessarily contradictory.

Hick also points out that all the world's major religions have some version of the golden rule, which is central to the perennial philosophy and is represented by Jesus' Great Commandment. In this context, he suggests that the basic criterion for judging religion is 'soteriological' – as evidenced, that is, in the personal transformation of 'the saints of all traditions'. By contrast, 'all or nothing christologies', as exemplified by the Chalcedonian definitions, run the risk of reifying religion and shutting it off from the life-enhancing energy expressed as generosity, kindness, forgiveness – the combination of *agape/karuna* that is more important than cosmological and eschatological speculations about which we can never be certain.

BE, 27–8

8.

By the Christ-principle, then, I mean all that effects reconciliation and the freeing of life by making reality known to itself and others. This knowledge penetrates even to the heart of the material creation; as Origen says, the Christ principle is evident in innumerable ways according to the need creation-able-to-be-set-free has of it. Already we know it heaving its way through the slow moraines, and the drifting continents are organized under its hand. We find it in the blind worm's struggle at the bottom of the sea for light, and in the artery pulsing in our brain, seeking its own light. It courses through the intelligent stars and the stillness where a touch of consciousness, unlikely, knows itself to know. And knowing itself also knowing the world divided, it becomes the warrior of incarnation, his temples crimson and his side torn out, riding his wooden ship across the borders of our nightmares. Incarnate, he knows the world as well as his mother's body, and his own: the child with meningitis is himself, the starving woman feeding pebbles to her babies, the drowning fisherman, the desolate, the old. Nor does he cease until the universe is a flame of brightness, a tower of ivory clothed with the sun, knowing itself as it is known. As William Law declares, in all this is nothing unnatural, for atonement lies in overcoming enmity not only in ourselves, but in the seas and storms, in plague bacilli, worms that thrive within a heart, the loss of love. Learning affliction, the Christ then seeks through every unity of speech and being, word and thing, until matter is found again in the spirit to be what it really is. And this is what is meant by the resurrection body.

OC, 11–12

THE ENCOMPASSING AND THE PERENNIAL PHILOSOPHY

Unbelievers in transcendence often prefer to affirm that the conditions of ordinary life are sufficient, and we should accept these conditions together with their limitations. This position is well stated by Derek Parfit, whose conclusions about ethics nonetheless share a great deal with the Perennial Philosophy in general and with Buddhism in particular, as Parfit himself points out.

9.

Among Western philosophers, David Hume in the eighteenth century argued against the independent existence of a substantive self, and among twentieth-century philosophers in the Humean line, Derek Parfit (*Reasons and Persons*, corrected ed. [Oxford: Clarendon, 1987]) links Hume's conclusions to the Buddha's and maintains that the Buddha was right about the soul, though Parfit's Buddhist critics scold him for putting his own twist on what the Buddha actually thought.

Basically, Parfit argues for the quite modest proposal that we are not separately existing entities 'apart from our brains and bodies, and various interrelated physical and mental events'. Persons do indeed exist as thinkers and agents with complex lives and relationships. But there is no essence or soul or 'deep further fact' separate from the thoughts, actions, experiences, and relationships making up the life of the individual in question, whose identity is not fixed and immutable, but indeterminate and capable of change.

IM, 84–5

From within the intense particularity of his painterly practice, Vincent van Gogh looked for some new, post-Christian way to express the perennial spiritual truths that he hoped to realize in his own life. In proposing that art provides something of what once was supplied by religion, he offers a striking example of one main component of the modernist sensibility. In this context, he insisted that, out of its own incompleteness, art points beyond itself to the un-nameable mystery of the source, of which art gives a real intimation.

10.

In Arles, Vincent wrote to Theo about Tolstoi's *My Religion*, suggesting that it describes the conditions under which 'a new religion, or rather, something altogether new, will be reborn, which will have no name but which will have the same effect of consoling, of making life possible, that the Christian religion once had' (686/4:282). Although he had not yet read *My Religion*, Vincent was confident about what he took to be its main message, and this was so not least because the ideas he attributed to Tolstoi reproduced the main lines of his own thinking about what we might loosely call a spirituality that would be as comforting as the old religion but not constrained by dogmatism or formal observance.

As we have seen, aesthetic and religious concerns remained closely interrelated for Van Gogh, and many of the hopes, aspirations, and insights of Christianity continued to inform and inspire him, both as a writer and as a painter. This is clear, for instance, in a letter to Émile Bernard from Arles (June 1888) in which Van Gogh praises Christ as 'an artist greater than all artists', whose special gift was to create 'LIVING men, immortals'. The letter goes on to comment on Jesus's promise that 'heaven and earth shall pass away, but my words shall not pass away':

> *Those spoken words, which as a prodigal, great lord*
> *he didn't even deign to write down, are one of the*

highest, the highest summit attained by art, which in
them becomes a creative force, a pure creative power.

These reflections, my dear old Bernard – take
us a very long way – a very long way – raising us
above art itself. *They enable us to glimpse – the art*
of making life, the art of being immortal – alive.

Do they have connections with painting? The
patron of painters – St. Luke – physician, painter,
evangelist – having for his symbol – alas – nothing
but the ox – is there to give us hope. (632/4:154)

In this bold representation of Christ as primarily an
artist, Van Gogh confirms his own commitment to his
vocation as a painter, and so the main thing he admires
about Christ is the 'creative force' or 'pure creative power'
that characterizes Christ's special genius. But then Van
Gogh goes on to say that 'these reflections' also go a long
way towards *'raising us above art itself.* Here, the discussion
opens upon a further dimension: although Van Gogh does
not explain what he means by 'the art of being immortal',
he seems to identify it with the mystery simply of being
'alive' in the world. The conclusion then brings us back
to painting by way of St. Luke, the patron of painters,
who was also Christ's disciple. And so – the priority of
art notwithstanding – the dialogue between the aesthetic
and the religious continues, even as it points us towards a
transcendent mystery that encompasses both.

LV, 185–6

11.

Van Gogh returns frequently to the idea that, even though
grounded in nature, the creative spirit also soars above
it: 'That is the highest art, and *in that* art is sometimes

above nature – as, for instance, in Millet's sower, in which there is more soul than in an ordinary sower in the field' (298:2:229). Art, he believed, depicts things 'more clearly than nature itself' (152/1:242), and for true art, 'something else is needed when working absolutely from nature' (552/3:340). Thus, although Rembrandt remains true to nature, he 'goes into the higher – into the very highest – infinite' (534/3:291). And although art is produced by 'human hands', it is 'not wrought by the hands alone but wells up from a deeper source in our soul' and is 'something larger and loftier than our own skill or learning or knowledge' (332/2:316).

This kind of language occurs frequently in the letters, drawing attention to the idea that art is simultaneously rooted in nature and transcendent of it. Yet Van Gogh knew all too well that the conditions that best enable the production of art are often all the more desirable because of their absence. The nurturing home, or nest, the protective space that provides serenity and inspires confidence, the sympathy of fellow humans who are like-minded and cooperative remain, in large part, ideals to aspire to. As ever, the negative contrast supplied by the lives we actually live makes the ideals all the more desirable, even as we also come to understand how intractable are the impediments to their realization.

LV, 87

The following excerpts focus on the spiritual teachings of Western Christianity, and in this context I take the gospel story of Jesus' transfiguration to be an effective summary of the core principles of the Perennial Philosophy, as the disciples experience a revelation of the transcendent mystery but are called then to engage with the poor and afflicted at the foot of the mountain. The process of transfiguration, like the growth and development of persons, remains incomplete in the world as we know it, and calls for a compassionate engagement with others. I also include here a set of excerpts dealing with the Buddhist and Taoist traditions from which I have learned a great deal about the interconnection between enlightenment and compassion. In conclusion, I revisit what I have said about the Perennial Philosophy in general, drawing on the personalist perspectives of Jacques Maritain and Cuthbert Butler.

12.

By and large, the Augustinian spirit prevails in what Cuthbert Butler calls the 'Benedictine centuries' (extending roughly from 550–1150), during which time contemplation by and large is regarded as the fruition of ordinary prayer in which everyone participates. As Ernesto Buonaiuti says, the liturgy is dedicated to safeguarding the spiritual life of Christians as a whole, without individualism, and as Butler claims, this approach is the backbone of the Western spiritual tradition represented by such figures as Augustine, Gregory the Great, Bernard, and Bonaventure. This tradition is roughly equivalent to what has become known as the 'affirmative way', an approach to prayer stressing the positive contribution of language in our journey towards contemplation. Thus, we are to see in things a trace or symbol of the divine creator and allow this particular illumination to guide us upwards through imagination ('spiritual vision' Augustine calls it), leading to the one, unrepresentable source of all manifestation. In contrast, the 'negative way' operates by our cancelling out of experience and imagination everything that is less than God, until there remains only a darkness in which God's presence might be revealed, dark yet paradoxically brilliant.

Neither of these 'ways' can in fact exist in isolation. On the one hand, the way of affirmation needs a certain amount of order and discipline and must stop short of idolizing the creation. It needs to acknowledge that God is not present to us in the fullness of God's essence, and God must approach us freely. On the other hand, proponents of the 'negative way' also participate in the world and require some basic comfort and security. They do not encourage us to reject the creation, for God blesses what has been made and leaves in it a trace of the divine source. Still, there are two distinct tendencies here, and by and large contemplatives during the Benedictine centuries lean to the first, expressed in a corporate or communal spirituality, whereas the second comes to the fore during the second half of the twelfth century, together with a renewed interest in Dionysius the Areopagite.

PV, 168

13.

St. Teresa of Avila tells us that there always remains more to discover and to know about God. This point is repeated, for example, by Jacques Maritain and Cuthbert Butler. Maritain describes mysticism as an 'experimental knowledge of the deep things of God', and Butler as an 'experimental perception of the Being and presence of God in the soul'. The words 'deep things' and 'Being and presence' indicate a disclosure or revelation, but without claiming that God's essence is fully present. This principle is important to grasp if the varieties of spiritual experience are to be accorded their due: as David Knowles says, in dealing with mysticism we are not trying to define a truth of revealed religion, but to assess God's dealings with individual souls who are always led in a particular way.

Careful investigation of individual cases might suggest the outlines of a perennial philosophy, but describing such a thing calls also for discrimination and critical judgement whereby generic and particular elements are balanced. In effecting this balance, the literature of mysticism resembles other kinds of literature, entailing personal evaluation and critical reflection.

PV, 165

14.

At the beginning, with the martyrs, for instance, it is hard to tell if an ecstasy experienced while facing the beasts was due to anaesthetic terror or supernatural intervention. This is the case with Perpetua, who found herself wondering aloud about when she was to be gored and tossed, after these dreadful things had in fact been done. By contrast, among the early Fathers who lived also under threat of persecution, the formulation of theories demonstrating how Christians could think like Greeks was in part conciliatory because such theories suggested that Christians ought not to be persecuted as promoters of a dangerous, new-fangled ideology, given that *gnosis* was the aim and Stoic asceticism the method. Thus, Clement of Alexandria and his pupil Origen describe a Christian Gnosticism to which ascetic practice can lead, so that a person's ascent to true knowledge is through 'leaving all hindrances, and despising all matter which is distracting'. Origen also developed a theory of 'spiritual senses', and in his commentary on the *Song of Songs* began a tradition subsequently developed by St. Bernard and St. John of the Cross, describing our highest experience of the divine as a bridal consummation.

When the early persecutions of the Roman state ceased,

or abated, the intensities that these persecutions engendered were re-expressed as another kind of martyrdom, the 'white martyrdom' of the hermits and desert-dwellers: Methodius' *Symposium*, the first Christian work on virginity, states that virgins are martyrs. St Athanasius (d. 375), who followed Methodius' principle in his *Letter to the Virgins*, wrote a *Life of Antony* (c. 357) which stated that self-denial and seclusion are a means of restoring the original nature from which we have fallen. The martyrs' example was thus duplicated in ascetic practices which, as in Clement and Origen, were to precede *gnosis*. In this respect the example of Antony influenced Augustine, as we see in *The Confessions*, and through Palladius' (d. before 431) *Lausiac History* and Cassian's (c. 360–435) *Conferences*, the sayings of the desert fathers passed into Western tradition.

It is inviting to detect among these patristic writers adumbrations of future schemes and stages describing the mystical way, but it is easy also to ignore how tentative are the early instructions on the spiritual life. Still, one modification of the predominant binary scheme of *ascesis* and *gnosis* is worth mentioning: the proposal, that is, by Evagrius Ponticus (345–399), to subdivide contemplation, or *gnosis*, into lower and higher forms. Evagrius' threefold division was associated at a later date with a scheme developed in the writings of Dionysius the Areopagite, distinguishing purgation, illumination and union, the three-fold way of Western mysticism, which found a highly systematic expression in the *De Triplici Via* of St. Baonaventure.

Evagrius thus helped to provide a plan for the contemplative life which married Alexandrian tradition with the Dionysian 'negative way'. For the West, however, before the revival of the Dionysian tradition in the twelfth century, the wisdom of the desert was consolidated with patristic tradition not so much by Evagrius as by Cassian, who gave to the 'Benedictine centuries' a form of contemplative theology that was ascetic, clear-headed and intellectual. Like Augustine, Cassian stressed gradual perfection in the degrees of love under the influence of grace. Augustine, we recall, distinguished between corporeal, spiritual and intellectual vision, and described the soul's ascent through a 'song of degrees' from the variety of the material creation towards the One. He also described this ascent in terms of an intensification of love, through initial, progressing and perfect stages. The spirit of Augustine's approach passed, especially through Cassian, to Gregory and Bernard, constituting, according to Cuthbert Butler, the main tradition of Western mysticism.

In the twelfth century this tradition reached a highpoint, and in his controversy with Abelard, St. Bernard already found himself contending with a new set of issues brought about on the one hand by scholastic philosophy, with its penchant to classify and describe 'ladders of perfection', and on the other hand by the rediscovery of Dionysius. In Hugh and Richard of St. Victor, the combination of scholastic classification and the Dionysian language of 'divine darkness' (for which, scholars have now shown, Dionysius is indebted to Gregory of Nyssa) produced a dynamic account of the life of prayer not replacing older tradition, but providing it with new vigour. As St. Bonaventure makes clear, by the thirteenth century the Augustine-inspired idea of progress through beginning, developing and perfect charity had combined with Dionysian distinction between purgation, illumination and union to suggest that the Dionysian scheme could be seen also as a series of stages along the way of love.

With the rise of nominalism and the crises of the Renaissance and Reformation, a further blossoming of mystical writing turned the scholastic classifications increasingly inward and produced a literature of remarkable subtlety and psychological insight. Meister Eckhart (1260–1327), for instance, was a pupil of Albertus Magnus, as was Thomas Aquinas, but in Eckhart Dominican theology and scholasticism underpin a personal vision which was to exert widespread influence throughout Northern Europe. Likewise, the devotional poetry found increasingly in handbooks of meditation and manuals of spiritual direction offered a means for analyzing individual spiritual experience according to a variety of schemes catering for a diversity of psychological types. Not surprisingly, during this period one can distinguish between schools of thought which gave to mysticism the flavor of particular national cultures. For instance, the fourteenth-century contemplatives, Richard Rolle, the anonymous author of the *Cloud of Unknowing*, Walter Hilton, and Julian of Norwich, interpreted the common tradition in a manner distinctively English, marked by a practical turn of mind and a kind of Chaucerian energy and charm. Although Rolle's emotionalism on the surface seems quite different from the Dionysian theology of the *Cloud*, both authors write with comparable immediacy and the unaffected, idiosyncratic humour characteristic of the group.

In the Netherlands, a devotional tradition grew up in the context of pious communities that helped to disseminate the teachings of St. Bernard throughout the Low Countries. Consequently, strong elements of bridal mysticism characterize the Netherlands tradition, and John of Ruysbroeck (1293–1381), who founded the Abbey of Groendaal in 1350, wrote his best known work there, *The Adornment of the Spiritual Marriage*, subsequently popularized by his disciple, Henry Herp (d. 1477), and which in turn influenced the Spanish mystics as well as the French School. The Brethren of the Common Life, founded in the Low Countries by Gerard Groote (1340–1384), also influenced the course of European spirituality through the example of community life stressing an affective, apostolic imitation of Christ, the most famous account of this ideal being *The Imitation of Christ*, by Thomas à Kempis.

The Spanish spiritual tradition is also highly distinctive, exemplified by Luis de Granada, John of St. Thomas, Peter of Alcantara, Juan de Valdès, Bernardino Ochino, Ignatius Loyola. The well-known Carmelites, Teresa of Avila and John of the Cross, were also much concerned with church structure and reform, and submitted themselves repeatedly to examination by ecclesiastical authorities. Ignatius Loyola's keyword, 'obedience', became the hallmark of a militant and ascetic spiritual discipline by means of which the Jesuits became key figures in the Counter-Reformation. In general, there is a special dramatic intensity in Spanish spirituality, as doctrines of illumination contend with a disciple of obedience and self-abnegation.

The French, drawing on Spanish and Netherlands sources, developed the École Française, which, again, had a distinctive character. Figures such as Benet of Canfield, Pierre de Bérulle, Mme. Acarie, François de Sales, and Nicolas Malebranche explored a strongly theocentric form of devotion in response to the new and pervasive rationalism of the times.

LM, 133–7

15.

The transfiguration occurs when Jesus takes Peter, James, and John 'up into a high mountain', and the three main synoptic accounts (Mark 9:1–35; Matthew 17:1–27; Luke 9:28–48) tell how the disciples witness Christ's gloriously altered face and body. Jesus then asks his disciples to keep silent about what they have seen 'till the Son of Man were risen from the dead' (Mark 9:9; Matthew 17:9), a saying that the disciples do not understand.

Later, at the foot of the mountain, Jesus and the disciples are met by a crowd of people, including the father of an epileptic boy. The man asks for his son to be healed and the disciples try to oblige him, but fail. Jesus is exasperated by what he declares to be a general condition of faithlessness ('O faithless and perverse generation, how long shall I be with you? How long shall I suffer you?' [Mtt. 17:17]), and he performs the cure himself. When the disciples wonder why they were unsuccessful, Jesus says, bluntly: 'because of your unbelief' (Mtt. 17:20). He then predicts his own death and resurrection, and, according to Mark, the disciples 'understood not' (9:32) but were afraid to ask.

To grasp the broader significance of this sequence of events for the gospel narratives as a whole, we need to consider the story about curing the blind man at Bathsaida, which occurs directly before the transfiguration. This is the only two-stage miracle in the gospels, and Jesus begins by spitting on the blind man's eyes but manages only to effect a partial cure. ('I see men as trees walking' [Mk. 9:24] says the man, graphically, about his fuzzy vision). On the second attempt, Jesus succeeds, and afterwards asks his disciples, 'whom do men say that I am ?' (8:27). 'Thou art the Christ' (8:29), Peter tells him. But when Jesus goes on to predict his own death and resurrection, Peter is unable to accept what he is told, and Jesus turns on him so vehemently as to leave little doubt about his displeasure. 'Get Thee behind me, Satan', (8:33), he says, and we can only imagine the bewildered Peter's reaction to this excoriating rebuke.

The main point in this troubling exchange is that although Peter identifies Jesus as Christ, he cannot accept the news about Jesus' suffering, and so he fails to understand that the visionary experience on the mountain can not, without distortion, be separated from the suffering of people in the ordinary world. The transfiguration, about which the disciples are told not to speak, and the muteness of the epileptic boy who 'foameth, and gnasheth with his teeth' (Mark 9:18), can therefore represent the silence of transcendence and the silence of abjection as the limits within which effective human discourse and agency occur. Because the disciples do not grasp this point, they are unable to heal the sick. Here, it is important to notice that Jesus does not reason with the disciples or try to explain the suffering with which he contends in others and predicts for himself. Rather, the scandal of suffering is acknowledged for what it is, and we are to accept the full weight of the problem – including the lack of adequate explanation. This is part of what the cross itself means, and the cross in turn brings us to the stony silence of the tomb, against which the resurrection stands as a protest that remains inseparable from the tragic events preceding it. Although the resurrection is intimated by the transfiguration, the disciples who witness the event on the mountain still have a lot to learn about the tragedy of the cross. On the mountain, it is as if speech is silenced in the glorious fullness of the moment, but some kinds of suffering call meaning itself into question, and the disciples' response to the crucifixion was to flee in disarray and confusion – in abjection, as it were.

Consequently, tragedy, which thematises the silencing of dialogue before the unanswerable problem of unjust or disproportionate suffering, requires special attention in connection with whatever claims we might want to make about transcendence and about how meaning can be discovered and shared through dialogue.

DA, 57–8

The following excerpts deal with a sample of key themes shared by the literature of the Perennial Philosophy in the West and the wisdom traditions of the East. These are: the idea of a spark or seed of light, of illumination or epiphany; the idea of a transfigured, intense ordinariness; the fundamental importance of transcending the ego; the interdependence of novelty and stability; the difference between meditation and contemplation.

The final excerpts are from the novel *The Kung-Fu Diaries*. This resort to fiction as a last word in this section returns us to the idea that the self is a narrative and that thinking remains always closely bound up with imagination. In this context, the difference between the uses of imagination in meditation and the imageless experience of contemplation in Western spirituality serves to introduce the analogous teachings of the Taoist traditions influenced by Chan Buddhism, as old Master Quan explains in the story. The Chan Buddhist aspect of Master Quan's teaching is central to Ta Mo (also called Bodhidharma) and to the Taoist and Buddhist texts that Master Quan considers. Finally, a brief passage on the Bodhisattva ideal brings us to a core tenet of the Perennial Philosophy, stated in a pure form as an aspiration which remains as enabling as it is challenging.

16.

The spark or seed of light is not confined to self-consciousness. The whole of creation in varying degrees shoots forth its own rays of light, surprising evidences of the gratuitous glory of things bearing traces of the Source, traces on which the human intelligence can seize by way of a variety of illuminations whereby the inner being of things and the inner human self are grasped as a unity. Poetry and art also provide this kind of illumination, so that the mystic and the poet point us in the same direction.

At this point we might reflect that the term 'seed' implies not only energy, but also a process of cultivation and organic growth; if we receive the 'seed of light' as a gift we need to be prepared to cultivate the flower that grows from it. The idea of spiritual development typically deploys metaphors of light and energy to remind us that growth is a patient process and not only a matter of sparkling moments, however significant these are.

DD, 75

17.

The compassion to which the mystics call us is accompanied by an intensified appreciation of contingency. The surprising experience of 'intense ordinariness' in things that happen to cross our path can evoke a sense of wonder in which even banal occurrences are experienced as infinitely precious. The mystics insist that small things, however contingent, are far from being inconsequential. The tiniest particles, after all, unleash the most dynamic force.

DD, 155

18.

Humility requires the annihilation of self-will, but, ironically, wanting to be humble is itself not without the taint of self-regard. We cannot be pleased with ourselves on account of our own humility, though neither should we relinquish the vigilance required in disposing ourselves towards it. It seems that although we are free to admire humility in others, we cannot really claim this perennially recommended virtue for ourselves.

DD, 135

19.

The Church needs its mystics if it is to remain vital, just as mystics need the Church if they are to understand their experiences. Neither, it seems, can do well without the other. Novelty, surprise, illumination and variety without form, like surprise without context, is disorienting. If every experience struck us as novel, we could not so much as make our way to the front door, for we would lose our sense of direction in the sheer, unclassifiable immediacy of whatever our gaze or our touch happened to encounter. Too much novelty is nightmarish, and novelty is most pleasurable when it is, somehow, kept safe, as the mystics are (or should be) by the church. For instance, we are free to enjoy the excitement of a roller-coaster because we believe that the machinery is reliable. But the smallest mechanical failure – the merest suggestion that the machinery does not hold – turns our experience to terror.

DD, 176

20.

One major, generally accepted distinction is that between meditation and contemplation. Meditation is comparable to speech, which proceeds discursively, uses imagination, and is directed by our will and intelligence. Contemplation is comparable to sight, which grasps its object intuitively, does not resort to imagination, and is given to us rather than generated by us.

Mystical theology also sometimes distinguishes between higher and lower forms of contemplation. The lower develops from meditation and is guided by our own effort and will, which enable prayer to pass beyond images and discourse. In the higher form, we are elevated in a manner beyond our capacity to achieve, but the exact point at which our own seeking for the way passes over into the way finding us is difficult to define. It is not unreasonable to suggest that the complexity of the debate itself indicates how the point of transformation differs for people of different temperaments.

A small number of terms has now developed from this discussion, and they are part of a common vocabulary. The prayer of meditation is described as *active, acquired, imperfect* and *natural*. Contemplation, by contrast, is *passive, infused, perfect* and *supernatural*. In the elusive intermediate stage, these terms are frequently supplemented by others, and used in a sense best derived from the context. The first set of terms, however, suggests that we are the initiators of prayer which is within our capacity as free creatures; the second set makes clear that our own efforts are inadequate entirely to effect what we seek.

DD, 202–3

21.

Master Quan says that the work of meditation boils down to this: use *chi* to nourish *jing*, transform *jing* to refine *chi*; use refined *chi* to build up *shen*. When an experience of stillness occurs, I should understand it as the merging of conscious mind with its source. Such a thing can only be known by experience, and here Quan points to a brightly coloured tangka on the wall facing his desk, depicting the primordial Buddha, Samantabhadra, with his consort Samantabhadri. The seated Buddha is brilliant blue, and his consort, who sits on his lap, facing him with her legs around his waist, is pure white. They sit together on a lotus, surrounded by brightly coloured flowers. Their sexual union is the first thing I see, but then Quan says, 'This is what we are talking about.'

I wait for him to go on. 'The Buddha is blue because he is infinite. His consort is white because she is pure consciousness, without content. The marriage of pure infinity and pure consciousness that you see here is the condition itself of what we are calling, for want of a better word, the still meditation, the Sea of Tranquility. In such a state, conscious mind is not obliterated, but also it is not identifiable with the ego. Indeed, it is the condition itself of liberation from the ego, from the turmoil and anguish of the three fires of samsara. All our talk about *chi*, *jing*, *shen*, the Microcosmic Orbit, and so forth, is sometimes called 'internal alchemy'. But it is merely a means to an end, and eventually it is discarded. Think of it as a starting point to enable you to focus – like a branch against which a bird pushes off in order to take flight. Sensations, such as *chi* moving in your meridians and organs, lights dancing in your head, elation or dryness – these are signs along the way, but they are of passing interest and should not be sought after or held on to. In the last resort, they are of no more significance than the thoughts and images that float into your mind as you focus your attention on your breath. Your whole training teaches you that patient practice brings you in the end to a high level of skill beyond the techniques themselves, and, in the case of meditation, to new kinds of awareness and understanding'.

KD, 162–3

22.

Quan then suggested four texts that provide sufficient basic understanding of meditation within our tradition.

First, Ta Mo, as always, has much of value to teach even though his writings exist today only in fragments. At the heart of his thinking is the idea that there is no difference between self and other because all beings are 'identical to the True Nature'. Consequently, 'we clearly know that seeking nothing truly is practice of the path', even though most people are in a 'perpetual state of delusion' because they persistently mistake their own desires and attachments for real seeking. In the Dharma, however, 'there is no self', and so it is best to 'wish for nothing'. Liberation, equanimity of temperament, and freedom from anxiety follow from practicing the Dharma, which means being in a state of mind that is also no-mind, and in which we 'solicit nothing' and are 'attached to nothing'.

Quan's second text is the Buddhist *Diamond Sutra*. It also offers a radical critique of the grasping ego, going on even to suggest that, in the end, teaching is itself a futile activity. There is nothing to be taught because there is 'not anyone' who is liberated, and language is merely a means of conveyance, like a raft. As such, language is a mode of mind, but 'modes of mind are not mind', and so, in the spirit of no-teaching, we need to abandon the raft of language altogether. Otherwise, we will remain caught up in delusions, like the vast majority of people.

For Ta Mo and the *Diamond Sutra*, transcendence of the ego and the surrender of its cravings open upon the mystery from which we emerge when we are born, and to which we return when we die – or when we die to ourselves in meditation. Quan said that these texts are the foundation on which the entire practice of Chi

Gong and of Kung-Fu stand. He then moved to his third recommendation.

The Jade Emperor's Mind Seal Classic deals with the 'three treasures' of *jing, chi,* and *shen.* These are the means by which we create a spiritual embryo, and everyone is capable of doing this, because 'within each person is a mysterious female'. The embryo is also called a spiritual 'seed', which in turn is a medicine, or 'elixir' which cures us of suffering. 'It is not white and not green', which is to say, it transcends the opposition between the Green Dragon or yang force, and the White Tiger or yin force, and it has the power to open our minds to original mind. When this occurs we are to 'keep to non-being yet hold on to being' and here, again, we encounter the idea that there is a state of mind that is also no-mind, a mysterious communion of pure infinity and pure consciousness. Whenever we catch a glimpse of original mind, we are said to 'reverse the light', so that our mind remains aware even as it is taken up into its own primal sourse.

The fourth book is *The Secret of the Golden Flower.* Quan says I should read it often and think about it carefully because it contains the essence of Taoist alchemy (as in *The Jade emperor's Mind Seal Classic*) and of Chan Buddhism (as in Ta Mo and the *Diamond Sutra*). Also, it addresses the needs of people living ordinary lives in the world, rather than specialized adepts, whether Taoist sages or Buddhist monks.

The Secret of the Golden Flower uses a mix of Taoist alchemical ideas, such as *jing, chi,* and *shen,* the golden pill, the embryo, the pearl, and the yellow court, among others. Throughout, these terms are a way of engaging us with the governing idea of 'turning the light around', which, as in *The Jade Emperor's Mind Seal Classic,* occurs when consciousness becomes aware of and dwells in the source.

KD, 164–5

23.

'She is Kwan Yin, a revered bodhisattva; do you know what that is? No? Well, as bodhisattva is a person who has attained enlightenment and has escaped the perpetual cycle of life and death in our suffering world. Yet a bodhisattva chooses to be reborn and to return to the world, and will continue to do so until all the suffering in our world and every other world is healed.'

I remember thinking, *That is a tall order for those bodhisattvas* and then, also *What a noble and touching idea.* I asked for her name again, and what she was doing on the dragon.

'Her name is Kwan Yin. She is the bodhisattva of compassion. In her right hand she has a branch of willow to show how flexible she is, and her tears for the world are also those of the weeping willow. In her left hand she has a little vase. It is full of healing liquor, the nectar of compassion that she pours on us suffering creatures. Here, she stands on a dragon but she is not always depicted that way. In this case, she is calming the turmoil, the fierce energy at the source of creation. Yes, the world is a nightmare of suffering, but see how she stands tall, how the drapery flows, reflecting the shape – and also the meaning – of the willow.'

'It is a lovely idea.'

'Not just an idea. A fact. Try it and see.' He was laughing, perhaps with a touch of amused self-mockery, as he placed the statue back on the shelf.

Afterwards, I began to notice that there were

representations of Kwan Yin throughout the house, and as I got to know more, I came to see how, in her many varieties, she was in fact all around us. Also, as I thought about the statue in the library, I found myself thinking about Father Gilles. He too had talked about compassion. Christ's cross and Kwan Yin belong, somehow, together, and I felt this more – how can I say it – in my imagination, as a sort of personal, dawning awareness, rather than as something I could explain.

KD, 14

Six Modern Authors
"an important and illuminating book . . . it has the seeds of the future in it".

Barbara Reynolds. *Modern Language Review*

Reading the New Testament
"a mind and sensibility trained, to an exceptional degree, in both literature and philosophical theology . . . He is capable of organizing the complex resources of his mind in the service of a powerful idea: that innocent suffering, so far from refuting Christianity, is in fact central to any real understanding of it. It is, after all, the faith whose sign is the cross. Patrick Grant understands this better than almost any other writer I have read".

A.D. Nuttall. *Author of "Shakespeare the Thinker"*

Breaking Enmities
"coming hard on the heels of Patrick Grant's magisterial trilogy on 'Personalism' (1992, 1994, 1996), *Breaking Enmities* represents the accumulated reading-skill and wisdom of a long-established scholar whose work should be far better known"

Dennis Brown. *Critical Survey*

Literature of Mysticism
"This book, though difficult, has a prevailing integrity, sanity, and wisdom about it . . . his book becomes a trial of our culture, and that culture is found wanting".

Colin Thompson. *Times Literary Supplement*

Transformation of Sin
"profound and graceful".

Franklin R. Baruch. *Renaissance and Reformation*

Personalist Trilogy
"the itinerary is dizzying, and only the force of a magisterial and synthesizing intellect could make it tractable . . . almost by definition the construction of his 'solution' requires an encompassing reinterpretation of all that can plausibly be thought to bear upon the question it proposes to answer".

David Lyle Jeffrey. *English Studies in Canada*

Images and Ideas
"an unusual combination of philosophical understanding and critical acumen".

David Norbrook. *Times Literary Supplement*

Imperfection
"I can't think of another book that combines such spread of reference, such succinctness, and such depth of concern without losing weight, or resonance, notwithstanding – shall we say – wisdom".

John Wilson Foster. *Author of "Colonial Consequences"*

Out of Contradiction
"Learned. Scholarly, and personal, this is a book of poignant honesty summoning our attention less to itself or to its author than to its matter, which is human faith and life despite, or perhaps through, contradiction".

Jeffrey Burton Russell. *Author of "Radical Evil and the Power of Good in History"*

Self-Fashioning in the Letters of Vincent van Gogh
"a deep and creative inquiry suggesting meaningful structures for understanding the richness of the artist's life and work. Grant succeeds in bringing Van Gogh's letters into the domain of literary studies, and demonstrates that the effort opens exciting new ways of understanding".

Cliff Edwards. *University of Toronto Quarterly*